The Financial Crisis and the Regulation of Finance

This volume is dedicated with affection
to David Llewellyn
on the occasion of his retirement
from Loughborough University

The Financial Crisis and the Regulation of Finance

Edited by

Christopher J. Green

Professor of Economics and Finance, Loughborough University, UK

Eric J. Pentecost

Professor of Economics, Loughborough University, UK

Tom Weyman-Jones

Professor of Industrial Economics, Loughborough University, UK

Edward Elgar

Cheltenham, UK • Northampton, MA, USA

Published by
Edward Elgar Publishing Limited
The Lypiatts
15 Lansdown Road
Cheltenham
Glos GL50 2JA
UK

Edward Elgar Publishing, Inc.
William Pratt House
9 Dewey Court
Northampton
Massachusetts 01060
USA

A catalogue record for this book
is available from the British Library

Library of Congress Control Number: 2010934046

MIX
Paper from responsible sources
FSC® C018575
FSC
www.fsc.org

ISBN 978 1 84980 870 5

Typeset by Servis Filmsetting Ltd, Stockport, Cheshire
Printed and bound by MPG Books Group, UK

Contents

PART FOUR REGULATION OF FINANCIAL FIRMS

PART FIVE INFORMATION, SHAREHOLDERS AND PROJECTS

Figures

Tables

Contributors

Peter Andrews
Head of Economics of Financial Regulation, UK Financial Services Authority.

Morten Balling
Emeritus Professor, (formerly President of the School) Aarhus School of Business, University of Aarhus; Council Member of SUERF – the European Money and Finance Forum.

Claudio Borio
Deputy Head of the Monetary and Economic Department, and Director of Research and Statistics, Bank for International Settlements, Basel, Switzerland; formerly at the OECD.

Franco Bruni
Professor of International Monetary Economics, 'Paolo Baffi' Centre on Central Banking and Financial Regulation, Università Commerciale Luigi Bocconi, Milan; member of the European Shadow Financial Regulatory Committee, Council Member and former President of SUERF – the European Money and Finance Forum.

Forrest Capie
Professor of Economic History, Cass Business School, City University; and Bank of England; formerly a member of the Shadow Chancellor's advisory council and the Shadow Monetary Policy Committee.

Geoffrey Dennis
Global Emerging Markets strategist, Citigroup Investment Research and Analysis.

Robert A. Eisenbeis
Chief Monetary Economist, Cumberland Advisors; member of the Shadow Financial Regulatory Committee, and of the Financial Economists Roundtable; formerly Executive Vice-President and Director of Research at the Federal Reserve Bank of Atlanta.

Charles Goodhart
Professor Emeritus of Banking and Finance, London School of Economics, and Programme Director, Regulation and Financial Stability, LSE Financial Markets Group; Fellow of the British Academy, formerly Chief Economic Adviser at the Bank of England, and member of the Bank of England Monetary Policy Committee.

Christopher J. Green
Professor of Economics and Finance, Loughborough University.

Shelagh Heffernan
Late Professor of Banking and Finance, Cass Business School, City University; Director of the Centre for Banking Research, and Associate Dean of the School.

Shelagh Heffernan was determined to take part in this venture to celebrate David Llewellyn's work: she prepared her paper for this volume and delivered it at the June 2009 conference even though she was already very unwell. Sadly, she died on 14 December 2010 before publication. The many tributes that have followed her passing constitute an eloquent testament to her own contribution to banking and finance.

Richard J. Herring
Jacob Safra Professor of International Banking and Professor of Finance, Wharton School, University of Pennsylvania; Co-director, Wharton Financial Institutions Centre; Co-chair of the Shadow Financial Regulatory Committee, and Executive Director of the Financial Economists Roundtable.

Darrin Grimsey
Partner, Ernst & Young Project Finance Advisory, Melbourne; Associate of Melbourne Consulting and Custom Programmes, the University of Melbourne.

George G. Kaufman
John F. Smith, Jr. Professor of Finance and Economics, Loyola University, Chicago, IL; Co-chair of the Shadow Financial Regulatory Committee, Executive Director of the Financial Economists Roundtable.

Mervyn K. Lewis
Professor of Banking and Finance, School of Commerce, University of South Australia; Fellow of the Academy of the Social Sciences in Australia.

David G. Mayes
BNZ Professor of Finance and Director, Europe Institute, University of Auckland; formerly Advisor to the Board at the Bank of Finland; Chief Economist at the Reserve Bank of New Zealand, and member of the European System of Central Banks' Monetary Policy Committee.

Andy Mullineux
Professor of Global Finance, Birmingham Business School, University of Birmingham; Director of the Global Finance Research Group, formerly Head of the School of Social Sciences.

Eric J. Pentecost
Professor of Economics, and Head of the Economics Department, Loughborough University.

Reinhard H. Schmidt
Professor of International Banking and Finance at Johann Wolfgang Goethe University in Frankfurt, Germany; Chairman of the Finance Department; member of the European Shadow Financial Regulatory Committee.

Tom Weyman-Jones
Professor of Industrial Economics, Loughborough University.

Geoffrey Wood
Professor of Economics, Cass Business School, City University; formerly special advisor on financial stability to the Bank of England, and research adviser at the Bank of Finland.

Abbreviations

AC World	MSCI All-Country World Index
ARROW	Advanced Risk Responsive Operating Framework
B&B	Bradford and Bingley
BIS	Bank for International Settlements
BoA	Bank of America
BoE	Bank of England
bp	basis points
BPRI	bank performance related information
CAR	capital adequacy requirement
CDO	collateralized debt obligation
CDS	credit default swap
CEBS	Committee of European Banking Supervisors
CEO	chief executive officer
CMO	collateralized mortgage obligation
CRD	Capital Requirement Directive
DBFOM	design-build-finance-operate-maintain
DBOM	design build operate and maintain
DIDMCA	Depository Institutions Deregulation and Monetary Control Act
ECB	European Central Bank
EEA	European Economic Area
EIB	European Investment Bank
EMEA	Europe, Middle East and Africa
EU	European Union
Fannie Mae	Federal National Mortgage Association
FDIA	Federal Deposit Insurance Act
FDIC	Federal Deposit Insurance Corporation
FDICIA	Federal Deposit Insurance Corporation Improvement Act
Fed	US Federal Reserve
FISM	financial institutions, systems and markets
FRC	Financial Reporting Council
Freddie Mac	Federal Home Loan Mortgage Corporation
FSA	Financial Services Authority
FSB	Financial Stability Board
FSMA	Financial Services and Markets Act

GDP	gross domestic product
GEM	global emerging market
HF	hedge fund
HMT	HM Treasury
IMF	International Monetary Fund
IndyMac	Independent National Mortgage Corporation
IPO	Initial Public Offering
IRS	Internal Revenue Service
LBO	leveraged buyout
LIBOR	London Inter-Bank Offer Rate
LoLR	lender of last resort
LSE	London School of Economics and Political Science
MBS	Mortgage-backed security
MoU	Memorandum of Understanding
OECD	Organisation for Economic Co-operation and Development
OIS	Overnight Indexed Swap Rate
P&G	Proctor and Gamble
PCA	prompt corrective action
PEF	private equity fund
PPP	Public Private Partnership
RBNZ	Reserve Bank of New Zealand
RBS	Royal Bank of Scotland
RIA	Regulatory Impact Assessment
RMBS	residential mortgage-backed securities
ROE	return on equity
RTO	risk to our objectives
SEC	Securities and Exchange Commission
SEIR	Structured Early Intervention and Resolution
SME	small and medium-sized enterprises
SPV	special purpose vehicle
SRR	special Resolution Regime
SUERF	European Money and Finance Forum
SWF	sovereign wealth fund
UBS	Union Bank of Switzerland
VAT	value added tax

PART ONE

The financial crisis

1. Introduction

Christopher J. Green, Eric J. Pentecost and Tom Weyman-Jones[1]

DAVID LLEWELLYN

All of the chapters in this book are the product of a one-day conference entitled 'Financial Institutions, Systems and Markets: Structure, Performance and Regulation' held at Loughborough University on 16 June 2009 to celebrate the career of David Llewellyn and his contribution to the Department of Economics at Loughborough University.[2]

David was appointed as Professor of Money and Banking in the new Department of Economics at Loughborough University in 1976 at just 33 years of age, a post he has held for over 30 years. After graduating from the London School of Economics (LSE) in the mid-1960s David moved to Rotterdam to take up the post of economist at Unilever. He moved back to the UK one year later to work for HM Treasury where he advised on both domestic and external financial matters, before leaving to join the staff of Nottingham University in 1967. In 1974 David joined the Treasurer's Department of the International Monetary Fund (IMF) in Washington DC where he was responsible for the analysis of banking and capital markets and advising on the reform of the international monetary system.

Just five years after his arrival in Loughborough, David became head of the Department of Economics (1981–91) and from 1985–2004 was chairman of the Loughborough University Banking Centre, which with the aid of sponsorship from leading UK banks (especially the former Midland Bank, National Westminster Bank and the Halifax Building Society) made Loughborough a centre for the study of the financial system. David was one of the principal drivers behind this very first public-private initiative, and the banking centre was subsequently responsible for a number of important developments. In particular it was one of the main pioneers of the empirical study in the UK of bank and building society efficiency and competition. By the early 1990s sponsorship had been reduced nationally, and the banking centre staff merged with the Economics Department and the Business School at Loughborough. However, David had put Loughborough on the academic map as a centre for excellence in the area of the economics of banking and financial markets and this reputation continues to this day.

Reputations are not built on sponsorship alone and David was very active in research. His book, *International Financial Integration: The Limits of Sovereignty* (1981), was the first in economics which tackled the implications of financial integration long before the topic was fashionable. This was soon followed by an edited volume on *The Framework of United Kingdom Monetary Policy* (1983) and the Gilbart lectures on the *Evolution of the British Financial System* (1985). In this pre-research exercise era academics focused less on academic journal papers and more on books, but as the demands changed so did the direction of David's output. David has contributed, *inter alia*, to the *Journal of Financial Regulation and Compliance, Journal of International Banking and Financial Law, Economic Notes, Open Economies Review, European Journal of Finance, International Journal of Financial Regulation and Compliance, Journal of International Financial Markets, Institutions and Money, Journal of Development Studies* and *Journal of International Financial Markets*. In addition, David has served on the editorial boards of *International Journal of Regulation and Compliance*, *International Journal of Bank Regulation*, and *Banking and Information Technology* and, of course, there are numerous chapters in books and reports on various aspects of the banking and financial sectors all around the world.

Throughout his career David has been extremely active in consultancy work for both private and public sector organisations. This reflected his belief that economics should be of practical use, as well as his wide interests in real-world problems, and these activities contributed greatly to his reputation. Between 1994 and 2002 he was a Public Interest Director of the Personal Investment Authority (the UK regulator of retail financial services until it was superseded by the Financial Services Authority (FSA)). In 2004 he was appointed by the South African Minister of Finance to be a member of the task group to investigate competition in the South African banking industry. He has been a consultant to the World Bank and the IMF and is currently a member of an IMF international advisory committee on governance in supervisory agencies. David was also a member of the advisory board of the European Banking Report at the Italian Bankers Association. In 2004 he was a consultant to HM Treasury on governance in life mutuals (the Myners report) and was a member of the PricewaterhouseCoopers team investigating the macroeconomic impacts of the Basel II Accord for the European Commission. In 2005–6 he was a member of the Council of Management of the European Money and Finance Forum (SUERF), a network association of bankers, central bankers, financial practitioners and academics, and was president between 2000 and 2006. This was one of David's ideal roles: bringing together academics and practising bankers and getting both groups to learn from each other, for their mutual benefit and the benefit of the organisations that they served.

As remarked elsewhere in this volume, one of David's most influential papers was his overview of 'The Economic Rationale for Financial Regulation' (Llewellyn, 1999). Economically rigorous, but also addressed to a wider audience, especially those sceptical of state intervention in financial markets, this paper set benchmarks by which regulators could work and be judged in practice, and it has had a major impact on the thinking and work of the FSA, much of which has inspired regulators worldwide.

As if this activity was not enough, David has always undertaken a full teaching load – even into retirement! In this way David has been an outstanding colleague. Although for many years David taught first year macroeconomic principles, he is best known for his course on financial institutions, systems and markets (timetabled as FISMs) – the only course of its kind in the country. In this course David combined his natural talent as a presenter and lecturer with his intimate knowledge of the financial sector and how it operates in a way that was (and is) accessible to all students with only a basic understanding of economics. His lecturing style was very much of the old school: first and foremost a performance – a very entertaining performance as the nitty-gritty material was interspersed with anecdotes and short stories of his latest visits to foreign parts. This made the dry subject of banking regulation and financial markets fascinating, and many generations of Loughborough students are grateful for David's treatment of the subject. When we developed a suite of master's degree programmes in banking, economics and finance in the 1990s, needless to say David devised a postgraduate version of the long-standing FISMs course which became one of the core modules on this very successful programme.

With David's retirement, economics at Loughborough in many ways has lost, if not its founder (who was Denis Swann), its most well-known and influential figure. Given that the subject matter of much of academic economics has moved in the direction of ever increasing abstraction from the real world, it is likely that we will never again see David's like in a Department of Economics. To those of us who have directly witnessed the extraordinary impact of his teaching and thinking on generations of students at Loughborough, this is a sad reflection of the current position and possible future direction of academic economics, and one which may well reduce the popularity of the subject for study, and the viability of the discipline in times of financial stringency. However, those of us who have journeyed some of the way with David will be forever grateful for the experience.

THE CHAPTERS IN THIS VOLUME

As luck would have it, the June 2009 conference was arranged just as the financial system was feeling the full force of the extraordinary events whose seeds may have been planted years ago but which hit the major industrial nations during 2007–09. All the invited speakers naturally turned their full attention to understanding the crisis, its causes and implications, especially for regulation and private behaviour.

The chapters fall naturally into five parts. In part one, Christopher Green and Geoffrey Dennis outline the events in the run-up to and during the crisis. Green concentrates on its origins in the US mortgage market and the bailouts in the major industrial countries; Dennis looks at how emerging markets fared during the crisis. In part two the contributions provide a general overview of financial regulation. Peter Andrews explains how the FSA has used economic evidence to inform its regulatory thinking since its establishment, especially building on Llewellyn (1999). Richard Herring and Reinhard Schmidt ask how the crisis has or should have changed our view of regulation, especially to improve rather than eliminate it. Any type of intervention involves moral hazard and Charles Goodhart gives a classic overview of the many levels at which the recent interventions are likely to alter the moral hazards faced by regulators and the private sector in the future.

Part three is concerned with 'macro-prudential' regulation, a term which was used by only a few until recently but which is now recognised to be a critical issue in understanding the behaviour and regulation of financial institutions to limit systemic risk. In the first chapter, Claudio Borio sets out the key issues involved in macroprudential regulation. The chapters by Franco Bruni and by Forrest Capie and Geoffrey Wood are concerned particularly with the potentially ambiguous relationship between monetary policy and macro-prudential regulation. For example, lender of last resort activities by a central bank are part of monetary policy but may also be critical in times of financial crisis, and there may be conflicts between the two objectives. Bruni discusses the principles of the relationship between monetary policy and regulation, whereas Capie and Wood place the debate in its historical context.

The contributions in part four concentrate on the more traditional 'micro' aspects of regulation. David Mayes considers in depth the 'Prompt Corrective Action' model for winding up financial institutions and how it might operate in a European context, particularly in a setting where so many financial institutions operate across borders: a key problem in the crisis as many of our authors observe. Most of the contributors to this volume argue that some regulatory reform is essential, and while not necessarily dissenting from this principle, the chapters by Robert Eisenbeis and George G. Kaufman and by Shelagh Heffernan also offer a more cautionary view. Eisenbeis and Kaufman point out, with particular reference to Regulation Q, that many well-intended regulations passed in haste have unexpected and undesirable consequences. Heffernan argues that in the case of the UK at least, regulators had most of the necessary tools to prevent disaster but either failed to use them at all, or acted too late despite having adequate timely information. On this view, the regulatory process as much as the regulations themselves needs overhauling.

In the final part, our contributors turn to the users of the financial system. Morten Balling considers how far disclosure and European Union (EU) disclosure requirements in particular can be used to limit the asymmetric information endemic in financial markets. Andy Mullineux looks at the monitoring role of shareholders, particularly in the context of the range of specialised institutions operating in financial markets. The practical difficulty of shareholder oversight is just one of several considerations suggesting a radical rethink of the business of banking, with Mullineux drawing a parallel between the money transmission activities of banks and the basic business of utilities. In the final chapter, Darren Grimsey and Mervyn Lewis evaluate the prospects for public-private partnership financing. In the post-crisis environment, longer-term private financing is more scarce, particularly for large projects, and this suggests that the public sector may need to be more fully involved in the risk-sharing aspects of the finance than has hitherto been the case.

Much more remains to be written on the recent financial crisis and its implications for financial institutions, regulation and indeed the general public. Inevitably, events have moved quickly, and some of the material in this volume might have been rewritten several times between the conference and subsequent publication. However, the editors and authors concluded that the energy of the conference would be best preserved by a relatively light updating of the material so as to transmit effectively the immediacy of the arguments that were presented. In this spirit we hope that the chapters in this volume will make an important contribution to understanding the crisis, how we got here, and where we might go next. We believe that it is particularly fitting that a volume devised to celebrate David Llewellyn's career speaks both to economists and practitioners of the need to redouble our efforts to improve the functioning of the financial system: in difficult times as well as in normal times.

NOTES

1. We thank Denise Simpson for her help in organising the June 2009 conference and Ben Booth and his colleagues at Edward Elgar for their enthusiastic help in the preparation of this volume.
2. The papers by Green, Andrews, Mayes, and Eisenbeis and Kaufman were not presented at the conference but were commissioned beforehand as part of this volume.

REFERENCE

Llewellyn, D.T. (1999), 'The economic rationale for financial regulation', Financial Services Authority Occasional Paper Series 1, London, April.

2. 'The day the music died': the financial tsunami of 2007–09

Christopher J. Green[1]

THE MUSICAL CHAIRS THEORY OF MARKETS

'We all got up to dance,
Oh, but we never got the chance!
'cause the players tried to take the field;
The marching band refused to yield.
Do you recall what was revealed
The day the music died?'
Don Maclean, *American Pie*

Interviewed by the *Financial Times* on 9 July 2007, the chief executive officer (CEO) of Citigroup, Chuck Prince, told the newspaper that he

> '. . . dismissed fears that the music was about to stop for the cheap credit-fuelled buy-out boom . . . [He said] that the party would end at some point but there was so much liquidity it would not be disrupted by the turmoil in the US sub-prime mortgage market. "When the music stops, in terms of liquidity, things will be complicated. But as long as the music is playing, you've got to get up and dance. We're still dancing." '[2]

We all know what happened next, even if the details are fading. Four months later, Citigroup reported a fourth quarter loss of US$9.8 billion including an $18.1 billion write-down, mainly on sub-prime mortgage-backed securities, and Chuck Prince resigned as CEO.[3] Twelve months later Citigroup was part-nationalised as it entered into an agreement with the US government which guaranteed up to $306 billion in problematic assets and injected $20 billion of public capital into Citigroup '. . . to restore confidence in a bank that defines the term "too big to fail" '.[4]

The chapters in this volume are all concerned in differing degrees with the implications and lessons to be learnt in the aftermath of the financial tsunami of 2007–09, of which events at Citigroup formed one part. In this chapter, I have the more modest ambition of outlining the events that took place in the run-up to and during the worst of the crisis when scarcely a week went by without a new failure or bailout being announced. More detailed explanations and post-mortems are left for subsequent chapters; the emphasis in this chapter is on the proximate causes and the sheer scale of the write-offs and ensuing support operations. I concentrate on the US where the problems originated and the UK, and do not discuss emerging markets for, as Geoff Dennis emphasizes later in the volume, 'emerging markets have had a good crisis'. In the final section, I briefly consider a selection of issues which have been widely discussed in the immediate aftermath of the crisis.

The events of 2007–09 were preceded by a global boom in commodity and security prices which can be dated from about 2002–03 following a sharp reduction in world interest rates, particularly in the US in 2001.[5] A period of low interest rates and rapid industrialisation in China and India generated a sustained increase in world economic growth which underpinned the commodity price boom. In addition, cheap credit fuelled a worldwide boom in demand for housing, especially in the US where policy changes were designed to encourage an expansion in home ownership, particularly among minorities and lower-income households.[6] Mortgage lending grew in scale and scope and new techniques were developed to enable the financing of this debt.

Most attention has focused on sub-prime mortgages: loans for house purchases with characteristics that debar them from the highest credit rating that mortgages normally attract. These characteristics include borrowers with a lower than desirable credit score because of some combination of a poor credit history and low or variable income or employment history. They also include the loan itself, if it has a particularly high debt-value to property value ratio. As the housing and mortgage boom developed, loans with debt-value ratios of up to 125 per cent became not uncommon. Borrowers were attracted by apparently low interest rates and, in the US, the essentially unlimited tax-deduction on mortgage interest payments. Lenders were attracted by the higher interest rates, fees and longer lock-in periods on these riskier loans. The apparent contradiction between the perceptions of borrowers and lenders was reconciled in the market by innovations in mortgage lending practices. These included loans with an interest-only payment schedule for the first few years (two years being common) and hybrids in which the first few years' interest and capital payments were made at a low fixed rate (the teaser rate). In all cases, there was a very sharp increase in cost at the reset after the initial period, with payments often more than doubling. Low-income borrowers frequently did not understand the full nature of the obligations they were incurring.[7] However, lenders were not concerned about default risk as long as house prices were rising; indeed it could be argued that foreclosure ceased to be a weapon of last resort and moved well up the order of possible actions to manage delinquent mortgages. Furthermore, little or none of this sub-prime debt remained with the loan originator; it was virtually all sold on, particularly in securitised form: the originate and securitise model.

SECURITISATION

Securitisation dates back well before the current crisis and involves the pooling of a large number of mortgages (or other debt) to be sold as mortgage-backed securities (MBSs) with uniform features that can be traded in organised markets. A relatively new feature of the securitisation process in the run-up to the tsunami was collateralisation. Collateralised debt obligations (CDOs) involved a further repackaging of securitised debt into tranches of cash flows, each with different repayment characteristics which were attractive to different groups of investors. A typical structure for collateralised mortgage obligations (CMOs) is shown in Figure 2.1. Since each tranche can be tailored to a specific group of investors, it is more attractive to that group and can therefore be priced more finely than uniform non-collateralised debt, although the corresponding weakness that went unrecognised until much later is that this process necessarily reduces the size of the aftermarket in comparison with uniform MBSs. This made it more difficult for banks to reduce their exposure to CMOs in a controlled way when defaults began to mount.

A common form of mortgage collateralisation was to tier the tranches beginning with those that turn out to be prepaid last. Ultimate holders of these obligations are purchasing them for a reliable long-term cash flow. The risk of prepayment inherent in any mortgage implies that the creditors are simultaneously writing an option on early redemption. The tranche which is prepaid *first* is that closest to being in the money, and is therefore the *most* risky in terms of cash flow, provided that is, default risk is ignored. The first CMOs were based on Ginnie Maes which have a US government guarantee. Sub-prime mortgages are by construction not so guaranteed. In a CMO package consisting exclusively of sub-prime mortgages where default risk is not negligible, it is those that are prepaid *first* that are probably the *least* risky. Thus, in comparison with CMOs based on Ginnie Maes, those based on sub-prime mortgages at a minimum inverted the risk structure of the payments stream, and in practice modified the risk structure in ways that ultimate holders of allegedly highly-rated debt would find difficult to determine. This was exacerbated to the extent that some securities were repackaged more than once, thus further

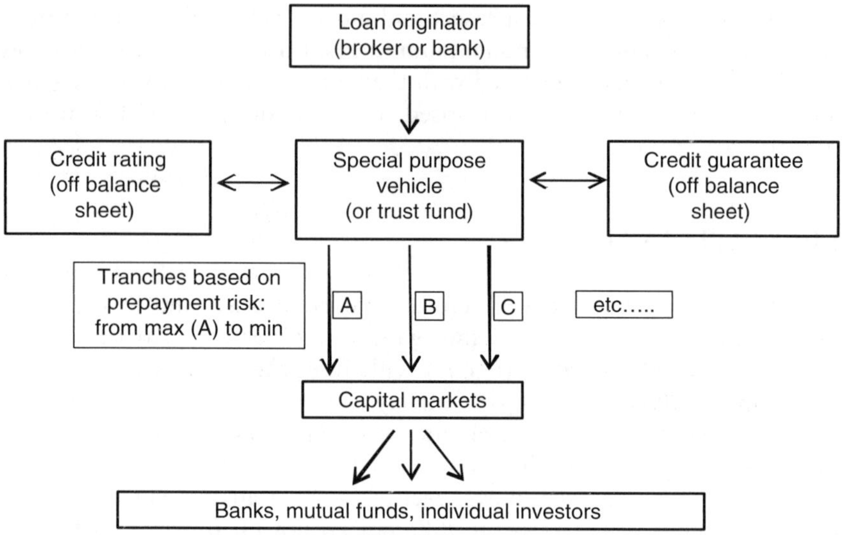

Figure 2.1 Collateralised mortgage obligations (CMOs)

obscuring the true nature of the underlying assets. It is clear in retrospect that this and other aspects of such contracts were not fully understood, or at least not explained to customers, by market professionals. Even where understanding did exist, many reports suggest that professionals chose to ignore them.[8]

Securitisation is one of many quarries in the hunt for the causes of the tsunami. The benefits of securitising illiquid debt are well-established. It pools and spreads the risks, increases market liquidity and therefore enlarges the pool of potential lenders and borrowers. Its bottom-line impact is to reduce the cost of capital for investments which may otherwise not have been made. It is difficult to see how securitisation *per se* can be blamed for the negligence and fraud which occurred in the sub-prime market. However, it is also clear that securitisation does pose general issues of monitoring and control which had not previously been fully appreciated. In the context of the mortgage market, the functions of obtaining, financing and repaying a loan were formerly under one roof, typically of a traditional bank or mortgage lender. Securitisation increasingly split these functions among at least four separate agents.

First, the loan origination company became a marketing organisation whose main objective was to maximise the number of mortgages created, as this maximised fee income, with the financing being provided elsewhere. Second, risk assessment was carried out on the CMO mortgage pool by credit-rating agencies. Academic research on credit ratings has until recently focused on the determination and implications of ratings. The moral hazard involved in an agency rating the debt of an entity which is contracting and paying for the rating was thought to be of second-order importance. However, it is not unlike a CEO or university vice-chancellor who seeks the opinion of employees about his or her own performance. The CEO may ask for an honest assessment but it is far from obvious that he will actually want, welcome or get one. Questions were asked about the rating agencies and the role of auditors in the wake of the earlier collapse of Enron, whose debt was still rated as investment grade three days before filing for bankruptcy, following a steady 15 month fall in the share price from $90 to just a few cents. On the face of it, the agencies wilfully ignored market evidence in rating the bonds, but little was done to mitigate this problem, and it re-emerged with still greater consequences in the failure of the agencies to adjust the ratings of CMOs in a meaningful and timely manner. The agencies claim that reputational concerns are sufficient on their own to ensure integrity, but the limited hard research evidence would suggest otherwise.[9] Third, oversight and management of the outstanding mortgage was largely in the hands of the managers of the special purpose vehicle and as long as house prices were rising they had little incentive to renegotiate the terms of repayment for borrowers who got into difficulties, as many sub-prime borrowers inevitably did. Finally, the ultimate holders of the mortgage were far removed from this process, since the claim was expected to be analogous to an (almost) risk-free annuity.

Overall therefore, the crisis raises important issues not necessarily about the underlying value of securitisation, but rather about its implementation and the need to improve substantially the monitoring process at all stages.[10] Of course effective monitoring is costly and it remains to be seen if the true costs of monitoring outweigh the benefits of securitisation itself.

THE BUBBLE BURSTS

In response to the inflationary pressures in the US economy, the Federal Reserve (the Fed) raised the discount rate in steps by a total of 425 basis points between mid-2004 and mid-2006. Housing supply overtook demand and, in the US, the boom in house prices and lending began to peter out. The first indication of the problems ahead came with the failure of the second largest US sub-prime mortgage lender-cum-broker. New Century was quoted on the New York Stock Exchange, but it collapsed rapidly in 2007, filing for bankruptcy in April, amid a criminal investigation and private law suits.[11] It was not just the bankruptcy, but the accompanying evidence of rampant mis-selling, falsification of documents and outright fraud, not just at New Century but elsewhere in the mortgage market, that should have set off more alarms than was the case.[12] Chuck Prince did not give his notorious interview until the summer of 2007 when he was largely dismissive of the sub-prime mortgage defaults, notwithstanding the size of Citi's exposure to the market at that time.

Prince had barely returned to his office when the pace quickened with the failure of American Home Mortgage, a large non-sub-prime lender,[13] and the provision by a group of major US banks of some $13.5 billion of emergency funding to Countrywide Financial, the largest mortgage broker in the country.[14] The problems at Countrywide and elsewhere led to a freezing of the short-term commercial paper market in mid-August. Securitisation requires mortgage originators to obtain and provide a continuous supply of temporary finance for the initiation of mortgages before they are securitised and sold. Concerns about the viability of mortgage originators following the collapse of New Century and the related problems at other mortgage companies were a major factor in causing a temporary freeze in short-term markets. Several funds whose investments were predominantly in sub-prime MBSs had to be given liquidity support by their parent company, Bear Stearns being the most prominent example. Banks rapidly became reluctant to rollover short-term credits, and short-term interest rate spreads widened sharply in America and in Europe: the LIBOR-OIS spread increased from effectively zero to 85 basis points by mid-September.[15] The Federal Reserve and European Central Bank (ECB) acted promptly to free up the market. The Fed reduced its discount rate by 100 basis points in two steps in August and September, relaxed borrowing terms at the discount window, and temporarily suspended restrictions on the amount banks could lend to brokerage companies. The ECB injected short-term liquidity but held interest rates unchanged.

The most dramatic effect of the August freeze was felt in the UK. Northern Rock, a former mutual building society, had floated in 1997 and subsequently expanded aggressively using the originate and securitise model. Unlike US mortgage brokers, Northern Rock was still a mortgage bank as it maintained a retail deposit base and did hold mortgages on its own books, but the ratio of mortgage loans to relatively stable retail deposits was far higher than for other UK mortgage lenders. Specialised mortgage brokers could halt originations in the face of a credit squeeze or freeze, but Northern Rock relied on continuously rolling over its money market borrowings to finance a substantial component of its assets. In August, during the credit freeze-up, there were little-publicised withdrawals of funds from Northern Rock by major institutions, effectively a run on the bank by informed depositors.[16] As rumours about the viability of the bank increased, Northern Rock turned to the Bank of England for support in the form of a special credit facility.

What happened next is still a matter of dispute. The Bank of England had adopted a markedly tougher stance than the Fed or ECB and declined to provide additional liquidity in the summer of 2007. Governor Mervyn King adopted a public 'no bailout' stance for any institution, arguing that adequate mechanisms existed to deal with instability and that the provision of special assistance would merely increase moral hazard to everyone's ultimate cost, a position he reiterated as late as 12 September.[17] The next day, the Bank of England was obliged to agree (publicly) to provide emergency funding to Northern Rock in the form of an injection of liquidity but this was already too late.[18] A full-scale run on Northern Rock began the next morning as retail depositors queued to withdraw their money, evidently unconvinced by the Bank's support or by the UK's deposit protection scheme which at that time only covered up to 90 per cent of UK £35 000. There was a pause over the weekend but the run continued on Monday morning, and late in the day the government guaranteed all deposits in Northern Rock. In February 2008 Northern Rock was taken into public ownership following several abortive efforts to find new owners. In evidence given later to the House of Commons, King argued that the Bank would in fact have been willing to provide substantial support to Northern Rock much earlier if it could have been done without publicity, along the lines of the 1973 'lifeboat' operation to support NatWest bank, but UK regulatory arrangements prevented this.

It was not immediately appreciated that the Chancellor's 17 September announcement effectively guaranteed *all* UK retail deposits, but the Treasury's accompanying statement made it clear that *any* UK bank which encountered similar difficulties to Northern Rock would be treated in exactly the same way.[19] A year later, Ireland was criticised for being the first EU country formally (and unilaterally) to guarantee all retail bank deposits (for two years), but the UK's much earlier decision essentially offered the same guarantee on a more open-ended basis for a very substantially larger deposit base.[20] It effectively superseded the UK's deposit protection system, and the decision in October 2008 to raise the deposit insurance limit to £50 000 was arguably pointless.[21] A further complication for UK depositors is that the degree of protection afforded depends on the number of separate registrations any bank holding company has with the FSA, with building societies permitted one only. Individuals may hold accounts at multiple institutions but, depending on the happenstance of registration, may be covered for any more-or-less random multiple of £50 000: in many cases exactly £50 000 and no more. The FSA has attempted to mitigate this issue by temporary rules which allow for separate protection up to £50 000 for funds held in a building society which has been merged during the crisis.[22] These rules are due to expire at the end of 2010 when new EU arrangements may be in the offing. At present, however, the UK's deposit insurance scheme fails any basic test of effectiveness or transparency.

THE LOSSES MOUNT: IN THE US . . .

The full scale of the problems facing the financial systems of the main industrial countries started to emerge more fully in late 2007, when Union Bank of Switzerland (UBS) reported a US$10 billion write-down of assets almost entirely due to losses in the sub-prime mortgage market.[23] Losses on this scale by a large international bank without any US retail base provided the first indication that the securitisation process had spread sub-prime risks much wider than to the immediate brokers and lenders who had already hit problems, and that spreading these risks had not thereby reduced them, as a simple-minded application of portfolio theory might suggest. UBS's fourth quarter loss was followed by Citibank's $18.1 billion write-down, an amount equal to the gross domestic product (GDP) of a mid-sized African country.[24]

Throughout 2008, attention shifted successively from one group of institutions to another as the impact of the initial write-downs and defaults spread through the whole financial system, first in the US and then to other industrial countries. The authorities' response was to support a series of ad hoc rescues. Bear Stearns, the investment bank that devised and came to specialise in MBSs, failed early in the year and was taken over by JPMorgan Chase. The takeover was underwritten by the Fed which provided a $29 billion guarantee in respect of Bear's less liquid assets: a written put option, part of whose value was promptly expropriated by Bear shareholders.[25] The Fed's actions were driven particularly by fear of the implications for counterparties in the CDO markets. Without rescue, there appeared to be a real possibility that Bear's entire portfolio would have to be liquidated with little likelihood that a meaningful sum could be raised from a fire-sale.[26]

Next to fall were the major US mortgage lenders: IndyMac, Fannie Mae and Freddie Mac.[27] IndyMac was taken over by the Federal Deposit Insurance Corporation in July and in September, in the then largest bailout in US history, Fannie Mae and Freddie Mac were taken into public ownership to be run by the Federal Housing Finance Agency.[28] One week later Lehman Brothers filed for bankruptcy. Last-minute attempts to sell Lehman to Bank of America or Barclays failed, but almost simultaneously, Bank of America was pressured by the US authorities into rescuing Merrill Lynch.[29] Merrill reported an annual loss of $19.2 billion in the summer and, like Lehman Brothers, effectively imploded as the scale of its bad debts and counterparty obligations mushroomed.[30] The problems at all these institutions varied in detail but by this time were familiar in outline: accumulating losses on repackaged mortgages and increasing counterparty failures following the bankruptcies, liquidations and restructurings that had already occurred, all implying a severe erosion of the bank's capital, exacerbated at the outset by an inadequate capital base in relation to the true level of potential liabilities. This created a loss of confidence reflected in a collapsing share price, followed by a more direct loss of confidence in the ability of a bank to borrow or roll over money on a day-to-day basis. For the investment banks, a further complication was the pyramid of commitments, contingent liabilities and counterparty risks, which made it virtually impossible to assess the true size of their liabilities.

The collapse in the value of MBSs and the widening impact of the failures among mortgage banks led next to the companies that specialised in guaranteeing credit. This business took several forms. Monoline bond insurers provide credit guarantees for municipal bonds and their business had expanded to include MBSs. The guarantee provides insurance against default and is therefore only effective if the credit rating and solvency of the insurer are not in doubt.[31] Bond insurers suffered credit downgrades during 2008, and bonds were increasingly priced as if uninsured. The Monolines survived, but it was the related business of credit default swaps (CDSs) that brought about the largest single failure in the whole tsunami: that of the general insurer, AIG. For most practical purposes a CDS is simply a generalised form of default insurance. However, whereas bond insurance is a specialised and regulated business, the CDS market was (and is) largely unregulated and it developed to cover a wide range of securities, including insurance against company bankruptcies. AIG became the dominant actor in a wide range of CDSs, especially in the sub-prime mortgage market. Its collapse followed a familiar pattern: the share price fell sharply in 2008; it lost $13 billion in the first six months of 2008; and on 16 September following the lowering of its credit rating, AIG was unable to borrow to post required collateral. Like Fannie and Freddie, AIG was effectively nationalised, with the US government taking an 80 per cent stake in the company. In addition, the Fed provided a credit line totalling $122.8 billion, much of which had to be used almost immediately as AIG posted a full-year loss of almost $100 billion but, like Bear Stearns, much of the put value was expropriated by the shareholders and management of AIG's creditors (Veronesi and Zingales, 2009).[32]

. . . AND IN THE UK, AND ELSEWHERE

In the UK, the run on Northern Rock was the first concrete manifestation of the crisis, but it was not long before the major banks had to bolster their capital. In April 2008, Royal Bank of Scotland (RBS) raised £12 billion following completion of its controversial takeover of Dutch bank ABN Amro with Fortis and Santander, and a subsequent asset write-down of £5.9 billion.[33] Barclays raised £4.5 billion in a placement with two sovereign wealth funds, and HBOS sought to raise £4 billion but almost the entire issue was left with the underwriters as the share price fell below the issue price.[34,35] As the UK's largest mortgage bank, HBOS was subject to periodic rumours about its financial stability throughout 2008. Shortly after the collapse of Lehman, but not obviously connected except by rumour, HBOS's share price began fluctuating wildly and on the same day, it was announced that Lloyds would take over HBOS, with the government waiving competition rules to make it possible: the combined entity would control almost 30 per cent of the UK mortgage market. Despite half-hearted public denials, it is generally recognised that Lloyds, as the only domestic bank not then requiring further capital, was pressured by the government to rescue HBOS. Eric Daniels, Lloyds' CEO, acknowledged later that the deal had been conducted in haste and that HBOS's balance sheet was in substantially worse condition than was believed at the time.[36] HBOS eventually reported a net loss of £11 billion in 2008. The UK's largest building society, Nationwide, fared much better as it had largely avoided the originate and securitise model. It was the government's rescue agent of first choice for other building societies, taking control of Derbyshire and Cheshire in September and Dunfermline early in 2009.

In other European countries the story was much the same. For example, in May 2008 UBS raised $15.5 billion in a rights issue. Fortis collapsed under the weight of its share in the ABN takeover; its Dutch part was taken over by the Dutch government, the rest being liquidated and sold. Santander fared better, largely because it sold on its share of the investment banking operations of ABN almost immediately. It was able to purchase Alliance and Leicester Building Society and the solvent parts of Bradford and Bingley after the latter had been nationalised. The Franco-Belgian bank Dexia was bailed out in September by a €6.4 billion capital injection by the Belgian, French and Luxembourg governments. Deutsche Bank reported a fourth quarter loss of €5 billion; and in October, the German government formed a consortium with a group of private banks to rescue Hypo Real Estate, a commercial property and bank holding company, by providing a credit line of €50 billion. One year later Hypo was nationalised.

RECAPITALISATION AND FISCAL BOOST

The impact of these events was not confined to the credit markets. Industrial production in the last six months of 2008 virtually collapsed, with every industrial economy recording the sharpest declines since records began (Figure 2.2). Ironically, it was the leading exporters, Germany and Japan, that were harder hit than the USA and UK, whose Anglo-Saxon capitalism many blamed for the disaster.

In October 2008, governments of most industrial countries made a more-or-less co-ordinated effort to halt the seemingly inexorable slide into financial collapse and a worldwide depression. The US passed the Troubled Assets Relief Programme (TARP) which allowed for the Treasury to purchase up to $700 billion of troubled assets and provided a further $400 billion of support for Fannie Mae and Freddie Mac.[37] By January 2010 some $574 billion had been committed to 828 companies (including automobile companies), and $334 billion was actually outstanding (net of repayments). Of this, ten companies had been paid a total of $373 billion, an amount approximately equivalent to 16 per cent of the UK's 2008 GDP, with AIG being by some way the largest recipient.[38] This support was followed early in 2009 by a fiscal injection worth $787 billion, on top of a $168 billion package passed by the Bush administration in February 2008.[39] Monetary policy was eased with aggressive cuts in the

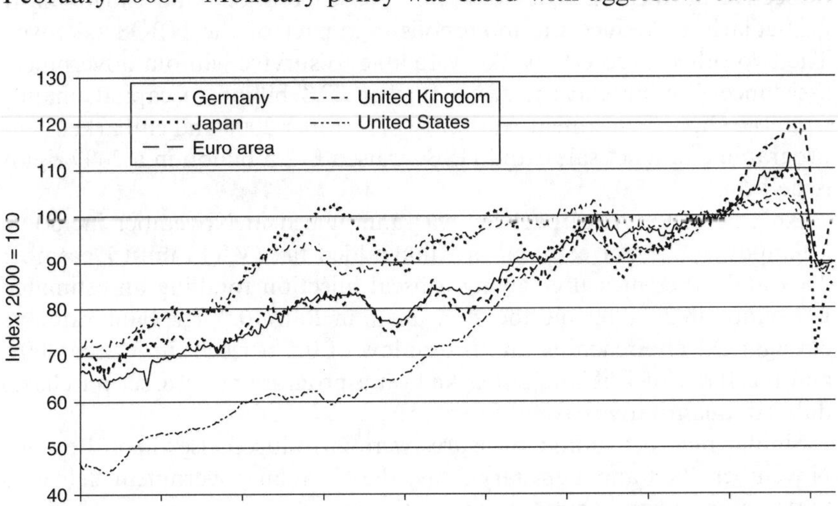

Source: OECD.

Figure 2.2 OECD: industrial production 1981–2009

discount rate which reached 0.5 per cent in December 2008, and the Fed embarked on a programme of buying a range of non-traditional assets from the banking system.

In the UK, banks were offered a recapitalisation package. RBS, which reported a UK record £24 billion loss in 2008, and Lloyds-TSB-HBOS accepted a capital increase totalling £37 billion in the form of rights issues which were underwritten and almost fully paid by the Treasury.[40] A further £350 billion was provided in Treasury loan guarantees and facilities under the Bank of England's liquidity scheme which was introduced to broaden the range of assets acceptable to the Bank in repurchase agreements.[41] Early in 2009 the government introduced a toxic assets insurance scheme in an effort to ring-fence the problematic parts of the banks' balance sheets. This was accompanied by a series of measures by both banks including asset sales and further capital injections: by the Treasury in the case of RBS, and by a combination of the Treasury and the private sector in the case of Lloyds. RBS obtained £44 billion more capital and Lloyds £25 billion.[42] By the end of 2009, the UK government owned 84 per cent of RBS and 43.4 per cent of Lloyds but, by its November rights issue, Lloyds had raised enough new capital to release the combined group from the government's asset insurance scheme and its associated costs.[43] RBS and Lloyds are expected to divest themselves of significant parts of their respective businesses: RBS to shore up its operations and Lloyds more particularly to reduce the monopolistic impact of the HBOS takeover. The two other large UK banks were able to survive without government assistance, but Barclays raised a further £7.3 billion in capital, mainly from the Qatar Investment Authority in October 2008 and embarked on a programme of asset sales, and HSBC raised £12.5 billion in a 2009 rights issue.[44,45]

An emergency fiscal package was announced in November including a temporary 2.5 per cent cut in value added tax (VAT) until December 2009 and other measures giving a fiscal injection totalling an estimated £41 billion in 2008/09 and the same again in 2009/10.[46] The bank rate was cut aggressively, reaching an historic low of 0.5 per cent in March 2009, and the Bank of England embarked on a programme of asset purchases dubbed 'quantitative easing'.[47]

Similar macroeconomic measures were introduced elsewhere. Between November 2008 and February 2009, the German government delivered three separate fiscal packages amounting to a total injection worth about €70 billion. between 2008 and 2010.[48] Japan introduced two supplementary budgets in October 2008 to provide a total boost of Y6800 billion (about $70 billion) and a further stimulus worth $81 billion in December for the 2009/10 tax year.[49]

ISSUES

The IMF has estimated that worldwide financial sector write-downs produced by this tsunami will total some $4 trillion.[50] This is a figure which is simply unimaginable to most people. Among the many questions to be answered, two are concerned with basic history: why did it start; and how did it get so large? There is obviously a vast range of other issues, especially the lessons to be learnt, and many of these are discussed elsewhere in this volume.

Some commentators have blamed policy failures for permitting a problem to escalate into a disaster of unprecedented proportions. It is generally agreed that Lehman Brothers' bankruptcy marked the point at which massive state intervention became inevitable, although the intervention did not finally occur until three weeks later. It has been argued that Lehman's bankruptcy could and should have been avoided, either by nationalising the bank or through a takeover by Bank of America or Barclays, the latter subsequently purchasing the rump of Lehman's US investment banking operations.[51] Henry Paulson, the then US Treasury Secretary later claimed that Lehman's could have been taken over by Barclays and later problems avoided were it not for the non-co-operation of the UK government.[52]

Paulson's claims appear to be largely an effort at self-justification, and others have taken a more realistic view.[53] First, it is clear that time was simply too short for proper due diligence to be carried out.[54] Given its subsequent problems with Merrill Lynch it is scarcely conceivable that Bank of America could have taken on both institutions, and the experiences of RBS with ABN, and Lloyds with HBOS suggest that any takeover ran the risk of fatally contaminating a second institution rather than providing for an orderly winding up of one. There is little reason to doubt that a full Barclays takeover of Lehman would have forced the bank into the arms of UK taxpayers along with RBS and Lloyds, with the consequent economic and political fallout: a substantial increase in the UK's rescue obligations and UK taxpayers bailing out a major American bank. From the viewpoint of the Fed, Merrill was much easier to save because its core business was still based on a large and solvent domestic retail brokerage operation, much as HBOS retained its retail deposit-taking business. Secondly, the alternative of the public ownership of a US investment bank would surely have produced political fallout in the US. This was not an issue for Fannie Mae and Freddie Mac as the latter were perceived as part of 'Main Street', whereas Lehman Brothers were equally evidently on 'Wall Street'. Finally, and perhaps most importantly, Lehman Brothers International constituted more than half the firm's business and it was doubtful whether any institution could either identify the size of its liabilities in the time available or take this operation over, even if it wanted to; and a takeover of the domestic bank alone was equally difficult given the obscure and interlocking nature of Lehman's assets and obligations, much of which emerged only gradually in the liquidation.

The sheer difficulty of dealing with international banks has been brought into sharp relief by the liquidation of Lehman's international operations. This is complicated by the fact that each part of the business in a different country has to be liquidated separately by different liquidators under different regulations. In some cases national law explicitly prohibits co-operation between liquidators who in any case typically have legal obligations which may be in conflict when crossing national boundaries. Given the uncertainty about the timing and amount of any payoff, Lehman's creditors' were effectively frozen indefinitely, with further knock-on effects in the rest of the financial system.[55]

Parallel problems within the EU have been brought out by the collapse of Iceland's banks. Icelandic banks enjoy the EU financial passport which permits financial services firms to operate across Member States while being regulated from their home country (normally an EU member), and Iceland adheres to EU deposit insurance regulations. The failure of most Icelandic banks and corresponding doubts about Iceland's willingness, and certainly its ability, to provide compensation to UK (and Dutch) retail depositors led the UK government controversially to use anti-terror legislation to freeze the assets of Landsbanki and related funds of the central bank and government of Iceland. At the time of writing, the dispute over responsibility for the banks' liabilities is unresolved: a proposal agreed by the three governments was overwhelmingly rejected by Icelandic voters in a referendum following the President's decision not to sign the required legislation amid reasonable concerns about its cost to Iceland. The dispute exposes serious deficiencies in EU cross-border regulatory arrangements, especially deposit insurance.

In February 2009, the UK passed a new Banking Act whose consideration predates the tsunami but whose content is supposed to reflect some of the lessons. The Act includes a new and much needed 'Special Resolution Regime' for winding up banks. However, this Act does not deal adequately with cross-border groups, and indeed could not do so without international agreement.[56] The brute fact is that international law and regulations currently provide absolutely *no* satisfactory or agreed mechanisms for the orderly and rapid winding up of a complex international bank, or for assured compensation of retail depositors in banks that are domiciled in another jurisdiction, even within the confines of the EU.

As to whether the crisis would have been less severe if Lehman Brothers had been rescued, the scale of the problems in the financial sector were already so acute that it is extremely difficult to believe that a rescue would simply have stopped subsequent developments in their tracks, including for example the collapse of banks like HBOS. Fannie Mae and Freddie Mac were taken into public ownership a week *before* Lehman Brothers declared bankruptcy, and the run on Northern Rock was a full year earlier. The financial system was saved not by decisions to wind up or rescue individual banks but by the comprehensive, effectively unlimited, and more-or-less co-ordinated guarantees provided by governments to their whole banking systems in all the affected countries in October 2008, supported by an unprecedented injection of cash through fiscal and monetary policy. To assert that this would all have been unnecessary if only Lehmans had been sold to Barclays, or any other, appears wilfully naive, more particularly in retrospect.[57] It needs to be underlined forcefully that the banks that remained standing did so, not through the heroics of their management, as is now bizarrely being claimed by some, but because of the put option provided by governments worldwide, a significant proportion of the value of which was promptly expropriated by management and shareholders of surviving banks (Veronesi and Zingales, 2009).[58,59]

Turning finally to the origins of the tsunami, economists have been obliged to engage in some navel-gazing as commentators have rushed to praise or condemn the subject and its practitioners for their influence, especially of efficient markets theory on bank behaviour.[60] Efficient markets theory suggests *inter alia* that asset prices are difficult, if not impossible to forecast, and to this extent it could be argued that the theory was validated, as few observers foresaw the scale of the problems or the extent of the rescue required, certainly Chuck Prince was not alone in his hubris in the early summer of 2007. On the other hand it is surely incorrect to claim as does Robert Lucas that: 'Until the Lehman failure the recession was pretty typical of the modest downturns of the post-war period.'[61] By this time, we had had the first UK bank run for 140 years, unusually high bankruptcy rates among US mortgage lenders, and the nationalisation of Fannie and Freddie prefigured early in July.[62,63]

In analysing derivatives disasters in the 1990s Miller argued that: 'What we really needed . . . was not more regulation of derivatives, but more understanding by top management of how to manage risk (and less hubris on the part of some corporate (and municipal) treasurers convinced they could forecast interest rates)'. Miller's central thesis was that losses in derivatives were largely redistributive in nature and so to this extent welfare neutral for the economy as a whole (Miller, 1996). Indeed, Miller argued for less regulation, although he was a long-time advocate of separating the money transmission from the lending functions of banks (Miller, 1995). However, even though headline losses may not represent true social costs, and some gains and losses may be redistributive in a purely accounting sense, it is hard to see how they cancel out in any useful economic sense. Most large-scale losses have multiplier-type consequences for the real economy which are unlikely to be offset. Lost output is a social loss, not a redistribution. One of the more direct consequences of recent bank losses is the requirement to rebuild capital. This can only be done by a combination of new capital subscriptions and higher interest margins. These divert scarce capital from other uses and increase the costs of capital and of intermediation in the economy as a whole: this unambiguously represents a consequential social loss.

In reviewing the succession of extraordinary losses resulting from transactions in complex securities over the last two decades, the two most persistent factors appear to be complexity and competence: far too much of the one and far too little of the other. Those involved have invariably argued, *ex post*, that the positions which ultimately led to the catastrophe were simply too complex to understand. One of the earliest such cases was Proctor and Gamble (P&G) versus Bankers' Trust in 1994–96, in which P&G sued Bankers Trust to recover approximately £200 million lost in interest rate swaps sold to them by the bank. P&G fought its case against Bankers' Trust not as a multinational corporation who had failed to exercise due diligence before entering a complex financial transaction, but as an innocent householder would claim she had been mis-sold an endowment mortgage by a group of spivs. Notwithstanding this positioning, P&G was essentially successful in all relevant details of the case.[64] UBS CEO Marcel Ospel's explanation for the bank's 2008 $10 billion write-down was that the bank's risk and finance unit did not understand the bank's sub-prime mortgage positions.[65] Nicola Horlick notoriously blamed the US Securities and Exchange Commission for her own admitted failure to carry out any kind of due diligence on the biggest Ponzi scheme of all: the Madoff funds.[66]

Banking and finance are now perceived as populated by highly-trained and mathematically sophisticated technicians. However, these technicians represent a tiny minority of total employment in finance.[67] Even among the technicians themselves, there seems to be astonishingly little appreciation of the differences between the laws of physics and the 'laws' of economics, pointed out *inter alia* by Wilmott (2000). Those who are not technicians invariably have little perception of what is involved in pricing straightforward securities, but nevertheless are employed in marketing them. Miller's claim that '. . .our financial markets and institutions are fully capable of recognizing and rejecting "toxic waste" without intervention by government regulators' (Miller 1996) appears simply to be false, and false on a grand scale. Furthermore, unlike the application of physical laws, applications of finance invariably take place in settings where severe asymmetric information is endemic. When this is combined with the potential for immense financial reward, the incentive for fraud can become overwhelming, especially when the borderline between fraud and honest error is practically impossible to draw, and is at best poorly understood either by insiders or outsiders. The carefully-worded examiner's report on Lehman's is nevertheless damning in its indictment of the integrity of Lehman's senior management: '. . . certain Lehman officers breached their fiduciary duties to Lehman and its shareholders by causing the company to file deficient and materially misleading financial statements, thereby exposing the company to potential liability. . .' (Valukas, 2010: 963) A financial system which fosters fraud and incompetence cannot be described as efficient. Furthermore, economists should not seek to escape direct consideration of the broad integrity of the system by undue resort to value-neutral terms such as rent-seeking.

At the point at which consumers encounter the financial system, the problems of complexity and competence recur. Since even a standard repayment mortgage and certainly most structured mortgage and savings plans sold to retail investors include an option component, which the over-the-counter retailer does not understand, the households at whom they are directed are never likely to be able to make more than a rough and poorly-informed guess at their true cost or value. More financial education would undoubtedly improve consumer awareness, but no amount of education is likely to limit significantly the risk of fraud and mis-selling of the many complex products which are routinely marketed to households.[68] Nor can we rely on institutions being careful to preserve their reputation for probity. The key financial products which play a major role in determining the lifetime well-being of most households are purchased once (pension rights) or a few times (mortgages) in a lifetime. If a reputation turns bad, it is far too late to return or replace the product. Households can never have any practical means of checking in detail the risks involved in these kinds of investments.

Finally, while we can sympathise with central banks and regulators who struggled to keep the system afloat in 2007–08 by encouraging the merger of failing institutions with those that had the good fortune to be among the upright dominoes, this strategy has produced fewer, larger institutions. Arguably, there are organisational diseconomies of scale in finance: complexity, conflicts of interest and monitoring problems all grow as the institution grows. Indeed it would seem that even the banks themselves have recognised some of this, although their recommendation is for an internally-financed insurance fund to shore up banks that are 'too big to fail'.[69] This misses the point completely: if a bank is too big to fail, it is too big, and should be broken up.

Without substantial reforms in all areas of finance, the long-term outlook for all of us is bleak. Next time I fear it will indeed be different, but only in being still larger, more costly and more intractable. To mix some metaphors: the music will stop and the orchestra will be inundated.

NOTES

1. The first use of the term 'financial tsunami' appears to be in a 2005 commentary by George Mullen in the *San Diego Union Tribune* on 9 June 2005, but it has come into much wider use since about November 2007.
2. Michiyo Nakamoto and David Wighton in the *Financial Times*, 9 July 2007.
3. David Wighton and Ben White in the *Financial Times*, 5 November 2007.
4. Greg Farrell and Henry Sender in the *Financial Times*, 24 November 2008.
5. The decline in US interest rates in 2001 was larger in magnitude than in 2008, although the 2008 cuts took place over a shorter period.
6. Carol Leonnig in the *Washington Post*, 10 June 2008; and Steven Holmes in the *New York Times*, 30 September 1999.
7. Bond, Musto and Yilmaz (2008).
8. See, for example, Alex Berensen in the *New York Times*, 7 August 2003.
9. Mathis, McAndrews, and Rochet (2009).
10. See, for example, Berndt and Gupta (2009).
11. Julie Creswell in the *New York Times*, 2 April 2007.
12. Mara Hovanesian in *Business Week*, 24 November 2008.
13. Associated Press in the *New York Times*, 7 August 2007.
14. E. Scott Reckard and Andrea Chang, in the *Los Angeles Times*, 18 August 2007; and Tom Petruno, in the *Los Angeles Times*, 25 August 2007.
15. LIBOR is the London Interbank Offer Rate for outright short-term interbank loans. OIS is the Overnight Indexed Swap rate; that is the rate for a swap between a loan for a specific term and a sequence of overnight loans for the same term. The crucial difference between LIBOR and OIS at any given maturity is that the latter does not involve any capital risk. The LIBOR-OIS differential is therefore a possible measure of the perceived credit risk in loans of that maturity, and is now commonly used as an index of bank distress.
16. Eisenbeis and Kaufman (2009), and Shin (2009).
17. Chris Giles and Scheherazade Daneshkhu in the *Financial Times*, 13 September 2007.
18. Peter Thal Larsen and Neil Hume in the *Financial Times*, 14 September 2007.
19. Peter Thal Larsen, Chris Giles and George Parker in the *Financial Times*, 18 September 2007.
20. John Murray-Brown and Neil Dennis in the *Financial Times*, 30 September 2008.
21. Patrick Hosking in *The Times Online*, 3 October 2008.
22. Moneymadeclear, Financial Services Authority, 2010.
23. Haig Simonian and Chris Hughes in the *Financial Times*, 10 December 2007.
24. For example, according to the World Bank (2009), Ghana's 2008 GDP was \$16.1 billion.
25. Bear Stearns traded at a high of \$172 a share in January 2007. Bear management initially agreed to be bought by JPMorgan for just \$2 a share, but following a shareholder outcry and the provision of Fed assistance, JPMorgan raised its price to \$10 a share. JPMorgan press release, 24 March 2008.
26. Chris Reiter, in *Reuters*, 24 March 2009.

27. IndyMac: Independent National Mortgage Corporation, formerly an offshoot of Countrywide with no connection to the US government. Fannie Mae: Federal National Mortgage Association; Freddie Mac: Federal Home Loan Mortgage Corporation. Fannie Mae was established in the 1930s as a government-sponsored agency to help low-income families buy homes. It was privatised in 1968 and Freddie Mac was set up in 1970 partly to provide competition to Fannie Mae. Although private companies from this time, their relationship with the US government remained ambiguous, and the severity of their problems stemmed in part from increased lending to low-income families following intermittent government instruction and suasion, beginning with the 1977 Community Reinvestment Act and reinforced in the 1990s.
28. Steven Holmes in the *New York Times*, 30 September 1999.
29. Larry Elliott and Jill Treanor in *The Guardian*, 3 September 2009.
30. Francesco Guerrera, Ben White and Krishna Guha, in the *Financial Times*, 18 July 2008.
31. *The Economist*, 26 July 2007.
32. Catherine Boyle and Elizabeth Judge in *The Times Online* 2 March 2009.
33. Maggie Urry in the *Financial Times*, 9 June 2008.
34. China Development Bank and Qatar Investment Authority; Amanda Vermeulen in the *Financial Times*, 18 July 2008.
35. Jane Croft in the *Financial Times*, 21 July 2008.
36. George Parker and Jane Croft in the *Financial Times*, 11 February 2009.
37. Nothwehr (2008).
38. At http://bailout.propublica.org/main/list/index taxpayers can discover the use of their money day by day.
39. Alan Beattie in the *Financial Times*, 11 February 2009.
40. Jill Treanor in *The Guardian*, 26 February 2009.
41. Peter Thal Larsen and George Parker in the *Financial Times*, 9 October 2008.
42. RBS obtained £19 billion following its participation in the toxic assets insurance scheme in March 2009 (Royal Bank of Scotland press release, 26 February 2009). The Treasury subscribed a further £25 billion in November together with £8 billion in a form of contingent equity (Patrick Jenkins and George Parker in the *Financial Times*, 3 November 2009). Lloyds raised £4 billion in an open offer in June 2009 and a further £21 billion in November in a rights-cum-convertibles issue (Lina Saigol, George Parker and Peter Thal Larsen in the *Financial Times*, 17 May 2009).
43. Jill Treanor in *The Guardian*, 2 November 2009.
44. Peter Thal Larsen in the *Financial Times*, 1 November 2008.
45. Bryce Elder and Neil Hume in the *Financial Times*, 12 March 2009.
46. Chris Giles and George Parker in the *Financial Times*, 25 November 2008.
47. George Parker and Norma Cohen in the *Financial Times*, 30 January 2009
48. Bertrand Benoit in the *Financial Times*, 5 November 2008 and 10 December 2008; and *Spiegel Online*, 13 February 2009.
49. Michiyo Nakamoto in the *Financial Times*, 31 October 2008; and Mure Dickie in the *Financial Times*, 8 December 2009.
50. IMF (2009). $1 trillion had been written down by April 2009, and almost half the exposure is outside the US.
51. Speech by Lorenzo Bini Smaghi, member of the ECB Executive Board, in Milan, 20 October 2008.
52. Larry Elliott and Jill Treanor in *The Guardian*, 3 September 2009; and 'The financial crisis, through Paulson's eyes', *New York Times Online*, 1 February 2010.
53. Cf Reinhart and Rogoff (2009), and McDonald and Robinson (2009).
54. Speech by Ben Bernanke reported in the *Wall Street Journal*, 15 October 2008.
55. Anousha Sakoui and Jennifer Hughes in the *Financial Times*, 13 September 2009; and Jennifer Hughes in the *Financial Times*, 26 May 2009.
56. Brierley (2009).
57. Reinhart and Rogoff (2009).
58. Daniel Gross in *Newsweek*, 19 October 2009.

59. Veronesi and Zingales (2009).
60. See the commentaries in *The Economist*, 16 July 2009.
61. Lucas in *The Economist*, 8 August 2009; responding to the commentaries in *The Economist* of 16 July.
62. Yalman Onaran in *Bloomberg.com*, 24 March 2008.
63. Charles Duhigg, in *New York Times Online*, 11 July 2008.
64. Forster (1996) and Wilmott (2000).
65. Chris Hughes and Haig Simonian, in the *Financial Times*, 12 December 2007.
66. Jasper Gerard in the *Daily Telegraph*, 8 May 2009; and John Kay in the *Financial Times*, 17 December 2008.
67. US Bureau of Labour Statistics (2009).
68. An example of this wishful approach is Bond, Musto and Yilmaz (2006, 2008) who argue that education is the best way to eliminate fraud in the sub-prime mortgage market.
69. Patrick Jenkins and Tom Braithwaite in the *Financial Times*, 30 January 2010; and John Kay in the *Financial Times*, 3 February 2010.

REFERENCES

Berndt, A. and A. Gupta (2009), 'Moral hazard and adverse selection in the originate-to-distribute model of bank credit', *Journal of Monetary Economics*, **56**: 725–43.

Bond, P., D. Musto and B. Yilmaz (2008), 'Victimizing the borrowers: predatory lending's role in the subprime mortgage crisis', *Knowledge@Wharton*, 20 February accessed 2 January 2010 at http://knowledge.wharton.upenn.edu/article.cfm?articleid=1901.

Bond, P., D. Musto and B. Yilmaz (2006), 'Predatory lending in a rational world', Federal Reserve Bank of Philadelphia working paper 06-2.

Brierley, P. (2009), 'The UK Special Resolution Regime for failing banks in an international context', Bank of England, Financial Stability Paper no. 5, July.

Eisenbeis, R.A. and G.G. Kaufman (2009), 'Lessons from the demise of the UK's Northern Rock and the US's Countrywide and IndyMac', in F. Bruni, D.T. Llewellyn (eds), *The Failure of Northern Rock, A Multidimensional Case Study*, SUERF Studies, 2009/1, pp. 73–96.

Financial Services Authority (2010), 'Moneymadeclear: UK banking and savings groups' accessed 2 January 2010 at www.moneymadeclear.fsa.gov.uk/about_the_fsa/compensation/uk_groups.html.

Forster, D.M. (1996), 'Derivatives: Procter and Gamble v Bankers Trust – an analysis of the holdings and their potential impact, *Journal of International Banking and Financial Law*, July–August: 320–25.

International Monetary Fund (IMF) (2009), *Global Financial Stability Report*, April, Washington, DC: IMF.

Lucas, R.E. (2009), 'In defence of the dismal science', *The Economist*, 8 August.

Mathis, J., J. McAndrews and J.C. Rochet (2009), 'Rating the raters: are reputation concerns powerful enough to discipline rating agencies?', *Journal of Monetary Economics*, **56**: 657–74.

McDonald, L.G. and P. Robinson (2009), *A Colossal Failure of Common Sense: The Inside Story of the Collapse of Lehman Brothers*, New York: Crown Business, Ebury Press.

Miller, M.H. (1995), 'Do the M & M propositions apply to banks?', *Journal of Banking and Finance*, **19**: 483–89.

Miller, M.H. (1996), 'The social costs of some recent derivatives disasters', *Pacific-Basin Finance Journal*, **4**: 113–27.

Nothwehr, E. (2008), 'Emergency Economic Stabilization Act of 2008', University of Iowa Center for International Finance and Development, December, accessed 2 January 2010 at www.uiowa.edu/ifdebook/issues/bailouts/eesa.shtml.

Pro-Publica (2010), *Eye on the Bailout*, accessed 29 January 2010 at http://bailout.propublica.org/main/list/index.

Reinhart, C.M. and K. Rogoff (2009), *This Time is Different: Eight Centuries of Financial Folly*, Princeton, NJ: Princeton University Press.

Shin, H.S. (2009), 'Reflections on Northern Rock, the bank run that heralded the global financial crisis', *Journal of Economic Perspectives*, **23**(1): 101–19.

US Bureau of Labour Statistics (2009),'National employment matrix, occupational employment by industry, 2008', Table 1.9, accessed 2 January 2010 at http://www.bls.gov/emp/ep_table_109.htm.

Valukas, A. (2010), *Report of Anton R. Valukas, Examiner to the United States Bankruptcy Court, Second District of New York In re Lehman Brothers Holdings Inc., et al., Debtors*, Chapter 11, Case No. 08-13555 (JMP), Vol. 3, Jenner & Block LLP.

Veronesi, P. and L. Zingales (2009), 'Paulson's gift', University of Chicago working paper, October.

Wilmott, P. (2000), 'The use, misuse and abuse of mathematics in finance', pp. 63–73, accessed 2 January 2010 at www.jstor.org/stable/2666776.

World Bank (2009), World Development Indicators Database, 7 October, accessed 2 January 2010 at http://siteresources.worldbank.org/DATASTATISTICS/Resources/GDP.pdf.

3. An emerging markets perspective on the recent crisis

Geoffrey Dennis[1,2]

'A GOOD CRISIS'

The global economy is likely to suffer its worst downturn of the post-war period in 2009 with, on current Citigroup estimates, real global GDP contracting by 2.5–3 per cent. World trade is also likely to fall sharply with the deviation of global exports from trend in 2009 likely to be the most severe by far since 1945.

This has been (and remains) a severe financial and economic crisis of the *developed world*. Beginning with the first hint of the sub-prime crisis in the US in early 2007, the current episode has led to the collapse of major US investment banks (Bear Stearns in March 2008 and Lehman Brothers in September 2008), the complete restructuring of the financial system in the US (and elsewhere, such as the UK) and has culminated in the worst global recession since the 1930s.

And yet, the emerging markets have held up relatively well during this crisis, despite its depth and longevity. Most powerfully, with global emerging markets (GEMs) as a group still expected to grow in 2009 (albeit very slowly), even as the global economy contracts sharply, GEMs are expected to account for more than 100 per cent of global growth in 2009 for the first time ever; we have not been able to find a year previously when the emerging markets have shown positive growth while the global economy as a whole (and, therefore, developed economies) has contracted. Citi's forecast is that industrialized world GDP will contract by around 4 per cent in 2009.

To be sure, this positive growth outlook for the emerging markets in 2009 is far from evenly spread. Our forecast for GEMs growth of around 0.5 per cent in 2009 is attributable to only a few, generally large, economies such as China (forecast to rattle along at over 8 per cent GDP growth in 2009) and India (close to 7 per cent)[3]. Whole regions are expected to contract in 2009, such as Latin America (−2.7 per cent) and Emerging Europe (−5.9 per cent). Therefore, all of the growth in emerging markets in 2009 year is expected to come from Asia (around 4.5 per cent).

However, the net result is the same. The concept of decoupling, so vaunted before the current downturn hit and then ridiculed as the global economy collapsed in the fourth quarter of 2008, has been, in the end, partly vindicated. This is best illustrated by posing a simple question. If observers had known two years ago that the group of developed economies was set to contract by around 4 per cent in 2009, what would have been the forecast for emerging market growth: −5 per cent, −7 per cent or even worse? In the event, positive growth of any magnitude for the emerging markets in 2009 should be viewed as both impressive and unprecedented.

So why is this and what has occurred to cause this relative decoupling as we will call it? The argument of this chapter is that this impressive relative performance of emerging market economies in this crisis should be put down to two main factors: (i) improved macro policies across the emerging world compared to the widespread practice of the 1990s; and (ii) specifically, the adoption in recent years by most emerging market countries of more flexible exchange rate regimes. These two factors should be set against the background of the ongoing globalization process which has opened up more and more emerging economies and has led to the development of robust domestic demand in many of them.

THE WORLD IS CHANGING

One of the most important changes underway in the world economy this century is the growing importance of emerging markets. Emerging market countries accounted for 74 per cent of world population in 2007, up from 71 per cent in 1980, and their importance in the world economy has increased, in particular, since the start of the last economic cycle in late 2002 and early 2003. If there is a defining label that should be attached to the (shorter than usual) economic cycle of 2002–07, it is globalization, as exemplified by the rising economic power and influence of the BRIC economies (Brazil, Russia, India and China) and by surging commodity prices. This growing importance of emerging markets, which we expect to continue, may be shown in a number of ways.

First, the share of emerging markets (as defined today) in global GDP has increased from 5 per cent in 1950, to 14 per cent in 1980 and 26 per cent in 2008; this share should rise slightly further to 27 per cent of global GDP in 2009. In their seminal work on the growth of the global economy (which introduced the concept of the BRICs), Wilson and Purushothaman (2003) predicted that the four BRIC economies, by 2050, would be 55 per cent *bigger* than the G6 economies combined (US, Japan, UK, Germany, France and Italy).

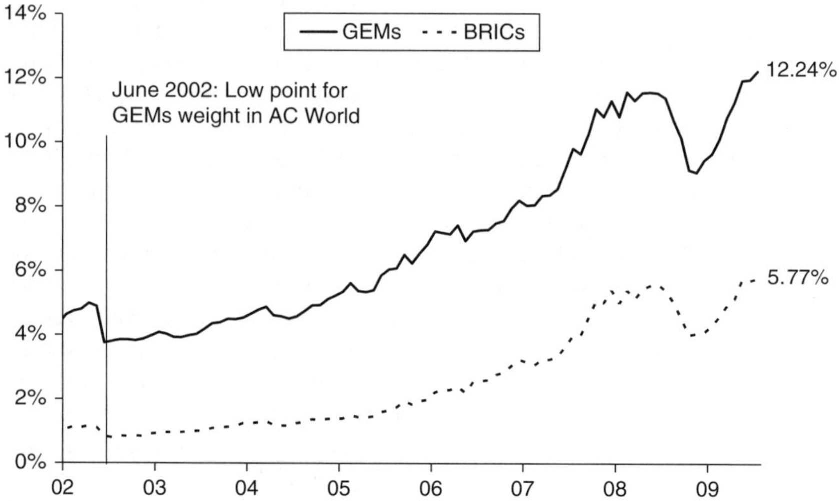

Source: MSCI, FactSet and Citi Investment Research & Analysis.

Figure 3.1 Weights of emerging markets in MSCI AC World (All-Country World) Index

Second, the weight of emerging markets in the MSCI All-Country World Index (AC World), the global equity investors' benchmark index has more than tripled from just 4 per cent at its trough as recently as mid-2002 to 12.2 per cent at the end of July 2009. Figure 3.1 shows, however, that this higher share of emerging markets has not occurred in a straight line. The initial peak of around 11.6 per cent in late 2007 was followed by a sharp pullback to just over 9 per cent during 2008, as emerging markets underperformed the developed markets during the global bear market in equities that began in late 2007. We argued, at the time, that this pullback was likely to be 'a correction in a secular rising trend', the latter being underpinned by the globalization process. The weight of the BRICs themselves in global equity market capitalization has shot up from around 1 per cent in mid-2002 to 5.8 per cent in July 2009. This increased weight of emerging markets in global market capitalization, over time, may be explained by: (i) better market performance; (ii) increased capital-raising activity in emerging markets; and (iii) increased float of existing equity issues.

Third, seven of the top 20 equity markets in the AC World index are now emerging markets: China, Brazil, Korea, Taiwan, South Africa, India and Russia (Table 3.1). These seven alone accounted for 9.5 per cent of

Table 3.1 Top 20 equity markets in MSCI AC World (2002, 2009)

Cycle Low (July 2002)					Current (July 2009)				
MSCI Free Float Mkt					MSCI Free Float Mkt				
	Market	Cap (US$, bn)	Weight (%)	# Co's		Market	Cap (US$, bn)	Weight (%)	# Co's
1	USA	7460.4	53.1	410	1	USA	8702.4	42.9	599
2	United Kingdom	1444.4	10.3	134	2	Japan	1913.1	9.4	347
3	Japan	1357.2	9.7	321	3	United Kingdom	1779.0	8.8	105
4	France	515.6	3.7	55	4	France	867.4	4.3	76
5	Switzerland	456.4	3.2	36	5	Canada	847.5	4.2	98
6	Germany	395.7	2.8	50	6	Germany	661.2	3.3	49
7	Netherlands	312.7	2.2	24	7	Switzerland	633.1	3.1	36
8	Canada	299.9	2.1	79	8	Australia	600.1	3.0	73
9	Australia	262.6	1.9	71	**9**	**China**	**465.7**	**2.3**	**103**
10	Italy	206.4	1.5	43	10	Spain	378.8	1.9	30
11	Spain	174.0	1.2	29	**11**	**Brazil**	**354.2**	**1.7**	**65**
12	**Korea**	**137.0**	**1.0**	**78**	**12**	**Korea**	**306.9**	**1.5**	**98**
13	Sweden	103.9	0.7	37	**13**	**Taiwan**	**294.7**	**1.5**	**121**
14	Finland	99.3	0.7	20	14	Italy	294.1	1.4	37
15	Hong Kong	97.5	0.7	28	15	Hong Kong	203.3	1.0	40
16	**Taiwan**	**86.9**	**0.6**	**91**	16	Sweden	202.6	1.0	30
17	**South Africa**	**76.6**	**0.5**	**38**	17	Netherlands	198.0	1.0	19
18	Belgium	57.7	0.4	17	**18**	**South Africa**	**180.0**	**0.9**	**44**
19	Singapore	53.5	0.4	35	**19**	**India**	**177.1**	**0.9**	**59**
20	Ireland	46.1	0.3	14	**20**	**Russia**	**137.1**	**0.7**	**27**
	Other	412.0	2.9	596			1084.5	5.3	340
	AC World	**14055.9**	**100.0**	**2206**		**AC World**	**20280.7**	**100.0**	**2396**

Source: MSCI, FactSet and Citi Investment Research & Analysis.

the AC World index at the end of June 2009. By contrast, going back just seven years to July 2002, only three emerging markets made it into the top 20 markets in AC World: Korea, Taiwan and South Africa, accounting for just 2.1 per cent of the global index at that time. In particular, note that in 2002 not one of the BRIC markets was in the top 20 list; now all four are, accounting for 5.8 per cent of the total index weight.

Fourth, the ratio of market capitalization to GDP (a conventional measure of the evolution of equity markets) is currently 35 per cent for

Table 3.2 Top 20 banks in the world (by market capitalization), July 2009

	Bank	Country	Market Cap (US$, bn)
1	IND & COMM BK-A	China	248.68
2	CHINA CONST BA-H	HK (China)	173.91
3	BANK OF CHINA-H	HK (China)	151.46
4	HSBC HLDGS PLC	United Kingdom	150.90
5	JPMORGAN CHASE	USA	142.23
6	WELLS FARGO & CO	USA	120.33
7	BANK OF AMERICA	USA	112.15
8	BANCO SANTANDER	Spain	101.72
9	GOLDMAN SACHS GP	USA	80.31
10	BNP PARIBAS	France	73.35
11	MITSUBISHI UFJ F	Japan	66.44
12	BANK OF COMMUN-H	HK (China)	62.88
13	ROYAL BANK OF CA	China	61.07
14	ITAU UNIBANCO BA	Brazil	59.74
15	BARCLAYS PLC	United Kingdom	56.70
16	CREDIT SUISS-REG	Switzerland	55.65
17	BBVA	Spain	50.63
18	CHINA MERCH BK-A	China	49.18
19	COMMONW BK AUSTR	Australia	47.34
20	WESTPAC BANKING	Australia	47.12

Source: Bloomberg and Citi Investment Research & Analysis.

global emerging markets and 61 per cent for MSCI AC World (dominated by developed markets). This gap shows the extent to which equity markets in emerging countries are still relatively underdeveloped versus those in developed economies, due to a more nascent equity culture, lower savings ratios and a smaller captive source of funds to invest in equities (such as pension funds). The data also imply that emerging equity markets should still grow considerably in size versus developed markets (so extending the trends above) over and above future growth of GDP.

Finally, if we go to the heart of the current crisis, the changing of the guard in favour of emerging markets is shown most dramatically in terms of the banking sector. Currently, as many as seven banks from the emerging world are in the top 20 list of global banks (Table 3.2), of which six are from China and one from Brazil. In fact, the biggest three banks in the world by this measure are currently Chinese, albeit two of the three are listed in Hong Kong. Moreover, of this top 20 list, just four banks are from the US, and two from the UK. By contrast, 20 years ago (in 1989), none of the top 20 banks in the world by market capitalization were from emerging markets, with 11 of the top 20 being from the US and four from the UK.[4] The only banks to retain their status as top 20 banks comparing 1989 with today are HSBC (UK), JPMorgan Chase, Bank of America, Goldman Sachs, and Barclays. This growing relative positioning of emerging market banks may, to be fair, be partly a cyclical phenomenon, which may decline slightly when developed economies recover.

NOT SUCH A SERIOUS CRISIS

This extraordinary situation, whereby the developed world has suffered by far its worst economic crisis since the 1930s and a major restructuring of its financial system, while emerging market economies have held up much better than usual at such a time (and than expected at the beginning of the crisis), means that, in our view, the 'emerging markets have had a good crisis'.

In practice, this means that the 2008–9 downturn in many emerging market economies has not been as serious as several of the crises seen over the past 20 years.[5] The course of events, and even the collapse of financial markets in many emerging market countries at a time of the worst global economic conditions since the 1930s, pale by comparison with many earlier crises in the emerging markets. Let us set out some examples from some of the major emerging markets.

Brazil: Crisis, What Crisis?

The Brazilian economy is, on Citigroup forecasts, set to contract by 1.5 per cent in 2009, which would be the worst year for the country since 1990. In the current downturn, Brazil has suffered a short, sharp recession, with GDP contracting significantly in 2008 Q4 and 2009 Q1. And yet, in Brazil itself, this feels like a much less severe crisis than the one which hit in late 2002, when there were serious fears that the soon-to-be-elected President Luiz Inacio 'Lula' da Silva would be forced to default on his country's massive (and expensive to finance) debt burden. This fear was reflected in far weaker financial markets than today. Spreads on Brazilian sovereign bonds briefly exceeded 2000 basis points (bp) (over ten year US Treasuries) in late 2002; in the current cycle, the worst spread level was close to 700bp late last year and this has since narrowed again to under 250bp. In early 2003, the benchmark Selic rate shot up, at its worst, to 26.5 per cent while the peak in the current cycle was around half that (13.75 per cent); indeed, nominal interest rates in Brazil have recently fallen into single digits for the first time since the 1960s. In late 2002, the Brazilian real collapsed to R$4.00/US$, compared to a low this cycle of R$2.50/US$.

The factors that have protected Brazil in the current global downturn have been the strength of its banking system and the closed nature of its economy; Brazilian exports account for only 14 per cent of its GDP. With confidence returning and the Brazilian economy already on the recovery track, the worst it seems that the current crisis will throw at Brazil is already past and it was far less severe than the dislocation of the financial markets and the sense of crisis in 2002–3.

Mexico: A 'Conventional Recession'

The argument that Mexico is having a less severe crisis than in the past is harder to make. After all, we now expect Mexican GDP to contract by 7.4 per cent in 2009, even worse than the crash of the economy in 1995 (−6.2 per cent) in the so-called 'Tequila crisis', after the devaluation of the peso in December 1994. However, even for Mexico, an emerging market uniquely vulnerable to the current global economic downturn (a fairly open economy, by Latin American standards, and dominant trade links with the US), the current crisis actually seems less dislocating than that in 1995.[6]

For this is a conventional recession (in business cycle terms) in Mexico, not an economic crisis that has been made in Mexico and which has been accompanied by a currency crisis or a collapse of the domestic banking system (as in 1995). The result has been, as in Brazil, far more resilient financial markets in Mexico than during the Tequila crisis. In 1995, in the wake of peso devaluation, short-term interest rates hit 80 per cent (from a pre-crisis low of around 10 per cent), while in the recent crisis, the actual peak in rates was as low as 8.2 per cent in late 2008 and short rates have since fallen to below 5 per cent. Although the peso did depreciate sharply from August 2008 to March 2009 (by 36 per cent from P$9.8/US$ to P$15.5/US$), its decline was far greater in 1994–5 (52 per cent from P$3.41/US$ in November 1994 to P$7.15/US$ in March 1995) and had more of a sense of crisis about it, as the move involved the breach of allegedly immutable fixed exchange rate bands (see below). Overall, although the Mexican economy is expected to perform even worse in 2009 than in 1995, the sense of crisis is far less (and this, despite the swine flu scare last spring and the escalating drug violence in the country).

Russia: Bad, But Not as Bad as 1998

The Russian economy is expected to contract by 7.5 per cent in 2009, broadly in line with the fall in Mexican GDP. However, as with Mexico,

Russia has held up in 2009 far better than during its trademark crisis in 1998. Again, the contrast is most stark in terms of financial market performance, given that in 1998 Russian GDP contracted by 5.3 per cent, actually less than this year's expected result. As the Asian crisis developed in the second half of 1997 (see below), leading to a sharp rise in risk aversion and a flight to quality, the Russian rouble came under severe pressure from early 1998 onwards, exacerbated by a sharp fall in the price of oil, Russia's leading export. Eventually, despite attempts to support the markets (including a sharp rise in interest rates) and the negotiation of an emergency support package with the IMF, the crisis culminated in mid-August in a debt moratorium, a major devaluation of the rouble and a temporary halt to trading on the local stock market. This signature event for the emerging market crisis environment of the late 1990s eventually saw the rouble fall by over 70 per cent in 1998 (from RUB6/US$ to RUB20.6/US$) and the local stock market fall by 85 per cent in US dollar terms.

Whatever happens in Russia during this crisis, it will not be as disastrous as the crisis of 1998, although amongst the large emerging markets, Russia is still the country that has been damaged the most in this crisis, due to problems in its banking system and a lack of economic diversification. For sure, the local stock market fell by 80 per cent in dollar terms from May 2008 to January 2009; however, the rouble's decline, although at times seeming to be out of control, has only amounted to around 30 per cent (from RUB23.1/US$ to RUB33.4/US$), even while oil prices plunged in the second half of 2008 by close to 80 per cent, from $145/barrel to $31/barrel. Also, the government debt market has held up much better than in 1998, when outright default occurred. Given the severe weakness of the Russian banking system and relatively poor monetary policy, 2008–9 may seem a very difficult period for Russia, but the big differences with 1998 remain the absence of default and much less political uncertainty (compared to the waning presidency of Boris Yeltsin in 1998).

Asia: Without a Doubt?

Finally, it seems fairly clear that the leading Asian countries have steered their way through the recent global downturn much more successfully than during the region's trademark crisis in 1997–8. That episode, which began with a devaluation of the Thai baht in July 1997 and then spread like wildfire across the region to engulf Malaysia, the Philippines, Indonesia and finally, in early 1998, Korea with currency devaluations and massive economic dislocation, was triggered by an inability to finance large external deficits. These, in turn, were mainly caused by large imbalances of the corporate sector. Investment levels in Asia were far above savings rates, although this was not due to overly expansionary fiscal policies. As currencies plunged, much of Asia collapsed into recession in 1998, with GDP contracting by 13 per cent in Indonesia, 10.5 per cent in Thailand, close to 7 per cent in Korea, and just 0.6 per cent in the Philippines. However, Asia as a whole actually grew in 1998 (according to IMF data) by 4.1 per cent, due to ongoing robust economic growth in China of 7.8 per cent, India of 5.6 per cent and, interestingly, also in Taiwan of 4.3 per cent. Developing Asia ex-China and India contracted by 4.5 per cent.

These data for 1998 have some remarkable similarities with the outlook for 2009, given that, as noted above, we expect China and India to continue to grow strongly this year, as they did in 1998. Also, several leading Asian emerging markets face sharp GDP contractions in 2009, such as Indonesia (−4.1 per cent), Malaysia (−3.4 per cent), Thailand and Korea (both −2 per cent); Taiwan has turned from a contributor to regional growth in 1998 to a drag in 2009, as GDP is forecast to fall by 4.4 per cent. As a whole, we expect emerging Asia to grow by 4.6 per cent in 2009 and, ex-China and India, to contract by 1.0 per cent. The best interpretation of these data is that Asia is having a bad year in 2009, except in China and India. So, the similarities with 1998 seem greater than at first glance. However, as with Russia and Mexico, we would argue that 2009 represents a less severe crisis for Asia than the late 1990s. Despite the collapse of the global economy, there have been no major currency crises in Asia, corporate debt defaults, nor banking system breakdowns. Most importantly, in those countries where GDP fell in 2009, the contraction was less severe than in the late 1990s.

INCREASING GLOBALIZATION AND POLICY SHIFTS

One of the standard results of equity market cycles is that a new sector and a new theme tend to emerge to drive every new bull market phase. In the 1990s, supported by the longest economic up-swing of the post-war period, with strong and sustained growth of business investment across the developed world (especially in the US), the technology sector drove the equity bull market. From September 1990 to March 2000, the AC World index rose by 235 per cent in dollar terms, with by far the best performing sector being technology. In the US itself, while the S&P Composite rose by 417 per cent over the 1990–2000 period, the Nasdaq Composite, which is dominated by technology names, surged by an astonishing 1450 per cent.

Following the collapse of the tech bubble after March 2000, a prolonged bear market in global equities followed (which lasted two and a half years) and a recession marked by a collapse of business investment; but once the next bull market in equities began in late 2002, a new driver emerged. Whether the ongoing globalization process drove the surge in commodity prices and emerging markets in the new cycle or whether the emergence of several critically important emerging markets (a proxy, if you will, for the concept of globalization) fuelled the globalization process itself, and so the surge in commodity prices, does not much matter.

The point is that global equity markets had a new driver, with the result that the briefer than usual bull market of 2002–7 had as its defining characteristic a commodity price bubble and emerging market outperformance.[7] In almost exactly five years to the day, from mid-October 2002 to late October 2007, the MSCI Emerging Markets index rose by 425 per cent, while the developed world-dominated AC World index rose by 145 per cent and the US S&P Composite by just 92 per cent. Over this same period, the benchmark index of commodity prices (the CRB index) doubled and actually kept on rising until July 2008, for an eventual full cycle gain of 172 per cent, even as emerging equity markets, notably in commodity-importing Asia, began to roll over.

Clearly, these events went hand-in-hand. The globalization process saw the gradual emergence of a newly wealthy middle-class, as more and more emerging countries opened up to trade, with their own domestic demand drivers leading to strong growth and soaring commodity prices. However, rising economic power need not mean rising importance in global investment terms. For this, economic policies are needed as well. Over the rest of this chapter, we argue that the key driver for all of this process has been much better economic policies in the emerging world. There are two aspects to this: better macro policies and more flexible exchange rates.

BETTER MACRO POLICIES

As noted earlier in this chapter, emerging markets suffered a series of crises in the second half of the 1990s. After explosive gains in stock markets in the early part of that decade, many Asian stock markets still remain (over 15 years later) well below their peaks of late 1993. The excess demand and bubble-like conditions that built up led to unsustainable current account deficits and, typically, fiscal deficits from over-expansionary policies. With adjustment of currency values constrained by the existence of fixed rate pegs of one sort or another, the pressure built up (without any opportunity for release) until exchange rate pegs literally blew up one after another: Mexico (1994), Asian countries (1997–8), Russia (1998), Brazil (1999) and, finally and most symbolically, in Argentina (December 2001) where the so-called Convertibility Plan had even been written into law.

If one common theme of this period was an attraction to fixed exchange rates, which ultimately proved unsustainable, the other theme was generally poor macroeconomic policies.[8] In fact, the existence of a fixed exchange rate peg, which protected the dollar value of a country's output until it didn't, allowed a country to pursue bad policies for longer than if the cold blast of market competition had been in place throughout to police economic policy (through a declining exchange rate).

Therefore, the late 1990s was characterized by over-expansionary, and ultimately unsustainable, macro policies within the emerging world. Fiscal and current account deficits were widespread and inflation was higher than it is today. The illusion of being able to pursue these unsustainable policies was supported by the existence of fixed currency arrangements.

The result of these bad policies was that when fixed pegs eventually collapsed and severe dislocation followed, these countries were forced to go cap in hand to the IMF, World Bank and other multinational organizations for financial support. IMF programmes to support individual emerging economies were so common in the second half of the 1990s and at the start of the new decade that there were even fears that the IMF would effectively run out of money. Along with these IMF support packages came conditionality and required adjustments of economic policies in these countries. These were often very severe and painful. The so-called Washington consensus involved fiscal tightening, monetary discipline, privatizations, the liberalization of internal markets, an end to price controls and the like. The overriding conclusion was that emerging markets were pursuing the wrong policies and needed to be disciplined: excessive fiscal and current account deficits were bad. Although these policy strictures (imposed by external creditors in return for financial support) were frequently criticized within the emerging countries themselves as overly punitive, they were often very necessary and, in the end, as we now know they worked.

Now, fast forward to the present day. One characteristic of the current global downturn and the cycle that preceded it (2002–7) has been that much better macro policies have been pursued by emerging markets as a block. Current account deficits have been reduced, and in some countries have turned into surpluses (for example, most of Asia and, for a time, much of Latin America), and fiscal balances have also improved. This is clear from Figure 3.2, which compares current account and fiscal balances for emerging markets as a whole in 1994–9 and 2003–08. While the improvement in the fiscal accounts this past decade has been less significant, the turnaround in current account balances has been dramatic. This

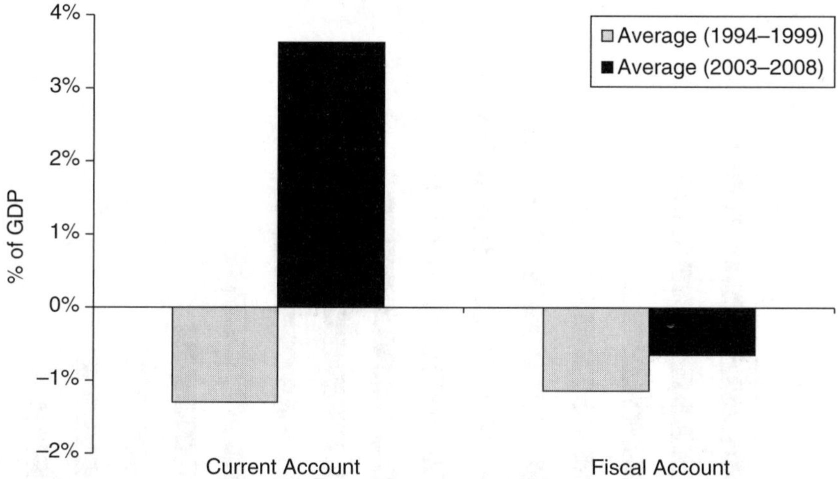

Source: IMF/World Bank and Citi Investment Research & Analysis.

Figure 3.2 Emerging markets: improvement in current account and fiscal balances

reflects the improvement in macro policies and, in turn, helps to explain the relative absence of major emerging market crises in the past ten years.

An impressive indicator of the impact of this improvement in fundamentals over the past ten to 15 years is the sharp reduction in the external debt obligations of emerging markets – from around 40 per cent of emerging markets' GDP in the late 1990s, to 27 per cent in 2007 and just over 23 per cent in 2008. Prosperity is self-feeding. Better policies which lead to improved fundamentals are then followed by reduced financing commitments, which in turn increase the flexibility of economic policies to deal with new crises. This has been the story for emerging markets in the recent severe global recession.

This later period has also been notable for the abandonment, in general, of fixed exchange rate systems by emerging markets (below). Better policies have protected these economies through the current global downturn both directly and through their ability to allow counter-cyclical macro responses when economies have come under pressure, and have allowed the emerging markets to 'have a good crisis'. Indeed, there has never been a period in history when so many emerging markets have been able to use macro policy to lean into the wind against economic weakness in this way.

As always, there are exceptions to this general rule of better policies in the emerging world. Most attention has been paid to the weak policies

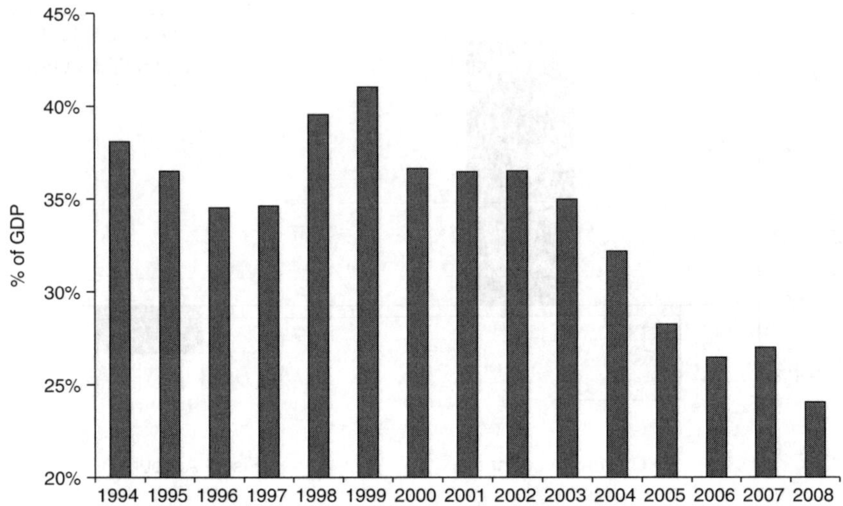

Source: IMF/World Bank and Citi Investment Research & Analysis.

Figure 3.3 Emerging markets: fall in external debt obligations

pursued by certain emerging markets in the Europe, Middle East and Africa (EMEA) region: higher budget deficits and often an unwillingness to tighten monetary policy sufficiently to deal with any inflation threat. Notable examples include Hungary, Russia, South Africa, Latvia and Ukraine and, to a lesser extent, Poland and Turkey. In our view, the sense that policies have been weaker in these countries than elsewhere in the emerging world has been compounded by the pursuit of more stable exchange rates with the Euro before the macro economic pre-conditions for this were in place. Examples here include Hungary, the outright fixed pegs adopted by Latvia, Bulgaria and Croatia, and for some countries, ultimately, membership of the euro itself.

An even better example of a country doing poorly in this environment is Argentina.[9] However, this has been for different reasons. Poor policies since 2002 and economic isolationism culminated in the recent expropriation by the government of the local pension fund system and taxation of the country's very important and highly competitive agricultural exports. This converted Argentina into a pariah for emerging market investing and, latterly, demoted it even to frontier market status. The result is that there are some emerging market countries, such as those within the EMEA region and Argentina, that have seen much worse macro performances during the recent crisis.

However, there is a final irony to this turn of events. If better policies have afforded emerging markets some policy flexibility in the current crisis via stronger fiscal balances and current account surpluses, they have also had another less desirable, unplanned effect. The switch of emerging markets as a group to large external current account surplus coincided (almost, by definition) with the explosive growth of current account deficits in certain developed economies, notably the US, but also the UK. As these surpluses built up in emerging markets (notably in Asia), reserve holdings exploded. This money had to be invested somewhere, and very frequently it was simply poured back into US Treasury bonds. This recycling of dollars, in effect, allowed the US (and others) to sustain their own consumer booms for much longer than would otherwise have been the case.

One result is that, after being criticized for running current account deficits in the late 1990s that led to a series of disruptive currency crises and a certain amount of global dislocation, emerging markets are now being criticized for running current account surpluses and, de facto, for contributing to the overleveraging of the US consumer and the size of the US housing bubble. We regard this critique as totally unfair and unreasonable, but perhaps an inevitable consequence of the much better policies now being pursued by emerging markets.

ADOPTION OF FLEXIBLE EXCHANGE RATES

The other macro policy improvement in the emerging world so far this decade has, in our view, been the effective abandonment of fixed exchange rate pegs and their replacement by more flexible exchange rates. It is almost as if emerging market countries, as a group, decided to distance themselves from the run of cathartic currency crises of the 1994–2001 period, determined to improve their macro policies and let floating exchange rates effectively police those policies day by day. It is clear to us that the increased flexibility of currency regimes operated by emerging market countries in the past few years has been every bit as important as the good policies themselves in allowing then to hold up so well during the recent global downturn.

As noted above, there have been exceptions to this new behaviour, notably in the pursuit by several EMEA countries (notably the Czech Republic, Hungary and Poland) of closer links to the euro. However, there is another even more important variant on (if not exception to) this behaviour: China. It has a currency that is not subject to full convertibility and clearly manipulated by the Chinese authorities – in other words far from a fully floating currency. However, keeping a comparison with the 1990s in mind, the Chinese Renminbi (RMB) is not held on a fixed peg to the dollar or even a fixed, but adjustable, peg either. The recent Chinese official policy of allowing a steady, but very slow, appreciation of the RMB against the US dollar is most akin to the old-fashioned idea of a 'crawling peg'. The latter arrangement does afford some of the policy freedom that is not available under a fixed peg and should clearly not be prone to the sort of dramatic adjustment so familiar under fixed pegs in the 1990s. In short, Chinese currency policy may not be ideal, but it is nearer to the emerging market norm of today than to the fixed peg approach of the late 1990s.

The general recent shift toward more flexible exchange rates is best seen by comparing the behaviour of emerging market currencies around the crisis periods of the late 1990s with that during the recent global downturn. Figures 3.4 to 3.7 show this for Mexico (comparing 1994–5 with the past two years) and Russia (1998–9 with today). The crisis periods of the late 1990s were characterized by currency stability for a time and then complete collapse; the recent crisis saw currency weakness for sure, but in a more controlled, less disruptive and, ultimately less extreme way. Weakness and currency pressure may be unavoidable, but they can be less dramatic and less of a 'crisis' if they occur under a floating currency regime.

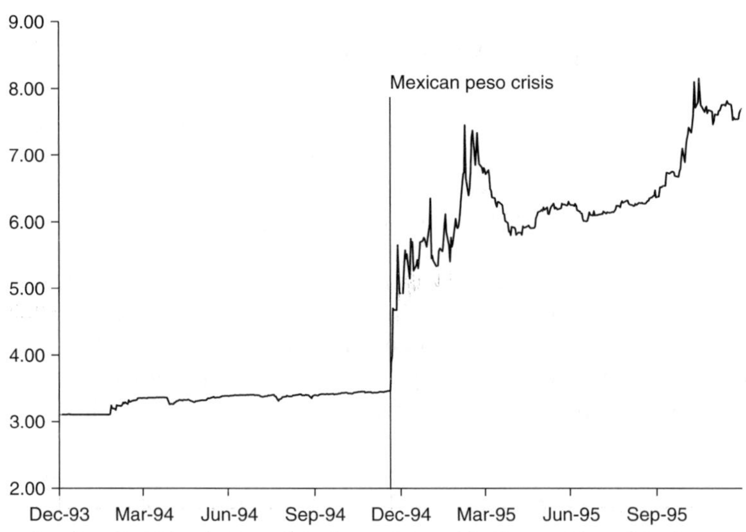

Source: Datastream and Citi Investment Research & Analysis.

Figure 3.4 Mexican peso/US dollar: 1 January 1994 – 31 December 1995

Source: Datastream and Citi Investment Research & Analysis.

Figure 3.5 Mexican peso/US dollar: last two years

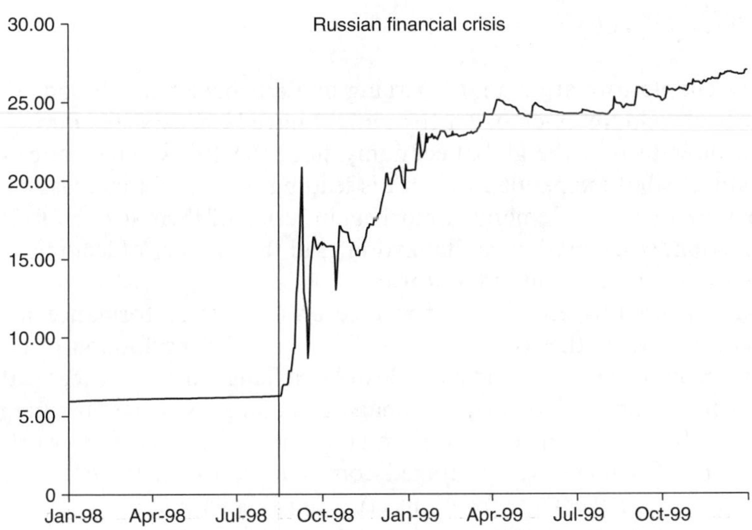

Source: Datastream and Citi Investment Research & Analysis.

Figure 3.6 Russian rouble/US dollar: 1 January 1998 – 31 December 1999

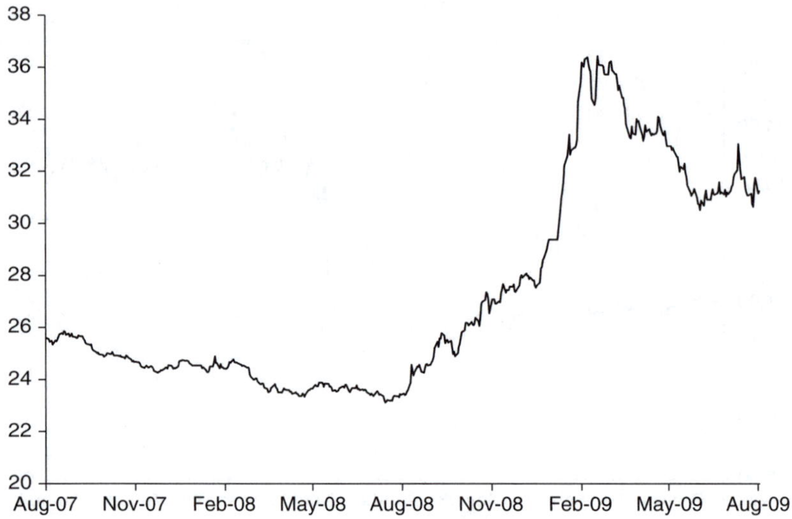

Source: Datastream and Citi Investment Research & Analysis.

Figure 3.7 Russian rouble/US dollar: last two years

CONCLUSIONS

In this chapter, we argue that emerging markets have had a 'good crisis'. They have held up much better than might have been expected during the worst downturn in the global economy since the 1930s. This better performance is both explained by, and is leading to, a rapid increase in the global importance of emerging markets in terms of their shares of GDP, population, stock market capitalization, and the number of leading stock markets and banks around the world.

We explain this growing importance and better performance in the current decade by the spread of globalization and the adoption of better macro-economic policies and more flexible exchange rates. Another feature has been the absence of major damage to banking systems in emerging markets during the current crisis (in contrast to the developed world) – the result of a much less leveraged consumer sector in these countries. Therefore, as they emerge from this crisis, most emerging market banking systems are better capitalized than they have been in the past and also far better capitalized than many developed market banking systems at present.

In our view, all these developments and this analysis can be summed up, albeit simplistically in one diagram. Figure 3.8 shows that there is a

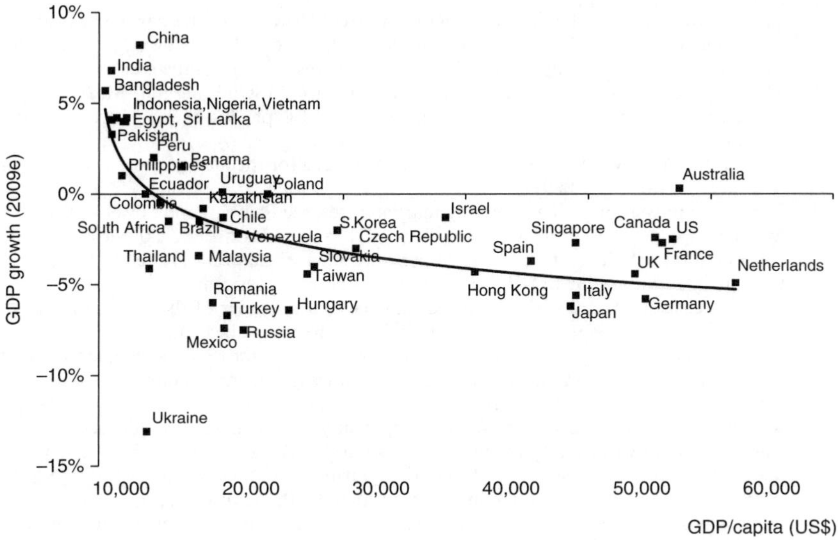

Source: IMF/World Bank and Citi Investment Research & Analysis.

Figure 3.8 GDP per capita vs. GDP growth 2009 (estimated)

fairly close, non-linear relation between the GDP per capita of individual countries around the world and forecasts for those same countries' GDP growth in the downturn year of 2009.[10] This has been a crisis of excessive credit creation and leverage, fuelled by over-expansion by banks. The higher a country's GDP per capita, the greater the likely credit penetration within that country (Credit/GDP) and, therefore, the greater the GDP contraction (or the slower the growth) in 2009 as the great de-leveraging began and banking systems around the world began to be restructured.

This lower credit penetration within emerging markets, in most cases leading to less damage to the countries' banking systems, has been another benefit for emerging market economies at the expense of developed economies. These improving trends of emerging markets' economic performance are unlikely to be quickly reversed. Emerging markets are on the march and the developed world had better take notice.

NOTES

1. The author is Global Emerging Markets Strategist at Citigroup Investment Research and Analysis.

2. The author wishes to thank Alonso Rios, Andrew Howell and the participants at the Financial Institutions, Systems and Markets conference at Loughborough University for comments on earlier drafts and Jason Press for research assistance.
3. The only other countries included in the benchmark MSCI Emerging Market index expected to record positive growth in 2009 are Egypt, Indonesia, Peru and the Philippines.
4. The author acknowledges Peter Marber as the source for the idea of presenting data in this way (see Marber, 2009).
5. For a full analysis of earlier emerging market crises, see Roubini and Setser (2004).
6. Mexico exports around 30 per cent of its GDP and sends around 80 per cent of its exports to the US. Therefore, some 24 per cent of Mexican GDP is exports to the US; the equivalent figure for Brazil, for example, is under 2.5 per cent.
7. For reference, I have already projected that the logical leader of the next bull market will be financials, given how far the sector fell in the recent bear market, and that the defining feature of the current economic collapse has been the extreme damage suffered by the financial sector in many developed economies (see Dennis, 2009).
8. This period saw many apologists for fixed exchange rates as the optimal policy choice for emerging market economies, including many so-called supply-side economists. Their argument was that by fixing its currency to the dollar, an emerging country tied itself to the (presumed stable) policies of its currency partner, so protecting the hard currency value of its output, income and, ultimately, its wealth. The flaw is this argument is that a country's wealth is ultimately determined by a country's own wealth-creating policies and, if these are not sound enough, a country's short-term higher standard of living gained by being tied to the dollar, for example, will prove illusory as the currency peg finally proves unsustainable, so eventually inflicting massive wealth losses on the country after all.
9. For one of the best descriptions and analysis of the build-up to, and aftermath of the Argentine collapse, see Blustein (2005).
10. The correlation coefficient between the two series in Figure 3.10 is −0.43.

REFERENCES

Blustein, P. (2005), *And the Money Kept Rolling In (and Out) Wall Street, the IMF, and the Bankrupting of Argentina*, New York: Public Affairs.

Dennis, G. (2009), 'The next bull market', *Citigroup Latin America Strategy Notebook*, April.

Marber, P. (2009), *Seeing the Elephant: Understanding Globalization from Trunk to Tail*, Hoboken, NJ: John Wiley.

Roubini, N. and B. Setser (2004), *Bailouts or Bail-Ins: Responding to Financial Crises in Emerging Economies*, Washington, DC: Institute for International Economics.

Wilson, D. and R. Purushothaman (2003), 'Dreaming with BRICs: the path to 2050', Goldman Sachs Global economics paper, no. 99, October.

PART TWO

Regulation in retrospect and prospect

4. Economic evidence and financial regulation

Peter Andrews[1]

INTRODUCTION

This short chapter summarises the main roles of financial regulators and draws attention to the important economic trade-offs that financial regulators have to make. It shows some of the ways in which the UK Financial Services Authority (FSA) has gathered the economic evidence needed to make these trade-offs in an informed way. It identifies an Occasional Paper, written for the FSA by David Llewellyn soon after the FSA was established, as an important catalyst for the FSA's ground-breaking work in this area. It sets out the statutory context for using economic evidence in UK financial regulation and summarises the concepts laid down in the Occasional Paper. It then describes the FSA's use of these concepts in its own approach to the economics of financial regulation. It briefly discusses criticisms of the FSA's approach and a few of the results obtained by the FSA from using it. It identifies the further challenges that lie ahead if the FSA is to continue to improve the quality of its decisions by learning more about the interactions between financial regulations and financial markets that determine whether or not regulation is beneficial in practice.

THE TRADE-OFFS FACING FINANCIAL REGULATORS: WHY THEY NEED ECONOMIC EVIDENCE

Financial regulators face extremely difficult choices. Typically, financial regulation involves mandating prudential standards for financial firms, rules for market conduct and disclosures to be made to consumers. The first of these activities aims mostly to combat the negative externalities of firms' failure.[2] The third aims mostly to reduce information asymmetries between financial firms and consumers, often in the difficult territory characterised as two-sided markets.[3] The second activity may have an important role in reducing negative externalities and information asymmetries.[4] We look briefly at each activity to establish the nature of regulators' problems and the implication that economic evidence can help financial regulators very much.

If financial regulators increase the capital requirements on banks, they may reduce the probability of bank failure. This could in turn reduce the loss of national output that tends to arise when banks fail and a crisis ensues. But increased capital requirements may also increase the cost of borrowing, and more costly borrowing may reduce national output.[5] Unless financial regulators are not at all accountable for the major negative impacts on society that may arise from their actions, they need to form a view about whether their calibration of capital requirements is likely to increase or decrease output.

Similarly, financial regulators are required to make rules with a view to achieving orderly conduct in markets on which securities, derivatives and other instruments are traded. Again, difficult trade-offs are involved. The costs of such rules may be huge, as was demonstrated in the case of the European Commission's Market in Financial Instruments Directive.[6] Also, there needs to be a return to investing in the acquisition of information if this activity is to occur in a quantity sufficient to generate informationally-efficient markets.[7] On the other hand, potential users of markets need to feel confident to enter them and, absent regulation, they would do well to be fearful.[8]

Why is this confidence important? If some market participants are consistently better informed about market developments than less informed investors, less informed investors may face a systematic disadvantage when trading. This can undermine confidence in the fairness of the market and reduce the willingness of the less-informed to participate. This lack of participation is in turn likely to be costly not just for those whose objectives would be best-served by participation but also for society more widely. The problem for regulators, then, is to make these markets safe to enter but not to do so at such cost that trading is reduced to levels significantly below socially optimal levels. It is also to make markets informationally-efficient in the sense that information is quickly available to all concerned and yet not to disincentivise unduly the investment needed to generate the information that is necessary for efficient markets.[9] A further complication for regulators to consider is that the level of trading might exceed socially optimal levels, as pointed out by FSA Chairman Lord Turner.[10]

The third activity considered here is the reduction of information asymmetries between firms and consumers or mitigation of the effects of these asymmetries. Again, financial regulators have to make difficult trade-offs that can be informed by economic evidence. For example, in the context of packaged investment products, mandating that consumers be given lots of information might improve consumers' ability to protect themselves but it also increases the costs borne initially by investment service providers. These costs are likely to be passed through to consumers and therefore to reduce the returns on the investments made, after deduction of charges and other expenses.[11] Indeed the costs of investing have been high enough materially to diminish investors' returns.[12]

Is the increased cost of investing outweighed by better decisions based on the improved information? The answer is not straightforward, partly because financial consumers are not necessarily rational agents.[13] In fact they may lack confidence in dealing with perceived experts and take dangerous short-cuts in decision-making.[14] A further complexity for financial regulators to consider in the trade-off arises from the fact that provision of additional information may improve the efficiency of competition, leading to a *lowering* of prices.[15]

A point worth drawing out of the references quoted above is that the UK's financial regulator, the FSA, has published several pieces of evidence about economic aspects of its regime and that the first of these is David Llewellyn's occasional paper 'The economic rationale for financial regulation'. This paper may be seen as a catalyst for the FSA developing its use of economics in regulatory policy to an extent that has not happened in many, possibly any other financial regulator around the world. In consequence, the FSA has already completed an assessment of the effects of higher prudential standards on the UK economy (see endnote 4), while other countries are seeking to use its methodology or similar ones to satisfy the Financial Stability Board's (FSB) commitment, on behalf of the G20, to explore the likely impact of reforms to the Basel standards:

> The planned quantitative impact assessment of the proposals will take careful account of the cumulative effect of all elements of the proposed Basel II changes. The FSB will assess the macroeconomic implications of the implementation of the proposed regulation. The Basel Committee will take this assessment into account in framing the appropriate transitional arrangements.[16]

THE UK STATUTORY CONTEXT AND SOME OBSERVATIONS ON IT

Under the Financial Services and Markets Act (FSMA) 2000, the FSA is required to publish an estimate of the costs and an analysis of the benefits that will arise if it makes rules.[17] It was also required to publish such an estimate and analysis if it issued general guidance.[18] This latter requirement was, however, removed by statutory instrument in 2007.[19] This provided that when the FSA publishes a draft of proposed guidance for consultation, it is no longer required to produce a cost-benefit analysis, an explanation of the purpose of the proposed guidance or an explanation of the FSA's reasons for believing that making the proposed guidance is compatible with its general duties under section 2 of the FSMA. In addition, the amendment meant that the FSA will not be required to follow the procedural provisions in section 155(5) to (9) in relation to proposed guidance. The rationale for the legislative change was that some guidance needs to be made quickly and simply, and the original requirements of section 157 could impede this. In practice, the possible costs of this statutory change – widespread imposition of guidance without consideration of whether they would pass a cost-benefit test – have not arisen because the FSA committed publicly to publish cost-benefit analyses whenever general guidance is expected to have a material impact on markets.[20]

Certain features of the requirement in section 155 of the FSMA are worthy of note. First, the requirement to publish information about costs and benefits is set firmly in the context of consultation: the information, which is typically based on extensive pre-consultation with firms, is published along with draft rules. This gives stakeholders the chance to correct it and, if appropriate, to challenge the FSA on the grounds of proportionality. Draft rules may be changed or dropped in the light of these responses, and this has happened many times.[21]

Of course this statutory approach recognises the reality that, in relation to costs, firms know far better than the FSA (or any other regulator) what compliance costs they will incur in order to comply with new regulations. Moreover, a somewhat similar situation applies in relation to the other costs and benefits of new regulations. The regulator may be able to use economic theory to predict the new equilibria that may arise in relevant economic markets from the incentives created by the regulations. Firms, however, know how they plan to respond to the regulations and may even have some information about how their rivals plan to respond – as a result of working together on trade associations' responses to the FSA's consultations, for example. Thus the sometimes large differences between the estimated costs of proposed rules as stated in the FSA's consultation papers and the revised estimates presented in further consultations or in policy statements are largely driven by developments in firms' thinking about how they will change their business practices in response to the proposals.[22]

Another aspect of the statutory link between consultation and cost-benefit analysis is that it incentivises the FSA to use its scarce economic resources on *ex ante* cost-benefit analysis (that is the analysis of proposals) rather than on *ex post* cost-benefit analysis (analysis of what specific regulations actually achieved). Accountability could be enhanced by a requirement for *ex post* analysis. Also, the results of such analysis are likely to be more reliable since the need to forecast market responses and interactions is avoided. Instead, event study approaches can be used and, if the regulations have been well-designed, data to measure their effects will have been specified and collected.[23] Of course, the problem of controlling for other relevant and contemporaneous changes remains.

Secondly, section 155 of the FSMA does not require the FSA to publish a full social cost-benefit analysis of its proposals along the lines set out in economic text books.[24] The requirement to analyse rather than estimate benefits has in practice enabled the FSA for the most part to ignore difficult issues such as shadow prices and income distribution. Section 155 also seems not to necessitate a consideration of the general equilibrium effects of regulatory changes. Such consideration would seem not to be a sensible use of scarce regulatory resources given, for example, that most of the FSA's rules changes involve no more than small adjustments to the cost functions of firms that are not necessarily operating in highly competitive markets. Certainly, a review of the impacts of the FSA on competition in financial markets that was undertaken for HM Treasury found little evidence of distortion caused by the FSA's regime.[25] On the other hand, where the FSA's proposals are likely to have very substantial effects on the economy as a whole, the FSA has abandoned its partial equilibrium approach and carried out the appropriate analysis.[26]

Thirdly, section 155 is very specific about the costs and benefits to be considered. It refers to those that will arise if the rules are made, compared with the situation if the rules are not made. This is presumably to make the point that the FSA is not to speculate about the beneficial effects it might achieve by intervention in markets. Rather, the analysis needs to be disciplined and the claims well founded. The background to this may be the situation described by Baldwin and Cave, for example, who suggest that hostility to cost-benefit analysis in the British civil service may be associated with a culture that places a heavy emphasis on administrative judgement about what may be in the public interest.[27]

The FSA has not necessarily shared the culture of the British civil service because its staff had highly varied backgrounds in, for example, the legal and accounting professions, predecessor regulatory organisations and the financial sector, as well as in the civil service. But an organisation whose main tasks were to set rules and then detect and punish breaches of those rules inevitably did not have a strongly economic culture. Thus meaningful implementation of the statutory framework for cost-benefit analysis described above required some positive steps to be taken, especially as only one of the FSA's predecessor organisations had any track record of undertaking cost-benefit analysis and foreign financial regulators provided no useful models in this area. The FSA publicly committed at a very early stage in its development to make 'cost-benefit analysis an integral part of our standard setting processes', signalling a willingness to go beyond its statutory requirements.[28]

THE ECONOMIC RATIONALE FOR FINANCIAL REGULATION

One of the FSA's first practical steps in this area was to establish an appropriate intellectual framework by asking David Llewellyn to write Occasional Paper 1, 'The Economic Rationale for Financial Regulation' (1999). This introduced almost all of the concepts that have in practice proved to be important in underpinning the FSA's work in the economics of financial regulation. It also provided useful responses to a number of the arguments then commonly made against financial regulation by free-market economists.[29] The main points in the paper may be summarised under its own headings as follows:

1. Externalities of firms failing and related systemic issues: regulation for systemic reasons is warranted when the social costs of failure of financial institutions (particularly banks) exceed private costs and such potential social costs, are (as is generally the case) not incorporated in the decision-making of the institution.
2. Other market imperfections and market failures: regulation is justified where the benefits of alleviating the effects of deviations from perfectly competitive markets are lower than the cost. Information asymmetry between consumers and financial firms is a key market failure here.
3. The economies of scale in monitoring that are achievable by regulators relative to individuals may justify regulation, especially as extensive monitoring is required in relation to financial contracts in which almost all of the supplier's performance takes place some time after the contract is agreed.
4. The problem of quality uncertainty in products, and how this can lead to low quality offerings crowding out higher quality offerings that are more expensive to produce, thereby undermining consumer confidence, unless regulators credibly set minimum quality standards.
5. The grid lock problem, in which firms may choose to adopt dubious practices because they have no confidence that their competitors will

not do so (in some circumstances the influence of peer group pressure may be greater than the incentive to invest in quality and reputation). Regulation can solve this kind of problem, which others have termed a nasty Nash equilibrium, by mandating minimum standards that all firms know will apply equally to all competitors.[30]

6. Moral hazard may arise from the existence of insurance and deposit protection schemes, leading to undue risk-taking behaviour by firms and consumers. Regulation can be constructed to offset this behaviour.
7. Consumers demand regulation for a variety of sensible reasons, for example reflecting risk-aversion. Thus, to the extent of rational demand, the costs of regulation are not deadweight costs and provision of regulation can be welfare-enhancing. Demand for regulation may, however, be excessive because regulation can appear from a consumer perspective to be costless when in fact it is not. This is a justification for cost-benefit analysis of regulation.
8. The competitive and other advantages of mandatory over voluntary disclosure of price and product information.[31]
9. Financial products and contracts are different from many of the other items bought by consumers because they are often credence goods bought under incomplete contracts and therefore subject to high transaction costs, including costs of search, bargaining, monitoring, enforcement, verification and redress. In principle, the costs of regulation may be lower than the decrease in consumers' transaction costs that regulation secures.
10. Market imperfections are more pervasive in retail than in wholesale business, implying that differentiated regimes of regulation are needed for these two types of market.
11. In financial markets regulation may be justified because consumers' lack of information and understanding, the high cost of switching, the long-term nature of many contracts and the lack of clarity of outcome for many years tend to undermine standard market disciplines such as reputation and competition.
12. Financial regulation need not be a zero-sum game or a transfer of rents from producers to consumers. It is possible that improved confidence in markets due to regulation can also make firms better-off.
13. Regulation and competition need not be in conflict. If properly constructed, regulation can enhance competition and, for example, deliver consumer protection through improvements to competition.
14. Much of the debate about alternative approaches to regulation is based on false dichotomies. For example, rules and principles are not in opposition. Each has properties that make them more suitable for

addressing certain problems and less suitable for addressing others. The main issue is to optimise the overall regime of regulation by making use of the best possible combination of instruments.

THE FSA's APPROACH TO THE ECONOMICS OF FINANCIAL REGULATION AND SOME OF ITS RESULTS

Following from the Occasional Paper summarised above, the FSA set out its own approach to cost-benefit analysis.[32] This involved a practical six-part impact analysis covering the FSA's own costs, compliance costs, the quantity, quality and variety of services, and the efficiency of competition.[33] These headings were designed to capture all material impacts likely to arise from FSA rule-making and to satisfy the FSA's statutory requirements in this field. As such, they captured the issues arising under the 14 headings of the Occasional Paper summarised above. Also, as the FSA's experience of undertaking cost-benefit analysis grew, it published further material on the topic.[34]

A significant difficulty with cost-benefit analysis is that the timetable for policy-making, for example in response to public or political concerns about financial malpractice or risk-taking, may be too short for robust, empirical economic analysis to be undertaken. Thus, since 2003, the FSA has sought to undertake a programme of economic research that is relevant to policy issues that are likely to emerge.[35] For example, following the emergence of the financial crisis in 2007, the FSA started work on banks' response functions to prudential standards, in order to inform itself about the possible economy-wide impacts of higher standards. Some of the results of this can be seen in the FSA's Occasional Papers series.[36,37]

Another potential disadvantage of cost-benefit analysis in practice is that it leads to a focus on what can be measured easily, for example compliance costs, because measurement often requires more resources than do other forms of assessment. Also, cost-benefit analysis typically requires a non-trivial level of resources and therefore tends to be carried out on near-final policy options rather than as part of the process of determining the best policy option.

Consequently, the FSA, given its public commitment to use economic insights to optimise policy, decided to supplement its cost-benefit analysis by making use of market failure analysis as a mechanism for assessing whether policy projects are worth pursuing. This has some important advantages. In particular, by making a clear distinction between market failures and market imperfections, market failure analysis can increase the likelihood that resources are not wasted on projects that have little prospect of yielding net benefits and that momentum does not build behind such projects before their likely outcome is appreciated. This strong emphasis on market failure as a filter for action seems not to be shared by many other agencies and the FSA considered its guide to Market Failure Analysis to be ground-breaking when, in the interests of transparency, it published its internal document.[38]

The distinction between market failure and market imperfection is addressed at the start of the guide in a quote from then FSA Chairman Callum McCarthy. He says that all real-world markets have some imperfections but that this is not a justification for regulatory intervention in them. The question is whether intervention is likely to be net beneficial and there are several reasons why it might not be. First, the nature of the imperfection may be such that it is in principle not possible for intervention by a government or other authority to correct it. In other words, perhaps the imperfection cannot sensibly be called a market failure; it is just a fact of life.[39] Secondly, even if there is a market failure, and therefore a chance that regulation can improve on whatever the market's own solution to its imperfection is, any regulatory intervention has a probability of failure. Thirdly, any regulatory intervention has a cost. Thus 'Identification of a market failure should not lead to the assumption that regulatory failure is less likely, or less costly. It is an open and empirical question, which needs analysis on a case by case basis'.[40] (Hence the case for cost-benefit analysis.)

The FSA's approach is not without its critics. For example: 'The market failure approach to regulation is vacuous – it is literally empty of meaning. . . . It cannot be known what the outcome of a perfectly competitive market process would have been in the absence of the process of competition, since there are undiscovered opportunities for increasing welfare.[41] Therefore, government action cannot correct market failure because government does not know the objective which it is seeking to achieve'.[42] Various arguments against this line of reasoning have been made.[43] For example, the argument seems to depend upon the idea that the purpose of using market failure analysis is to produce the (unknowable) outcome of a perfectly competitive market. While that may be an ideal objective of regulation, it is not one that is familiar in the statutes that set objectives for financial regulators.[44] For most regulators, a more realistic objective is to improve on the current state of the market.[45] The value of market failure analysis will then lie in whether it can help them to achieve that objective.

Certainly, one consequence of the FSA's use of market failure analysis is that, when challenged by the House of Lords to provide evidence of how its approach to regulation avoided unhelpful interventions in markets, it has had a ready list of cases in which regulatory action has been considered but rejected in the light of market failure or high-level cost-benefit analysis. This was submitted to the House of Lords Select Committee on Regulators in 2007, in the form of a follow-up memorandum to oral evidence. At the same time, the London Investment Bankers' Association (now AFME) commented favourably on the FSA's approach in its evidence to the House of Lords on economic regulators' use of Regulatory Impact Assessments (RIAs):

> Overall, our experience is that on all of the Committee's questions on RIAs, the FSA sets the standard, internationally and nationally, both in terms of thought leadership and increasingly as regards practical implementation. Although not without difficulties on some particular issues, since its inception the FSA has:
>
> - Increased the resources and seniority of its dedicated economic analysis team.
> - Developed rigorous methodologies and practical policy-making tools to support the development of evidence-based regulation. These go beyond the use of regulatory impact assessment and include the use of market and regulatory failure analysis to determine whether or not there is a 'prima-facie' case for regulatory intervention.
> - Increased the degree of senior challenge to policy proposals in the formative stages of the regulatory policy process: a senior FSA committee is tasked with ensuring that a convincing market failure analysis is part of the first stage of the policy process.
> - Made public commitments to undertake and publish market failure, impact and cost-benefit analyses, and these statements have enabled the industry to hold the FSA to account for its actions.
>
> Within the context of what is emerging as an exemplary approach to evidence-based policy making, there are two areas where further improvement could be expected . . .[46]

Some examples of the results of the FSA's work on the economics of financial regulation have already been cited in this chapter. A few more may be in order, one for each of the three areas of difficult trade-offs for financial regulators that were described above.

The following example relates to the reduction of information asymmetries between consumers and financial firms or mitigation of the effects of these asymmetries. The FSA was obliged by statutory changes to introduce a regime for regulating the conduct of mortgage business. It wanted to learn of the scale of benefits delivered by the regime. One aspect of this was an exploration of the market impacts of the regime through the use of data envelopment analysis to compare the efficiency of consumption before and after the regime was introduced. The results were not very positive, and can be seen in FSA Occasional Paper 27.[47] Following the introduction of the regulations, there was no increase in the particular measure of the efficiency of consumption that was made. These results may have contributed to the FSA's decision to pursue a further review of the mortgage market and its regulation.[48]

The FSA's work on estimating market cleanliness is an example of making rules with a view to achieving orderly conduct in markets on which securities, contracts for differences and other instruments are traded. This used bootstrapping and an event study methodology to estimate the proportion of takeover announcements and other trading announcements that are preceded by an abnormal price movement in the stock concerned. In the case of takeover announcements, the proportion turned out to be approaching one third.[49,50] This finding does not necessarily mean that insider trading is occurring before 30 per cent of takeovers but, understandably, it attracted significant media interest. It may have contributed to the FSA's decision to invest materially more resources in enforcement activities relating to market conduct.

An example was given in endnote 4 of research undertaken with the goal of helping to deliver an appropriate regime to combat the negative externalities of firms' failure. This work involved the use of three separate models: a credit sector which can be made to respond to regulation, a national macroeconomic model, and a crisis model. The crisis model is especially interesting because in principle it throws some light on the vexed question of the causes of the recent crisis. The crisis model published in FSA Occasional Paper 38 differs from many such models in the economic literature because it is based exclusively on data about developed countries. While it has subsequently been expanded to include a current account deficit variable, which turns out to be significant, its central finding remains intact, that by far the biggest determinant of crisis in developed countries is lagged growth in house prices. Strictly, this proves nothing about the cause of the recent crisis as the house price variable may be capturing other economically significant factors such as the quality of bank lending. On the other hand, the strong association between increasing house prices and crises suggests that the causes of house prices increasing, whether they be regulatory, monetary, fiscal or perhaps even a fact of life, deserve some attention.[51] But this is just one aspect of a complex story; Adam Smith might have seen the problem as lack of competition (in the sense that concerns the competition authorities) as well as a fact of life; certainly, he thought that banks should be small: 'By dividing the whole circulation into a greater number of parts, the failure of any one company, an accident which, in the course of things, must sometimes happen, becomes of less consequence to the public. This competition, too, obliges all bankers to be more liberal in their dealings with their customers, lest their rivals should carry them away.'[52]

FUTURE STRATEGY FOR USING ECONOMIC EVIDENCE IN FINANCIAL REGULATION

Economics provides a wide range of theories and tools that financial regulators can use to increase the evidence base on which difficult trade-offs are made and decisions taken. The FSA is very far from exhausting the possibilities.

In the area of reducing or alleviating information asymmetries between consumers and financial firms, it may be possible to design disclosures that exploit rather than are confounded by the decision heuristics that consumers use. It may also be possible to use the insights from game theory to design incentives for financial firms to co-operate with their customers. It may further be possible to make use of data about price, risk aversion and willingness to pay in order to achieve a more refined understanding of the suitability of a product for a consumer than has hitherto been seen. It is certainly possible in principle to use Data Envelopment Analysis to detect which firms or advisers tend to sell products with low-value features and high prices. In the area of achieving efficient and orderly markets, it may be possible to complement existing measures of cleanliness by using econophysics techniques such as the minimum spanning tree, or to develop new measures of efficiency.[53] In the area of combating the negative externalities of firms' failures, it will certainly be possible, with more time, to make substantial improvements to the modelling reported in FSA Occasional Paper 38, for example by making the crisis model endogenous to the national macroeconomic model and then estimating annual probabilities of crisis that reflect forecast economic developments. It may also be possible, for example, to develop useful models of networks such that network stability can be tested and then improved by policy.[54]

These possibilities are interesting and as a programme of applied economic research might significantly improve financial regulation but they do not amount to a strategy. In principle, however, economic insights could be used to produce three main types of strategy for financial regulation. Each of these types of strategy could complement the other two.

One of these types of strategy was mentioned in David Llewellyn's FSA Occasional Paper 1. This is optimising the mix of regulatory tools (such as principles, guidance, rules, outcome-focused rules, detection of breaches, prosecution of breaches, size and type of sanction) at each stage of the regulatory process; that is from authorisation to, in the extreme, the closure of firms or markets. An approach along these lines has already been developed for the Dutch Ministry of Justice.[55]

A second type of economics-based strategy is to draw on lessons learned about market failure and *ex post* cost-benefit analysis and to define an evidence-based policy cycle with respect to significant, relevant economic markets. In the case of the FSA, markets in which activities fall within the Regulated Activities Order associated with the FSMA could be identified and their operation assessed through research and analysis covering issues such as market failure, regulatory failure, efficiency and consumer outcome. Depending on the results, new regulatory measures or deregulation (subject, in the case of rules or material guidance, to *ex ante* cost-benefit analysis) could be implemented. After a suitable gap, the cycle recommences when further research in the form of *ex post* cost-benefit analysis is undertaken to determine the success or failure of the initiative and whether further action is warranted.

The third type of economics-based strategy is to develop a set of trackable indicators of the efficiency and effectiveness of the various components of the financial system. This could be approached from the perspective that the role of the financial system is to deliver effective and efficient financial intermediation at a low cost from cradle to grave; that is from the aggregation of capital from individuals, to management of the resultant funds, to allocation of capital to its users through capital markets, through banks and through other intermediaries, to returning capital to its owners, including through decumulation. To assess how well financial intermediation in this sense is working and the extent to which this is improved, or not, by financial regulation (after controlling for other factors as appropriate), one might need indicators in areas such as: the cost of investing; the costs of the creation and operation of collective investment vehicles, bond issuance, initial public offerings (IPOs), the creation and operation of trading venues, supply of information to those trading, and the supply of governance services for all of the above; market cleanliness (incidence of suspicious price movements); market efficiency; the cost of capital; the availability of capital; the availability of loans (which could be excessive or insufficient); consumption efficiency (quality-adjusted price); default rates (for example as an indicator of suitability); persistency of contracts (incidence of costly, early termination); and the quality of advice (a statistic on suitability). Indicators such as these could provide crucial management information for financial regulators.

At the time of writing, the future of the FSA is unclear. Whatever institutional framework is favoured, there is a case for ensuring that the commitment to evidence-based financial regulation that has developed from Occasional Paper 1 continues to grow.

NOTES

1. The opinions expressed in this chapter are those of the author writing in his personal capacity and should not be interpreted as representing the official views of the Financial Services Authority.
2. Llewellyn (1999).
3. Armstrong (2006).
4. See, for example, the literature reviews in FSA (2005) and FSA (2007).
5. Barrell et al, (2009).
6. FSA (2006a).
7. Grossman and Stiglitz (1980).
8. Pirrong (1995).
9. This does not mean a market that *always* prices efficiently but it does mean a market that gives high returns only if high risks are taken. See Malkiel (2003).
10. Turner (2010).
11. Carhart (1997).
12. James (2000).
13. Choi, Laibson and Madrian (2006).
14. De Meza, Irlenbusch, and Reyniers (2007).
15. James (2009).
16. http://www.financialstabilityboard.org/press/pr_100109a.pdf.
17. Financial Services and Markets Act 2000, section 155.
18. Financial Services and Markets Act 2000, section 157.
19. The Regulatory Reform (Financial Services and Markets Act 2000) Order 2007 No. 1973; Article 13.
20. FSA Policy Statement 07/10 (2007).
21. See, for example, FSA Policy Statement 10/6 (2010).
22. Again, this is demonstrated by the case of the Retail Distribution Review. See FSA Policy Statement 10/6 (2010).
23. MacKinlay (1997).
24. See, for example, Layard and Glaister (1994).
25. Office of Fair Trading (2004).
26. FSA (2009b).
27. Baldwin and Cave (1999).
28. FSA (1998).
29. For a powerful example, see Benston (1998).
30. Miles and Scott (2005).
31. See footnote 15 above; also: Andrews (2009).
32. Alfon and Andrews (1999).
33. FSA (2000).
34. Klumpes, Meeks, Simpson, and Andrews (2000).
35. See the FSA's research page available at http://www.fsa.gov.uk/pages/Library/research/economic/index.shtml.
36. Francis and Osborne (2009a).
37. Francis and Osborne (2009b).
38. FSA (2006b).
39. On the other hand, some scholars use a wide definition of market failure, although not in a policy-making context. For example: 'Typically, at least in allocation theory, we mean [by market failure] the failure of a more or less idealized system of price-market institutions to sustain "desirable" activities or to stop undesirable activities. The desirability of an activity, in turn, is evaluated relative to the solution values of some explicit or implied maximum-welfare problem'. Bator (1958).
40. Callum McCarthy, quoted in FSA (2006b).
41. See Hayek (1982).
42. Arthur and Booth (2007).

43. See Andrews (2007).
44. In the case of the FSA, see section 2 of the FSMA 2000.
45. Thoughtful regulators will consider not just the current state of the market but also whether there are signs of dynamic change within the market that will solve the problem concerning them.
46. Memorandum by the London Investment Bankers Association to the House of Lords Select Committee on Regulators (2007).
47. Monteiro and Zaidi (2007).
48. FSA (2009a).
49. Dubow and Monteiro (2006).
50. Leitterstorf, Monteiro and Zaman (2007).
51. One argument might be that, in the great moderation, increased retained profits and other forms of accumulated wealth, whether in banks or elsewhere, needed to be deployed and increased asset prices. It may be an interesting question whether this should be classified as a market failure, a regulatory failure or a fact of life.
52. Smith (1776).
53. See, for example, Aitken et al (2009).
54. See, for example, May, Levin and Sugihara (2008).
55. See http://www.it11.nl/it11/ and http://www.jh-co.com/our_history.html.

REFERENCES

Aitken, M.J., F.H. de B. Harris and S. Ji (2009), 'Trade-based manipulation and market efficiency: a cross-market comparison', paper presented at the 22nd Australian Finance and Banking Conference, November, accessed at: http://papers.ssrn.com/sol3/papers.cfm?abstract_id=1460992.

Alfon, I. and P. Andrews (1999), 'Cost-benefit analysis in financial regulation – how to do it and how it adds value', Financial Services Authority occasional paper 3, accessed 5 October 2010 at www.fsa.gov.uk.

Andrews, P. (2007), 'Are market failure analysis and impact assessment useful?', in Stephen Weatherill (ed.), *Better Regulation*, Hart Publishing.

Andrews, P. (2009), 'Did life and pensions disclosure work as expected?', Financial Services Authority occasional paper 32, accessed 5 October 2010 at www.fsa.gov.uk.

Armstrong, M. (2006), 'Competition in two-sided markets', *RAND Journal of Economics*, **37**(3): 668–91.

Arthur, T. and P. Booth (2007), 'Financial regulation, the state and the market: is the Financial Services Authority an unnecessary evil?', *Economic Affairs*, **26**(2): 22–30.

Baldwin, R. and M. Cave (1999), *Understanding Regulation*, Oxford: Oxford University Press.

Barrell, R., E.P. Davis, T. Fic, D. Holland, S. Kirby and I. Liadze (2009), 'Optimal regulation of bank capital and liquidity: how to calibrate new international standards', Financial Services Authority occasional paper 38, accessed 5 October 2010 at www.fsa.gov.uk.

Bator, F. (1958), 'The anatomy of market failure', *Quarterly Journal of Economics*, **72**(3), 351–79.

Benston, G. (1998), 'Regulating financial markets: a critique and some proposals', Hobart Paper no. 135, London: Institute of Economic Affairs.

Carhart, M. (1997), 'On persistence in mutual fund performance', *Journal of Finance*, **52**(1): 57–82.
Choi, J.J., D. Laibson and B.C. Madrian (2006), 'Why does the law of one price fail? An experiment on index mutual funds', National Bureau of Economic Affairs working paper no. 12261, May.
De Meza, D., B. Irlenbusch and D. Reyniers (2007), 'Information versus persuasion: experimental evidence on salesmanship, mandatory disclosure and the purchase of income and loan payment protection insurance', Financial Services Authority Economic Research, London, Financial Services Authority.
Dubow, B. and N. Monteiro (2006), 'Measuring market cleanliness', Financial Services Authority occasional paper 23, London, accessed 5 October 2010 at www.fsa.gov.uk.
Financial Services and Markets Act 2000 (c.8) (2000), accessed 5 October 2010 at www.uk-legislation.hmso.gov.uk/acts/acts2000/ukpga_20000008_en_1.
Francis, W. and M. Osborne (2009a), 'On the behaviour and determinants of risk-based capital ratios: revisiting the evidence from UK banking institutions', Financial Services Authority occasional paper 31, London, accessed 5 October 2010 at www.fsa.gov.uk.
Francis, W. and M. Osborne (2009b), 'Bank regulation, capital and credit supply: measuring the impact of prudential standards', Financial Services Authority occasional paper 36, London, accessed 5 October 2010 at www.fsa.gov.uk.
Financial Services Authority (FSA) (1998), 'Meeting our responsibilities', August London.
FSA (2000), 'Practical cost-benefit analysis for financial regulators, version 1.1', June, London, accessed 5 October 2010 at www.fsa.gov.uk/pubs/other/CBA.pdf.
FSA (2005), 'Trading transparency in the UK secondary bond markets', FSA discussion paper 05/5, London, accessed 5 October 2010 at www.fsa.gov.uk.
FSA (2006a), 'The overall impact of MIFID', London, accessed 5 October 2010 at www.fsa.gov.uk/pubs/international/mifid_impact.pdf.
FSA (2006b), 'Market failure analysis and high-level cost-benefit analysis', FSA miscellaneous publications, November, London, accessed 5 October 2010 at www.fsa.gov.uk.
FSA (2007), 'Disclosure of contracts for difference', FSA consultation paper 07/20, London, accessed 5 October 2010 at www.fsa.gov.uk.
FSA (2009a), 'Mortgage market review', FSA discussion paper 09/3, London, accessed 5 October 2010 at www.fsa.gov.uk.
FSA (2009b), 'Turner Review conference discussion paper', FSA discussion paper 09/4, London, accessed 5 October 2010 at www.fsa.gov.uk.
FSA (2007), 'Implementing the regulatory reform order in relation to guidance', policy statement 07/10, July. London.
FSA (2010), 'Distribution of retail investments: delivering the RDR – feedback to CP09/18 and final rules', policy statement 10/6, March, London.
Grossman, S.J. and J.E. Stiglitz (1980), 'On the impossibility of informationally efficient markets', *American Economic Review*, **70**(3): 393–408
Hayek, F. (1982), *Law, Legislation and Liberty*, London: Routledge.
James, K. (2000), 'The price of retail investing in the UK', Financial Services Authority occasional paper 6, accessed 5 October 2010 at www.fsa.gov.uk.
James, K. (2009), 'Regulatory reform and the cost of retail investing through life offices: 1998–2006', Financial Services Authority occasional paper 39, accessed 5 October 2010 at www.fsa.gov.uk.

Klumpes, P., G. Meeks, D. Simpson and P. Andrews (eds) (2000), 'Some cost-benefit issues in financial regulation', Financial Services Authority occasional paper 12, London, accessed 5 October 2010 at www.fsa.gov.uk.

Layard, R. and S. Glaister (eds) (1994), *Cost-Benefit Analysis*, 2nd edn, Cambridge: Cambridge University Press.

Leitterstorf, S., N. Monteiro and Q. Zaman (2007), 'Updated measurement of market cleanliness', Financial Services Authority occasional paper 25, London, accessed 5 October 2010 at: www.fsa.gov.uk.

Llewellyn, D.T. (1999), 'The economic rationale for financial regulation', Financial Services Authority occasional paper 1, London.

London Investment Bankers Association (2007), memorandum to the House of Lords Select Committee on Regulators, accessed 5 October 2010 at www.parliament.the-stationery-office.co.uk/pa/ld200607/ldselect/ldrgltrs/189/189we29.htm.

MacKinlay, A. (1997), 'Event studies in economics and finance', *Journal of Economic Literature*, **35**: 13–39.

Malkiel, B. (2003), 'The efficient markets hypothesis and its critics', *Journal of Economic Perspectives*, **17**(1): 59–82.

May, R., S. Levin and G. Sugihara (2008), 'Complex systems: ecology for bankers', *Nature*, **451**: 893–95.

Miles, D. and A. Scott (2005), *Macroeconomics – Understanding the Wealth of Nations*, Chichester, John Wiley & Sons.

Monteiro, N. and R. Zaidi (2007), 'Market impacts of MCOB', Financial Services Authority occasional paper 27, London, accessed 5 October 2010 at www.fsa.gov.uk.

Office of Fair Trading (OFT) (2004), 'Review of the impact of the Financial Services and Markets Act 2000 on competition', prepared by Oxera for the OFT, accessed 5 October 2010 at www.oft.gov.uk/shared_oft/reports/financial_products/oft714.pdf.

Pirrong, C. (1995), 'The self-regulation of commodity exchanges: the case of market manipulation', *Journal of Law and Economics*, **38**(1): 141–206.

Smith, A. (1776), *Wealth of Nations*, London: Methuen.

The Regulatory Reform (Financial Services and Markets Act 2000) Order 2007, No. 1973, accessed 5 October 2010 at www.england-legislation.hmso.gov.uk/si/si2007/uksi_20071973_en_1.

Turner, A. (2010), 'What do banks do, what should they do and what public policies are needed to ensure best results for the real economy?', Speech to the Cass Business School 17 March, accessed 5 October at www.fsa.gov.uk.

5. The economic rationale for financial regulation reconsidered: an essay in honour of David Llewellyn

Richard J. Herring and Reinhard H. Schmidt[1]

INTRODUCTION AND OVERVIEW

2009 was the tenth anniversary of David Llewellyn's classic work, 'The Economic Rationale for Financial Regulation' (Llewellyn, 1999). It was the first Occasional Paper issued by the FSA and provided a plausible rationale for what the new institution was designed to accomplish. Llewellyn gave a thorough and balanced assessment of the economic rationale for financial regulation, written with his characteristic clarity and elegance. This perspective of a well-respected, mainstream economist became widely cited and, indeed, often appeared on college syllabi.

Since the 1990s, financial instruments, markets, institutions, regulations and macroeconomic conditions have changed markedly. Notably, innovations in derivatives have increased and tended to blur the traditional lines between financial institutions. Capital markets have become much more important in the operations of large financial institutions, and large, complex financial institutions have become more numerous, even larger and even more complex. For example, the top five banks controlled 9 per cent of world banking assets in 1998; now they control well over 18 per cent. Moreover, the Basel I guidelines for capital adequacy have been adopted by more than 125 countries, often with the unexpected result of encouraging the growth of off-balance sheet transactions that substitute for more heavily regulated on-balance sheet assets. Basel II has replaced Basel I in several countries and has been extended to what were the five largest investment banks, with the unintended consequence of greatly increasing leverage. Moreover, accounting standards (which, although unacknowledged, have always been critical to any kind of international capital adequacy standard) have evolved from a hotchpotch of national, generally accepted accounting principles that sometimes differed within countries across sectors of the finance industry and usually differed across countries, to a fair value standard.[2] Yet, despite all of these innovations, most of which were thought to be advances in financial technology when they were introduced, the world has sustained the most damaging global financial crisis since the Great Depression.

While much of what Llewellyn wrote in the mid-1990s remains true today, we hope that he will revise his classic work to take account of what we have learned from these developments. We will be presumptuous enough in this chapter to offer him unsolicited advice about issues he may wish to consider for such a revised edition. The central challenge is to explain why the institutions overseen on the basis of Llewellyn's classic rationale for financial regulation failed to achieve the primary objective of financial regulation – systemic stability.

In the second section we will begin with a brief sketch of Llewellyn's original work, review some of the major changes in instruments, markets, institutions and regulations that have occurred since his paper was written, including a change in the nature of systemic risk. The concluding section will highlight the key issues we hope he will address in a new edition of his paper.

LLEWELLYN'S ECONOMIC RATIONALE FOR REGULATION AND FINANCIAL INNOVATIONS

For those who have not read Llewellyn's classic work recently we will begin with a very brief and necessarily superficial summary of his key arguments.[3] Llewellyn identified three key objectives for financial regulation: (1) to sustain systemic stability; (2) to maintain the safety and soundness of financial institutions; and (3) to protect consumers of financial services. While the first two objectives were once regarded as virtually synonymous, recent experience has served to heighten the differences between macroprudential regulation and supervision, and micro-prudential supervision. Indeed, if market participants assume that supervisors are ensuring the achievement of the second objective, the likelihood of systemic instability may be increased by undermining incentives for the monitoring and pricing of risk by market participants. Moreover, we have come to realize that monitoring the interconnections and correlations among institutions and markets is much more important to achieve systemic stability than focusing on the safety and soundness of individual institutions considered separately. The third objective, of course, has become much more complicated as the complexity of financial instruments has increased and the originate-and-distribute model has displaced much of traditional (buy and hold) lending where customer relationships were of utmost importance and the same institution originated the loan, underwrote the loan, serviced the loan, restructured the loan (if necessary) and held it on its books until it was repaid (or charged off).

Because of the heightened importance of capital markets for the activities of most major banks we would like to propose a fourth major objective: to maintain the integrity of financial markets. This would include attempts to improve the efficiency and transparency of the price discovery system, promoting market liquidity and ensuring the safety and soundness of the clearing and settlement processes.

Llewellyn also argues that regulators should prevent systemic problems associated with externalities and correct principal-agent problems and other market imperfections. Like most other economists at the time Llewellyn did not address the equally troublesome problem of how to motivate supervisory agents to act in the best interests of their taxpayer principals.[4] Although the recent crisis certainly revealed a number of egregious principal-agent problems within firms and among firms, particularly in the securitization process, it also highlighted the failure of most regulatory and supervisory institutions to undertake the kinds of precautions that might have prevented or at least mitigated the crisis.

Llewellyn also argues that regulators should take advantage of economies of scale in monitoring financial firms to promote consumer confidence. This is one compelling argument for gathering most financial regulatory and supervisory functions in one institution like the (then) newly created FSA. But to the extent it succeeds in promoting consumer confidence by placing greater emphasis on regulatory oversight it may lessen monitoring by the private sector. Moreover, it is difficult to argue that the integrated financial regulators have performed with greater distinction in this crisis than the traditional specialized regulators, which, of course, does not deny the potential merit of the idea.

Llewellyn argues that supervision and regulation can counter gridlock among financial institutions by reassuring counterparties that they are safe from adverse selection and moral hazard. This has proven much too great a burden for supervisors and regulators. That the sub-prime crisis caused such immediate and complete gridlock internationally indicated that financial institutions had very little confidence in the supervisory authorities or each other when faced with such a shock.

Finally, Llewellyn argues that financial regulation should counter the moral hazard associated with the revealed preference of governments to provide safety nets. After a crisis in which governments have risked trillions of dollars – more than 25 per cent of world GDP by one conservative estimate – in bailing-out and propping up financial institutions, it is clear that much remains to be done to make this worthy goal a reality.[5]

Llewellyn identifies two kinds of regulation and supervision: (1) prudential regulation, which focuses on the solvency, safety and soundness of financial institutions; and (2) conduct of business regulation. In his view they may overlap on systemic concerns.

First, with regard to prudential regulation, he views the key challenge as preventing systemic problems. But he also stresses that prudential supervisors must protect customers from being exploited by better informed financial institutions. In this sense, the supervisor plays a fiduciary role if consumers are unable to assess safety and soundness when they purchase a financial product or contract, which usually involves the customer paying cash now for the promise of a benefit that may not be realized until far into the future. If the post-contract behaviour of the financial institution determines the value of the contract, it can pass on the cost of hazardous behaviour to an insurance fund or compensation scheme if badly supervised.

Llewellyn argues that conduct of business regulation is necessary because financial intermediaries may exploit their fiduciary responsibility by rendering bad advice that benefits the firm but not the customer, or the financial intermediary becomes insolvent before the contract matures. Moreover, the contract may be misunderstood by the customer or there may be outright fraudulent misrepresentations. The failure of the US authorities to oversee the conduct of the mortgage business properly and, worse still, the urging of the Congressional overseers to lower normal lending standards to serve the housing aspirations of lower-income groups certainly contributed to the sub-prime crisis. This episode is a prime example of how badly conducted business can contribute to systemic risk.

Much to Llewellyn's credit, he foresaw one of the fatal weaknesses in the British deposit insurance system that made British banks especially vulnerable to runs in the wake of the Northern Rock liquidity problem, even though the UK had not experienced a run since the collapse of Overend and Gurney in 1866. He noted that the low limit of £2000 and the reliance on co-insurance in which the depositor must bear 10 per cent of the loss above a very low minimum, meant that deposit insurance in Britain could itself become a source of systemic risk. He clearly saw the credit risk implicit in co-insurance and low ceilings, but he did not articulate the additional burden that most deposit insurance systems (with the notable exception of the US Federal Deposit Insurance System) place on depositors in failed banks – liquidity risk resulting from the lag in repayment that can last, in some cases, until the bank is resolved. Since bank deposits are often a consumer's most liquid asset, this loss of liquidity can be as devastating as the credit loss and needs to be dealt with by whatever authority resolves the bank.

Llewellyn's concern about systemic risk focused on banks because of the pivotal position they have played in the financial system, especially in clearing and settlements and managing the payments system. Moreover, in most systems banks are the main source of finance for the majority of borrowers. Their highly leveraged balance sheet structure, in which illiquid assets are financed largely by short-term liabilities, many of which are payable at face value on demand, makes them inherently vulnerable to a loss of confidence and ruinous runs that may prove contagious. His main concern, of course, was contagion from one bank to others, either because of direct exposures (which may be large, opaque and rapidly changing) or because of suspected exposures to the same shock that caused the first bank to collapse.

Ironically, Llewellyn contrasted the fragility of commercial banks with the more robust structure of investment banks. He was not alone in this view. It was certainly shared by the primary regulator of investment banks, the Securities and Exchange Commission (SEC). The traditional US view was very much like Llewellyn's. It was assumed that investment banks do not pose systemic risk because they: (1) are unlikely to be subject to a run, since customer funds are not co-mingled with the firm's own funds; (2) they hold mainly high-quality, marketable securities and should be able to deleverage rapidly without suffering illiquidity costs in the event of a funding shock; (3) they do not have access to systemically important large-value clearing and settlement systems except through large banks, and thus the authorities could rely on indirect regulation by supervising banks.

Indeed, this view seemed justified by the collapse of Drexel Burnham Lambert, which for much of the previous decade had been the most profitable bank on Wall Street. Drexel had departed from the traditional investment banking model by financing with short-term funding bridge loans for less-than-investment grade borrowers in the expectation that Drexel could quickly replace the bridge loans with issues of high-yield (junk) bonds. They also financed a considerable inventory of junk bonds in the same way in order to maintain a liquid secondary market. When the market for junk bonds collapsed (at least in part because of the criminal indictment of Drexel and the removal from the market of Michael Milken, the chief architect of the junk bond market), Drexel found that it had inadvertently taken on the structure of a commercial bank operating without the safety net provided by deposit insurance and access to the lender of last resort. The bridge loans became bridges to nowhere because it was impossible to issue new high-yield debt and the inventories of high-yield debt plummeted in price. When investors refused to roll over their claims on Drexel, the holding company was forced to declare bankruptcy even though the regulated broker/dealer and primary dealer were transparently solvent.[6] But there was no contagion to other institutions.[7] In fact, the stock market rose the day that Drexel declared bankruptcy.

Most other large investment banks (with the notable exception of First Boston) stayed with the traditional investment banking model of funding high-quality, liquid assets with short-term borrowing and repurchase agreements (repos). This gave them remarkable flexibility to respond to changing market conditions. Their balance sheets could expand or contract accordion style depending on the funding available. Because of the high quality of their assets they could shrink their balance sheets substantially without incurring illiquidity costs.

The EU had long held the contrary view and worried that US investment banks could be a serious source of systemic risk. This may have reflected the fact that many of the largest European banks have traditionally had a full range of investment banking powers or the fact that the largest US investment banks had established commercial banking operations in the EU. The EU insisted that the investment banks be subject to consolidated prudential oversight comparable to that applied to large US banks or from bank-holding companies that would be subject to consolidated supervision in Europe. Rather than submit to regulation by the EU, the five leading investment banks agreed to become Voluntary Consolidated Supervised Entities subject to Basel II-like capital standards, supervised by the Securities and Exchange Commission (SEC). This turned out to be a prime example of the law of unintended consequences because when the investment banks applied Basel II-like capital standards they found that they had substantial amounts of excess regulatory capital (not unlike the case of Northern Rock) and their net leverage ratios more than doubled (see Figure 5.1).[8] This clearly made them more rather than less vulnerable to a shock as the EU had expected.

The fact that this programme was voluntary, which meant that it had to be carefully negotiated with those being regulated, is a prime example of regulatory capture. Llewellyn rightfully worries about over regulation because the cost of regulation is not priced in the market and thus consumers will demand too much. But he ignores the important countervailing force of the political market that determines regulations in many countries. Financial service industry lobbyists are often very powerful and, in the US, are the largest contributors to Congressional campaigns. Because regulators and supervisors have so many ill-defined objectives it is difficult to hold them accountable for any one objective. This problem is further exacerbated by the constraints of civil service pay scales, which do not usually permit incentives for the achievement of particular objectives. Moreover, the failure of a supervised firm is usually regarded as a

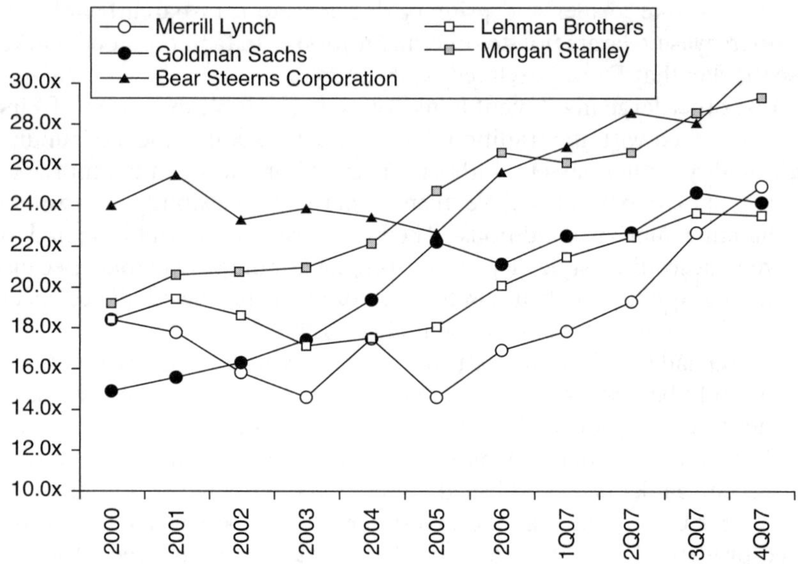

Source: Company disclosure, Bernstein Analysis.

Figure 5.1 Securities industry net leverage ratios

supervisory failure (even when it should be interpreted as effective supervisory discipline), while the waste of resources in letting an insolvent, zombie firm continue in operation is generally ignored. Thus supervisors often tend to forbear and hope that a change in conditions will restore the solvency of a troubled institution. Moreover, the 'ascent to heaven' is not an exclusively Japanese vice. Many SEC lawyers leave to represent institutions they formerly regulated (for much higher salaries) once they have gained sufficient experience at the SEC.

Over the last decade, the large US investment banks have adopted a new model (in addition to increasing their leverage). Their portfolios have shifted dramatically in favour of lower quality, less liquid assets that are inevitably much more difficult to sell without incurring an illiquidity cost in the event of a funding shock. (See Figure 5.2, for example, which shows the sharp rise in lending commitments to industrial corporations.) They have also become much more heavily involved in the derivatives business both as dealers and position takers. Although plain vanilla interest rate swaps and currency swaps are relatively transparent, the advent of credit default swaps introduced significant complexity in determining the credit exposures of institutions (in addition to helping them manage credit

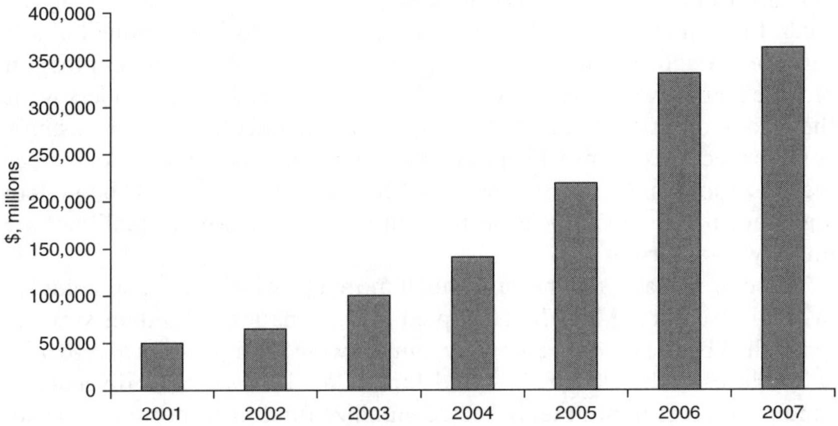

Source: Company disclosure, Bernstein Analysis.

Figure 5.2 Industry lending commitments

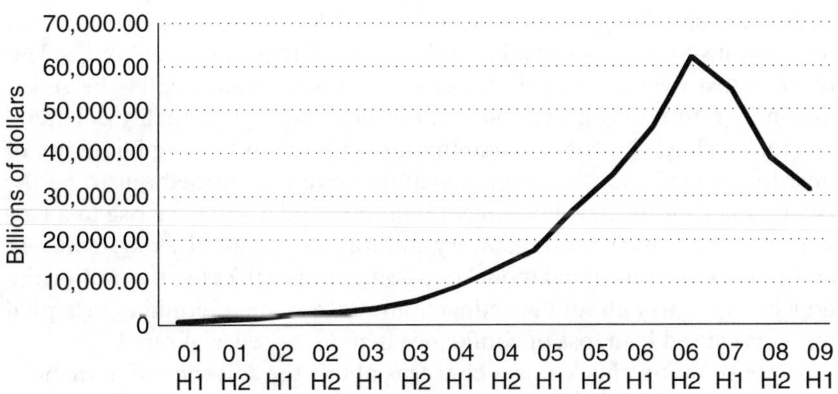

Source: International Swap Dealers Association, includes CDSs referencing single names, indexes, baskets and portfolios.

Figure 5.3 Credit default swaps outstanding, 2001 through first half 2009

risk more effectively than ever before). Figure 5.3 shows the exponential growth in credit default swaps until the crisis began. This rapid growth itself led to significant documentation problems as back offices struggled to keep up with the rapid velocity of trading. Moreover, the ability to separate the credit risk from traditional credit risk-bearing instruments meant that no firm (or regulator) could be sure who actually was assuming the credit risk. Simply knowing the identity of a firm's lenders or bond holders was not enough and might, in fact, give an entirely misleading impression of which entity would suffer loss in the event of a default, much less what the knock-on consequences might be. The introduction of increasingly complex securitizations which were often tranched, recombined with other securitizations and tranched again added further opacity to the system and made it virtually impossible to identify and evaluate the quality of the underlying securities.

These firms have also become much more global in reach and complex in legal structure. Most had adopted an international funding strategy controlled by the holding company, but drawing funds from broker-dealer subsidiaries in the US, the UK and Japan. While this greater diversity of funding sources undoubtedly helped stabilize funding in normal times, in the event of a shock, local regulatory authorities are inclined to ring-fence the parts of the group that they can control, exacerbating the funding (and capital management) challenge for the holding company.

One of the most remarkable changes in funding strategy was the growing reliance on tri-party repos to fund balance sheets.[9] In 1990, repo credit was 13 per cent of federally insured deposits. By 2007, repos were 60 per cent of federally insured deposits and two-thirds of the repos matured (or needed) to be rolled over overnight. If the buyer loses confidence in the seller, they may refuse to roll over the repo or demand higher quality collateral or more collateral. This, in combination with the increasing illiquidity of investment bank portfolios and expanded leverage, turned out to be the Achilles heel of the new investment banking model and gave rise to a new kind of risk, which the regulatory authorities regarded as systemic. In addition to the traditional model of a contagious bank run, the authorities now had to worry about the endogenous destruction of liquidity in capital markets caused by a loss of confidence in a major seller of repos.

Suppose that a shock raises concerns about the solvency of a financial institution heavily dependent on repos for liquidity. (With investment bank leverage ratios often above 30:1 and market price volatility during 2008 often approaching 40 per cent, it is not difficult to imagine the motive for a loss of confidence.) Figure 5.4 shows the two related mechanisms at work.[10]

First consider the 'margin/haircut spiral' in which counterparties lose confidence in a seller of repos. At first they are likely to react by imposing larger haircuts on collateral and demanding more collateral to roll over a repo. The seller of the repo can either react by providing more collateral or not renewing the repo, but this will result in a reduction in the size of its balance sheet. Either course results in a sale of assets. If the institution

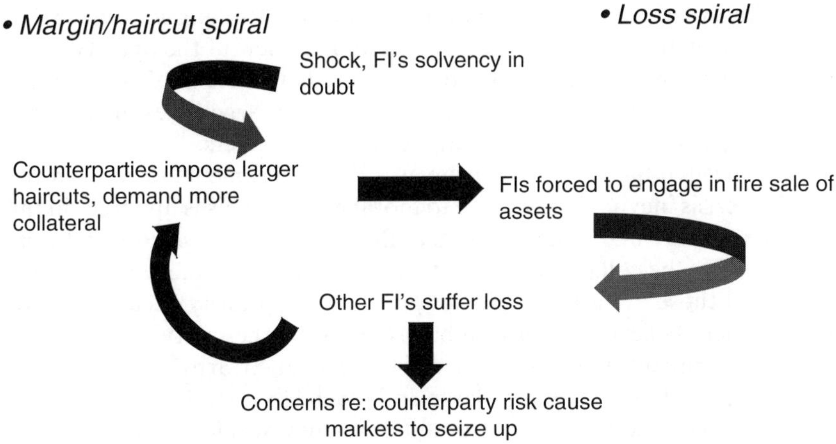

Figure 5.4 Systemic nightmare updated: the destruction of endogenous liquidity

has already repo'd its most liquid assets (which is highly likely since that provides the lowest funding cost), it will have no choice but to sell illiquid assets. This will drive down prices in the secondary market. Since investment banks are marked to market daily (so long as an active market exists), they will be forced to mark down the remainder of any position in that asset they may hold. This reduces equity and increases concerns about the institution's solvency, which will lead to greater haircuts, more demands for collateral or for better collateral, and ultimately to a refusal to deal with the institution at all. Like a bank run, this can become a self-fulfilling prophecy and can reduce the supply of intermediation quite rapidly.

The second channel is the transmission of the shock to other institutions holding similar positions. When the secondary market price of an asset falls, they too will be forced to mark down the value of their own holdings which reduces their equity and increases their leverage. Their counterparties may react just as in the previous case and another margin/haircut spiral may begin. When concerns about the sellers of repos become widespread, the market may simply dry up. But if an investment bank cannot meet its cash obligations when due, it must declare bankruptcy. Because of the size of these institutions and their opaque connections with the rest of the financial system, the first instinct of the regulators in the US was to stretch the safety net to protect investment banks. Bear Stearns was the first to succumb and a heavily subsidized, shotgun marriage was arranged with JPMorgan Chase to prevent any loss to creditors or counterparties that might cause further, uncertain damage to the financial system. The regulators simply didn't know what the consequences of a bankruptcy might be because they did not know the institution's exposures and, in view of the opacity of the instruments in which Bear dealt, could not predict where the damage might spread. To prop up confidence in the remaining large investment banks they set up a special discount facility for primary dealers.

As Llewellyn has noted, the propensity of governments to react in this way in a crisis inevitably gives rise to moral hazard. This is apparent in this case. There were many things Lehman Brothers could have done in the six months after the collapse of Bear Stearns to have strengthened its balance sheet, but those initiatives were not given a high priority because the top management believed the firm to be protected by the safety net. After all, if the government would intervene to save Bear Stearns, an investment bank that was less than half as large and much less complex than Lehman Brothers, there could be little doubt that they would do as much for Lehman. Indeed, this deduction was shared by a number of other market participants so that Lehman found that it could fund itself much more easily in the wake of the rescue of Bear Stearns. Some asset managers actually referred to the purchase of Lehman commercial chapter as a moral hazard play because they could pick up a bit more yield without incurring (they assumed) more risk.

The logic seemed plausible, but it was flawed. In the wake of the bailout of Fannie Mae and Freddie Mac, the authorities were loath to help Lehman when it came under pressure because of mounting losses. Moreover, they felt that the market had sufficient time to anticipate a Lehman bankruptcy so that those institutions that were heavily exposed would have hedged themselves appropriately. (They apparently took no account of Lehman's global network of subsidiaries.) It also neglected a lesson that policymakers should have learned from the Herstatt crisis in 1974. When a regulator does something unexpected that causes loss to creditors or counterparties, it may destabilize markets even if the institution itself is not especially large.[11] Moreover, whatever point they hoped to make regarding market discipline was completely undermined when two days later they bailed out AIG, ultimately injecting $180 billion to prevent it from causing loss to creditors or counterparties.

Both of these examples showed the damaging consequences that can occur when the authorities lack the appropriate tools to resolve a faltering institution in a way that will not cause damaging spillover effects or impose unwarranted losses on taxpayers. Moreover, the international complexity of Lehman's corporate structure, with hundreds of separate subsidiaries, showed that an effective resolution policy must be coordinated with resolution policies in other key countries to avoid destabilizing international spillovers. Llewellyn's 'Economic Rationale for Financial Regulation' was silent on the issue of resolution, but it has become clear that an effective resolution policy is essential to control moral hazard and prevent the distortion of incentives that arises when one group of firms is believed to have preferred access to official assistance in the event of a crisis. We feel certain that Llewellyn will have valuable insights on how resolution policy should be combined with the other tools of regulation and supervision.

CONCLUDING COMMENTS: SUGGESTIONS FOR A REVISED EDITION

We conclude by offering some specific suggestions for topics that Llewellyn may want to consider for a new edition of his 'Economic Rationale for Financial Regulation'. These suggestions are inspired jointly by three sources. One source is the general and far-reaching transformation of financial sectors in the course of the last ten years; the second is the evolution of political and academic thought about regulation and supervision; and the third is the experience of the ongoing financial crisis that started in 2007. Possibly the most important lesson from the crisis is that sound regulation and effective supervision of the financial sector are of paramount importance for the proper functioning of the financial system and that the hopes that were once associated with far-reaching deregulation are, in retrospect, not likely to be effective in the absence of a credible resolution policy that can prevent any failure from becoming systemic and encourage effective market discipline.

We hope a new edition of Llewellyn's 'Economic Rationale for Financial Regulation' would reflect on the changing structure of financial sectors and systems in recent years. The boundaries between banking, insurance and capital markets have largely disappeared. Many financial institutions and financial instruments have adopted a hybrid character. Derivatives and other sophisticated financial products have gained greatly in importance. Many banks have adopted a new business model known as 'originate and distribute'. And national borders have largely lost their former importance, except during a crisis when a systemically important financial institution must be resolved or more often, because of inadequate resolution procedures, bailed out.

Regulation and supervision of banking, insurance and capital markets must be integrated both in terms of their institutional design and in terms of their substance. This may take the radical form of creating one single relevant authority, as implemented in the case of the British FSA, or a more moderate form of separate but interrelated and cooperating institutions. One of the main challenges of financial regulation is to strike a balance between the advantages of specialization, which is better suited to the characteristics of individual institutions, and comprehensive oversight, which can take better account of growing interdependencies.

The tasks and objectives of any configuration of regulatory institutions must today be defined in a way that reflects the interdependencies between banks, capital markets and insurance firms. The aims of banking regulation and supervision must today include that of ensuring fair and efficient capital and insurance markets and insurance firms, and correspondingly capital market and insurance regulation and supervision should aim at simultaneously contributing to sound and safe banking.

Since financial activity is no longer confined to individual countries' territories, regulation and supervision of the financial sector has become more and more a supranational issue. Obviously, supranational regulatory and supervisory institutions appear to be better suited than national institutions to take cross-border aspects into account and to create a level playing field for competition across borders. But there is also the danger that they may be overly political and excessively bureaucratic institutions and that they are too far removed from where acute problems arise and where pertinent information is available. Moreover, as the current crisis shows, the step from supervising a bank to rescuing it can be small. Since the cost of bailing out a bank is ultimately born by a national government, there are limits to a policy of shifting the supervisory role to supranational institutions, in spite of the increasing role of cross-border activities and cross-border spillovers in the case of a crisis. As in the case of integrated versus specialized institutions, a sound balance between national and supranational institutions must be found and carefully implemented.

What makes relevant policy decisions so difficult with respect to these two institutional issues is the fact that they are interrelated. For instance, it may seem reasonable and appropriate to have national FSA-type integrated institutions in a number of large EU Member States, and at the same time one central European institution that would be responsible for regulating and monitoring the increasingly integrated European capital market. But this will work only if there is unprecedented, intensive cooperation between the national authorities and the supranational agency. The issue of the design of regulatory institutions should be taken more seriously than it was a decade ago.

One of the main lessons of the current financial crisis is that banks, including large and seemingly well-established banks, can easily get into serious financial trouble at least in part because of financial incentives to take excessive risks. Thus, there is a need to find ways of dealing with large banks once they are in trouble that does not exacerbate moral hazard incentives for risk taking. Bailouts may restore stability in the short-run, but only at the cost of increasing incentives for risk taking in the long run. Much more attention must be paid to resolution policies that limit spillovers, but deter excessive risk taking in the future.

Unfortunately, supervisors and governments cannot make a credible commitment to a 'no bailout policy' until they have developed resolution procedures that can be applied without creating intolerable spillovers. Of course, for this to be possible important changes in banking regulation are required which amount to creating a new and specific insolvency regime for large, systemically relevant banks.[12]

There are many more aspects of financial regulation and supervision that need to be seen in a new light after the crisis, and that require political action. Because of space limitations, we must confine ourselves to merely naming a few. One new area concerns enhanced transparency, such that in a crisis the relevant authorities would be in a position to assess if a given financial institution is really 'systemically relevant' and how risk is distributed throughout the financial system. A second, and related area is the transition from micro-prudential to macroprudential regulation and supervision. Indeed, it is extremely important that financial sector policy complements its current focus on the stability of individual financial institutions with a focus on how the various elements of the financial system are related and how a failure in one part of that system could affect the other parts and the system as a whole.

NOTES

1. Richard J. Herring: Jacob Safra Professor of International Banking, The Wharton School, University of Pennsylvania (herring@wharton.upenn.edu); and Reinhard H. Schmidt: Professor of International Banking and Finance, Johann Wolfgang Goethe University, Frankfurt (Schmidt@finance.uni-frankfurt.de).
2. The process of convergence between International Financial Reporting Standards and US Generally Agreed Accounting Principles is, however, far from complete.
3. Of course, we urge you to read the original for a complete and clearly articulated treatment (Llewellyn (1999)).
4. A notable exception is the work of Ed Kane who has repeatedly emphasized this theme. See, for example, Kane (1989).
5. See, Haldane (2009).
6. Substitute sub-prime related securitizations for high-yield debt and you have a striking parallel to part of the recent crisis.
7. The Bank of England and the Fed had to serve as honest brokers in unwinding Drexel's balance sheet to prevent creditors from attempting to seize Drexel's assets in the clearing and settlement process as they were liquidated.
8. This is likely to be a substantial underestimate of intra-reporting-period leverage because there is significant evidence of window dressing to disguise leverage at the end of each quarter. (See the report of Anton Valukas (2010), the court-appointed examiner in the Lehman bankruptcy case describing 105 and 108 repo transactions.)
9. A tri-party repo is a natural outgrowth of the traditional two-party repo in which the

collateral is held by a neutral third party to reduce counterparty risk and administrative costs. A repo is like a secured loan in which a borrower sells a security with a simultaneous agreement to buy it back from the lender at a fixed price and date. Unlike a secured loan, however, legal title to the security passes from the seller to the buyer. The third party in a tri-party repo is generally a custodian bank that acts as intermediary. The custodian is responsible for the administration of the transaction including the allocation of collateral, marking the collateral to market and, on occasion, substituting collateral. As part of the collateral management agreement the buyer and seller agree on an eligible collateral profile that reflects the buyer's appetite for risk.

10. For additional discussion of this mechanism, see Brunnermeier et al (2009).
11. Herstatt was closed in June 1974 at the close of business in Germany, but in the middle of the clearing and settlement process in New York where several banks that had sold Asian or European currencies to Herstatt earlier in the day expected to be paid in dollars in New York. This demonstrated, just as the Lehman case did, that the authorities who close an institution can shift losses to foreigners by picking a time that disadvantages foreign creditors. Since it is normally assumed that the regulatory authorities will take a more cosmopolitan view of their responsibilities (as, indeed, most have done after Herstatt and before Lehman Brothers), when these expectations are disappointed, key participants withdraw from the markets until they feel they once again understand the rules of the game. In the wake of the failure of Herstatt, trading in the dollar/Deutsche mark market, the most active foreign exchange market at that time, nearly ceased for several weeks and the failure of a relatively small German bank caused an international financial crisis.
12. A detailed proposal of how such a strategy of allowing bank restructurings without inducing moral hazard might work, has recently been proposed by Krahnen and Sieckmann (2010) in a paper published by the policy platform of the House of Finance.

REFERENCES

Brunnermeier, M., A. Crockett, C. Goodhart, A. Persaud and H. Shin (2009), *The Fundamental Principles of Financial Regulation*, London: Centre for Economic Policy Research accessed at www.cepr.org/pubs/books/P197.asp.

Haldane, A. (2009), 'Banking on the state', presentation to the 12th Annual Federal Reserve of Chicago International Banking Conference, 25 September, accessed at www.bankofengland.co.uk/publications/speeches/2009/speech409.pdf.

Kane, E. (1989), 'Changing incentives facing financial services regulators', *Journal of Financial Services Research*, **2**: 265–74.

Krahnen, J.P. and H. Siekmann (2010), *Rescue Strategies without Moral Hazard*, House of Finance policy platform, Frankfurt, Germany: Goethe-University.

Llewellyn, D.T. (1999), 'The economic rationale for financial regulation', Financial Services Authority occasional paper series 1, April.

Valukas, A. (2010), 'Report of Anton R. Valukas, Examiner to the United States Bankruptcy Court, Second District of New York In re Lehman Brothers Holdings Inc., et al., Debtors', Chapter 11, Case No. 08-13555 (JMP).

6. Moral hazard

Charles Goodhart

INTRODUCTION

In their efforts to forestall and to limit the financial crisis, central banks and their governments have extended the safety net to a much wider range of bank, and banking-type, liabilities. With the downside risk of loss thereby limited, the potential for moral hazard is enhanced. We discuss in turn what this may mean for deposits, bank holdings of liquid assets, subordinated debt, equity and remuneration.

I discuss the implications, and possible countermeasures, in each instance. Only in the case of equity holders has there been significant loss. Here the problem is not one of moral hazard, but rather how banks can generate a large enough return on equity (ROE) to satisfy investors, at the same time as being constrained by tougher regulation, including limits on leverage. The difficulty of doing so may have significant effects on the future structure of the financial sector.

The proponents of narrow banking would have us believe that the only essential elements of a financial system are the payments system and retail deposits. But developments in the recent crisis have revealed that the wider system of credit provision to the private sector is also regarded as crucial to the effective functioning of the economy. Neither Lehman Brothers, Bear Stearns, Fannie Mae, or AIG in the USA, nor IKB, or HRE in Germany were retail deposit banks, or had much direct contact with the payments system. Yet all were rescued, bar Lehman Brothers, and allowing the latter to slide into bankruptcy is now generally regarded as a glaring error of policy.

Clearly the boundary of the safety net, at least in crisis conditions, extends far beyond the ambit of narrow banks, despite the widespread clamour for a return to narrow or utility banking. One reason for the enthusiasm for narrow banking is that the wider the safety net is, the greater the scope for moral hazard. In so far as agents are protected against failure, but get the benefit of success (that is that they have a convex pay-off function), they will be induced to take additional risk

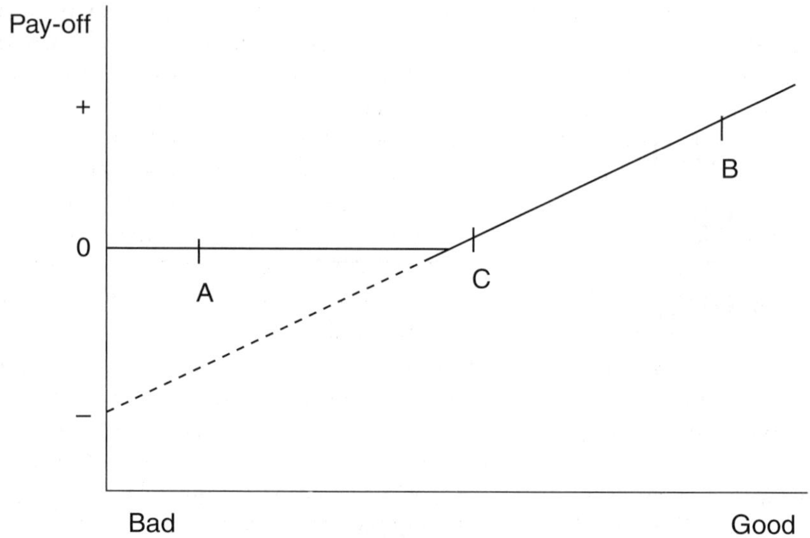

Figure 6.1 Mean expected returns

because with such a function that increases the mean expected return. Thus in Figure 6.1 a 50 per cent chance of getting either A or B gives a mean expected return greater than C.

The archetypal convex pay-off institution is the limited liability of shareholders. So, rather than encouraging managers to reduce risk, large shareholders are likely to be urging them onwards to riskier bets. Northern Rock was the darling of the London Stock Exchange until quite well into 2007! What is, to a historian, remarkable is that so few commentators recalled, in the crisis of 2007–09, the methods which prior generations had used to check moral hazard, which was to cut out, or at least to dilute, limited liability of shareholders; nor to appreciate the reasons why this mechanism was abandoned.

In the earlier years of the nineteenth century, and before then, managerial and owners' risk-taking with borrowed money was constrained by making their liability unlimited (the dashed line in Figure 6.1). Depositors had a claim against managers/owners down to their last object of value until their deposits were repaid in full; and in the several early bank panics, many bank owners were thereby ruined (an event which was central to much early British literature). The last such major occasion was the City of Glasgow Bank failure in 1878.

The reason why limited liability for bank equity holders was introduced then was that the apparent risks of bank equity holding had become so obvious that no one would invest unless the expected ROE was extremely high. To achieve such an ROE would require a huge spread between deposit and lending rates, very costly intermediation and a small banking system. This latter was, correctly, perceived as being inimical to growth and to international competitiveness *vis-à-vis* France, Germany, and others. Note that in the present clamour to make banking safer, little immediate attention is being given to the question of the effects of such measures on bank (required) ROEs, margins and spreads, or to the likely shape of future intermediation.

The Victorians realised, of course, that the switch from unlimited to limited liability would enhance moral hazard. Their immediate answer was to call for more transparency. I particularly like this quotation from Rae's *The Diary of a Country Banker* (1885, pp. 154–5):

> Even a Board of financial lunatics, with a maniac for Manager, could not pile up such a mountain of loss, if they had a whole decade, without detection or disturbance, to do it in.
>
> But they would not go undetected nor undisturbed for a tenth part of that time. Within the compass of the first twelve months of their maladministration, these gentlemen would find themselves, under the new order of things, put in financial durance by the auditors, to await the verdict of their shareholders.
>
> No doubt there will be banking losses in the future; but they can never attain to vast and overwhelming totals again, because hereafter they will be checked in time. There can never again be successful concealment of evil-doing stretching over periods of time. You will have to render an annual account of your stewardship, and that account must henceforth be verified by the sharpened vision of skilled accountants. The nursing of doubtful accounts by means of fraudulent book-keeping to figures more and more portentous, year after year, will no longer be possible. The enormities of our banking past, can never be re-enacted; the banking misfortunes of the future will be trifles light as air, compared with the devastating experiences of the past.

There are, of course, several contributing reasons why transparency can never be a sufficient (nor perhaps even a necessary) guard against bank failures and panics, but the main one is that the future cannot be accurately forecast. Since bank assets are claims on future cash flows, their value inevitably depends on uncertain expectations, subject to fluctuations in risk aversion, Keynesian fashions, and so on. Only those believing fervently in the efficient markets hypothesis, a dwindling bank of acolytes, could still believe that there is, at any time, some Platonic true version of the current value of a bank.

If we cannot rely on transparency, or rely on that sufficiently, we have to think of alternative mechanisms to limit moral hazard. The need to do so is now all the greater since the scale and scope of the safety net has been so extended in the current crisis. For example, deposit insurance has been made not only 100 per cent (from the prior 90 per cent between £3000 and £30 000 in the UK) up to a prospective much higher cap; but also the range of bank assets either accepted as collateral against central bank lender of last resort loans, and more recently insured directly by government, has been progressively widened. After the mayhem attending the Lehman failure, most bank subordinated debt is effectively guaranteed. Even bank equity holdings are treated gingerly. Governments are, for a variety of reasons, reluctant to take banks, which may be insolvent under some criteria, into complete public ownership and wipe out the equity holders. What has caused the greatest public outrage, of course, has been that the chief executives of banks, who have presided not only over failure but also have caused sizeable taxpayer burden, have escaped not only unpunished but even with massive leaving payments and pensions.

So moral hazard has advanced wherever we look. In the rest of this chapter we consider how this may now be held in check in the areas of deposits, liquidity, subordinated debt, equity, and remuneration.

DEPOSITS

The main enhancement of moral hazard in respect of bank deposits has been the extension of deposit insurance, following the run on Northern Rock in September 2007. As stated in my book *The Regulatory Response to the Financial Crisis* (Goodhart, 2009: 45–7), amended slightly to account for subsequent events,

> A question that is too rarely asked is 'What is the purpose of deposit insurance?' In fact there are two quite distinct purposes. The first is to allow an insured institution (a bank) to be closed by the authorities with less social hardship and less consequential political fuss. This can, it has been widely thought, be done by insuring all small deposits 100 per cent, and medium-sized deposits with some partial co-insurance up to some limit, or cap. The second is to prevent (politically embarrassing) runs by depositors. This latter requires both 100 per cent deposit insurance, and a very rapid payout, preferably next working day, to succeed.
>
> If a deposit insurance scheme of the second kind is introduced, it will also serve to meet the objectives, i.e. facilitating closure, of the first type of insurance. But it also carries with it an extra disadvantage, in that it makes the character and conduct of her bank of no consequence whatsoever to the depositor. Any such 100 per cent insured bank, irrespective of how awful its reputation may become, can always meet its bills and stay in business, simply by paying marginally over the odds for extra deposits. The moral hazard becomes enormous, whereas the partial co-insurance system does not suffer, at any rate, to anywhere like the same extent, from that serious disadvantage. And it is a serious disadvantage as experience in the USA during the S&L crisis and

empirical studies from the World Bank have clearly shown, see Demirgüç-Kunt and Detragiache (2002), Demirgüç-Kunt and Huizinga (2004), and Demirgüç-Kunt and Kane (2002).

Anyhow the UK system was initially clearly of the first kind. It was first introduced in 1982, and then revised in 1995 in the aftermath of the BCCI crisis of 1991, a bank which clearly had to be shut, but for which the political and legal reverberations continued for many years. It was never intended, nor expected, to prevent runs, since that was not its purpose. Indeed the likelihood of a bank run occurring in this country was not then perceived as a realistic possibility. When, nevertheless, such a run occurred, the current deposit insurance scheme was immediately dismissed as faulty and insufficient, and the plan became to jump directly to the second kind of scheme, 100 per cent insurance, though issues still remain on the coverage and possible cap of the scheme.

There are two problems with this. The first is that the question of what kind of deposit insurance scheme to have, and its coverage, cap and speed of payout, really ought to be European, if not world wide, in answer and resolution. Yet the UK has been rushing towards a unilateral conclusion for itself. Apart from being, typically, non-*communautaire*, this is likely to cause grief in the context of an increasingly cross-border banking system.

The second is that the, seriously disturbing, impetus to moral hazard that the switch from type 1 to type 2 deposit insurance scheme brings with it made it absolutely imperative to introduce at the same time arrangements to allow the authorities to close 'bad banks' before they can pile up potentially huge losses and debts to the insurance fund, that is early closure schemes which go under the generic name of 'prompt corrective action' (PCA). Particularly in view of the switch in the category of deposit insurance scheme, but even without that, Mervyn King, the Governor of the Bank stated that the introduction of such an early closure, PCA, scheme was the most important reform that needed to be introduced (House of Commons Treasury Committee, January 2008, p. 81, Q1608), as was achieved in the Banking Act of February 2009, establishing a Special Resolution Regime Act (SRR) for banks.

There are, at least, three concerns with the current (post-2009) regulatory position. The first is that the scope of the application of the SRR has been limited to banks and building societies, (against the advice of some experts in the prior consultation process, who had argued for a wider remit to all systemically important financial intermediaries). After the experience in the US with both Lehman Brothers and AIG, the authorities there, both Geithner at the US Treasury and Bernanke at the Fed, asked Congress (March 2009) for the ability to extend the special insolvency regime, and PCA, to a wider range of systemically important financial intermediaries. This was done in the Dodd-Frank Act of 2010. The US example suggests that the scope of the UK Banking Act of 2009 may be drawn too narrowly to avert potential difficulties.

The second concern also relates to boundary problems. The first aspect of this relates to branches of foreign banks. These are legally part of the home bank, and covered by the home bank deposit insurance, which, if less generous than the UK insurance arrangements, can be topped-up to the UK level under the UK Financial Services Compensation Scheme, if so chosen by the bank concerned. The problem is that the home country may be unable (or unwilling) to meet its obligations should a domestic bank which is too-big-to-rescue fail. While the FSA can, at least in theory, refuse entry to banks' branches from countries where this might be a problem outside the EU, this cannot be done with banks from EU countries since they have a passport. This (*ex ante* improbable) event actually occurred in the UK with the collapse of Landsbanki HF in October 2008.[1] Adair Turner argued in his review of March 2009 that, unless a harmonised European system of deposit insurance could be introduced, the FSA should have the power to require branches to become fully capitalised subsidiaries of the host country.

I am far from sure, however, that this latter would fully solve the problem. If the home/headquarter bank fails, it is unlikely that the host country subsidiary can survive, however well supervised. There are limits to the extent that host country supervisors can, or should, ring-fence foreign subsidiaries' assets to cover domestic liabilities. Thus, although the local depositors will be protected, the domestic deposit insurance fund will have to rely on the home country government meeting the shortfall, which could be very large. Where the home country gives its domestic depositors preference in cases of insolvency, as in the US or Australia, the loss to the taxpayer (deposit insurance fund) in the host country could be large, even with local supervision of the subsidiary.

The third concern relates to the ability of the FSA to use its power of PCA to close down a bank quickly enough. Take the case of Northern Rock. As of September 2007 its mortgage assets, on an historic basis with default rates up to that point, were assessed as good quality. Yet in view of the prospects for the UK housing market and the effect of that on related residential mortgage-backed securities (RMBS), wholesale depositors were engaged in a quiet run. If Northern Rock had offered well over the odds for additional retail deposits, to fill the funding gap, would the FSA have closed it? Probably not, if only because of the threat of a law suit. By later, in 2008, with the worsening housing market and values of RMBSs, Northern Rock would have become patently insolvent, but its shortfall would by then, almost certainly, have been much greater. Thus the ability to offer 100 per cent insured deposits, and thus often avoid insolvency through inability to meet due payments, could delay the onset of bankruptcy, and make the resultant collapse bigger. In those cases where accountants/auditors can be leant upon (as with Bernie Madoff and Alan Stanford), bankruptcy can be deferred for years, while losses mount.

So the new extended 100 per cent deposit insurance scheme gives bad banks, already established in the UK, much greater scope to defer bankruptcy. Whether the FSA will have the courage and strength of character to shut them down, in the face of threatened law suits, before they can rack up huge uncovered debts has yet to be seen. At the very least the FSA should produce a listing of all banks offering deposit rates significantly above average, and be ready to explain to the Treasury Select Committee what steps they had taken to verify that the business of such banks was in each case acceptably prudent.

LIQUIDITY

The provision of liquidity was the field in which moral hazard first showed in the recent crisis. There are two main aspects of liquidity, funding liquidity and market liquidity. Funding liquidity relates to the ability of banks, and of other borrowers, to raise additional cash by borrowing in (wholesale) markets on reasonable terms (relating to interest rates and duration). Market liquidity relates to the ability of banks, and of other intermediaries, to raise additional cash by selling their assets into the market on reasonable terms (relating to the price adjustment needed to absorb such extra sales).

Both aspects of liquidity had been allowed, by the regulators, to worsen markedly in the years and decades prior to 2007. Banks were increasingly funding their loans, both directly and via off-balance-sheet entities, by means of (short-term) wholesale funding. Loan to deposit ratios, which had been below 100 per cent as recently as 2000, often rose to 150 per cent by 2007. Regulators took no effective steps to check this, perhaps believing that wholesale markets were so efficient that banks capable of meeting their Basel II capital adequacy requirement (CARs) could always access such markets.

The situation with respect to market liquidity had worsened many years earlier. Prior to the 1970s, banks in the UK at least, would typically hold some 30 per cent or more of their assets, directly or indirectly via balances at the discount houses, in public sector debt. Indeed the main prudential ratios at that time related to liquidity, cash or liquid asset ratios, not to CARs. This changed in the 1970s and 1980s as the greater availability of funding liquidity, enhanced competition, and a switch of regulatory focus away from liquidity to capital requirements, took hold.

There was an abortive attempt in the mid-1980s by the Basel Committee on Banking Supervision to agree an accord on liquidity, as a companion to the Basel I Accord on CARs, but it failed. The decline in bank holdings of highly liquid, mostly public sector assets continued, so by the time that wholesale funding markets closed up, from August 2007, the banks had minimally few traditional liquid assets left on their books. So when such banks came to their central bank for liquidity support, they had few traditional liquid assets to pledge as collateral.

The initial reaction to this differed between central banks, and between economists. Some central banks, such as the Bank of England, felt that the banks had misbehaved by leaving themselves so exposed to liquidity shocks. Thus, to lend freely against less liquid assets would be to condone and to reinforce bad behaviour. So the Bank of England was initially reluctant to widen the scope of its Lender of Last Resort (LoLR) support. In contrast the ECB was, from the outset, prepared to lend against a much wider, catholic range of assets, including high-quality RMBSs. It remains unclear, however, whether this was a serendipitous result of including in its set of acceptable assets whatever had been so accepted by any of its initial national central banks, or whether this was the outcome of a conscious choice. The US Federal Reserve System was somewhere in the middle.

Similarly some economists, such as Buiter and Siebert (2007), argued that just as it was the Good Lord's *métier* to pardon and have mercy on sinners returning to the fold, so it was a central bank's *métier* to create liquidity against any asset, so long as such an asset could be reliably priced, so that the central bank could apply an appropriate discount (haircut) to protect itself against loss. Against this, other economists, such as myself, argued that such a generous policy put all the downside of liquidity risk onto the central bank, leaving the commercial banks with the upside benefits; and that the price volatility of less liquid assets would be such that accepting these as collateral could lead the central bank into loss.

In the event, the prospect of contagious financial failure and the economic disasters that could engender, forced those concerned about moral hazard to give way, step by grudging step, until a whole raft of additional non-liquid assets could either be exchanged for liquid assets or pledged directly against cash from the central bank. Similarly and especially, in the US the range of financial intermediaries who could apply to the central bank (Fed) for liquidity support progressively widened. As a generality, though no doubt subject to qualification, the more that a central bank restricted its liquidity support in this crisis out of concern over moral hazard, the worse it performed.

This does not, however, imply *ipso facto* that such concern was, *ex ante*, wrong and misplaced. But it does imply that this experience has shown that, in the event of a crisis, central banks are likely to feel forced, *ex post*, to extend liquidity on the basis of whatever commercial banks, and other systemic financial intermediaries, have available to offer them. So the mere threat of withholding such support, or constructive ambiguity, will not prevent banks from adopting illiquid strategies in pursuit of profits.

What this does imply, therefore, is that there will have to be other (pecuniary) incentives and sanctions in order to encourage banks to adopt more liquid, less illiquid balance sheets. There are various ways of doing so. An original proposal, put forward by Persaud, one of the authors of the Geneva Report on 'The fundamental principles of financial regulation' (Brunnermeier et al., 2009), is 'mark to funding', whereby the accounting procedure to value assets depends on the duration of the liabilities supporting them. A more standard approach, also mentioned in the Geneva Report, is to vary a bank's CAR in line with its liquidity, as measured by its maturity mismatch ratio for example.

Both of these proposals have been criticised, the latter on the grounds that conflating capital and liquidity requirements together is confusing, and puts excessive regulatory weight on time and state-varying CARs. The more mainstream approach is to see LoLR as a form of insurance against liquidity shocks, and to propose that this be financed by insurance premia.

Some would advocate, and hope, that such insurance might be provided by the private sector. That is, in my view, not possible. Only the central bank can, *in extremis*, create liquidity; a liquidity crisis is a tail event with a largely unknown probability; the private sector tends to be myopic in cases with long runs of normal, good outcomes, very occasionally interspersed with disastrous bad events; private insurance would just shift risk from one part of the private sector to another with uncertain effects on its concentration and control (AIG is the obvious example).

Having thus excluded private sector insurance, the remaining solution is public sector insurance. Under this rubric, the central bank imposes a liquidity premium on each bank according to its individual measured liquidity and at the same time lists the terms and conditions on which it will make liquidity available on a wide range of assets (and perhaps more widely to a range of financial intermediaries other than just banks).

SUBORDINATED DEBT

One of the measures of the default risk of a bank has been the price at which its subordinated debt stood, and more recently the price of its credit default swap (CDS). Unlike equity holders, debt holders suffered downside risk, with no potential benefit from upside profit. Whereas equity holders would benefit from the option characteristics of equity, and hence would welcome volatility and gambling for resurrection, bond holders would not. Hence there was a drive by some economists, notably

Calomiris, to require banks above a certain size to issue such subordinated debt *and* to have regulators and supervisors adjust their control measures in line with either the relative (or absolute) pricing of such debt.

But such a line of argument implies that such subordinated debt holders are reliably subject to loss when their bank runs into trouble. This assumption has not been maintained during the recent crisis. The record has been patchy. The subordinated debt holders of Fannie Mae and Freddie Mac were protected, even though their shareholders were effectively wiped out. These debt holdings were so large, and held by such strategic lenders as foreign governments, that default might have adversely affected the credit standing of all US institutions. In the case of Lehman Brothers, the subordinated debt holders were not protected. This resulted in the incipient run on US money market mutual funds. More generally the resulting panic and widespread increase in risk spreads caused governments around the world to guarantee not only all deposits but all debt liabilities including subordinated debt.

In a crisis, when market funding is disappearing, (and wholesale nationalisation of the whole, or a large proportion, of the banking system is not the desired option), any source of additional funding will be welcomed, and further debt issues will then depend on government guarantees on repayment. Thus Tim Bond, the head of asset allocation at Barclays Capital, wrote in the *Financial Times* on 24 March 2009:

> The main objective of government assistance is to prevent a generalised bank run, thereby giving banks sufficient stability to earn their way through the bad debt cycle. This objective is achieved by maintaining confidence that banks can pay their debts.
>
> Any action that hurts the interests of senior bank bond holders would be opposed to this objective. Senior bonds are a necessary source of funding for banks. They supply longer-term liquidity and thus play a valuable role in reducing the vulnerability of banks to the maturity mismatch between long-term loans and short-term funding, the Achilles heel that has caused the downfall of several institutions.
>
> In most European jurisdictions, senior bank debt explicitly ranks *pari passu* with deposits. So any government action that might hurt senior bank debt holders would also hurt depositors, achieving the precise opposite to the presumed intention. In the US, although senior bank bonds rank below deposits, exactly the same arguments apply. Any default to senior note holders is tantamount to allowing the bank to fail, an eventuality that can have, as we saw in the case of Lehman and during the Great Depression, cataclysmic economic effects. As such, the risk that governments might opt for such a policy is virtually zero. In effect, credit markets began to discount a thoroughly implausible outcome to the credit crisis.

Even before the onset of the recent crisis CDS (and bond prices) were somewhat affected by expectations of government rescues in bad circumstances, so that the debt (or CDS) of larger and more systemic institutions would trade at somewhat higher prices, see Völz and Wedow (2009). In the aftermath of the crisis the debt, and CDS prices will be thoroughly polluted by such considerations. This certainly does not mean that such market prices will contain no information; rather that the information content is likely to become much more difficult to interpret. So the proposals to tie regulation/supervision more closely to subordinated debt have probably become derailed.

Meanwhile, and perhaps partly as a consequence of such guarantees, the focus of market attention has been shifting from the wider tiers towards core tier one, excluding even the hybrid forms of capital, such as preference shares. Thus the market is now paying most attention to pure equity and retained earnings as a measure of bank strength.

EQUITY

Indeed equity has had less support from government intervention than other forms of bank liability. It is true that much of such intervention has provided generalised subsidies to banks, and that governments and taxpayers have recapitalised banks. Without such support the banks would either have failed, or would have had to be nationalised. In that sense the equity holder has benefited from government support. But the recapitalisation has led in many cases (such as Lloyds and RBS) to massive dilution, and the decline in bank equity prices from 2007 until March 2009 has been brutal. Bank equity holders have suffered.

The problem in this instance is not an enhancement of moral hazard; it is rather the reverse. Given the apparent increase in risk, how can the banks generate sufficient ROE to support any recovery in bank intermediation. Consider the following. In the aftermath of the crisis, and the greater realisation of the risks involved in banking, investors may be looking for a higher return on equity, than hitherto. Yet required core tier one ratios will be rising, and there are likely to be limits on leverage. So banks are unlikely to be able to generate the ROE that investors will be seeking. The resolution is likely to involve a considerably smaller traditional banking system with much wider margins (spreads) between deposit and lending rates, and probably charges on transactions such as cheque payments.

Such wider spreads are likely to encourage the incursion of alternative, non-traditional forms of banking and disintermediation of banking services, perhaps into markets. In the past bank supervisors, especially in the US, have sought to enforce the separation of banking and non-financial business. There is at least a question whether, in future, retail banking will be combined with retail supermarkets. Perhaps Walmart will become the main rival to Citibank, Tesco of HSBC and Carrefours of BNP; could the Post Office Bank make a come-back?

Increasingly the extension of retail credit, such as car loans and loans to small and medium-sized enterprises (SMEs), is being done on the basis of simplified, standardised, credit scoring systems, accessed electronically, with minimal personal interaction between banker and borrower. But if the personal touch of the banker is no longer required, or used, why have such intermediation at all? Electronic markets can develop enabling lenders both to diversify and to out-source pursuit of defaulting borrowers, a kind of retail borrowing/lending e-bay. ZOPA is one example that already exists. Until the advent of this crisis, I had regarded the business plan of electronic market alternatives to bank intermediation as unlikely to succeed, but the prospective widening of loan/deposits spreads may just hand such markets a golden chance to get established.

It is difficult to envisage either what the future shape of financial intermediation will look like, or what it should look like. My view, however, is that two common sets of proposals – that banks should have much tighter and more restrictive regulation, and that there should be a return to more narrowly focused retail banking – may well be mutually inconsistent. The reason why these may well be inconsistent is that there may be insufficient profit in regulated retail banking to sustain its continuation. What is, perhaps, more likely is that retail banking and money market mutual funds become almost indistinguishable with both providing (mainly electronic) payment and transactions services and both investing in safe, short-term assets, from both the public and private sectors.

In contrast, whereas securitisation is currently regarded as malign, I believe that it will play an increasing role in future finance. The electronic markets for retail lending, which may partially replace banking, will depend on a form of securitisation, whereby lenders will hold claims on a pool of borrowers, and will be able to sell such claims in the market. Similarly securitisation of residential mortgages was an excellent idea; it was just that the quantitative modelling on which it was based was irredeemably flawed.

So, on this view, most retail lending will move out of banks into markets, where such loans will be securitised, and sold onto final investors, both institutional and personal. There will, however, also be special cases for borrowing, including some forms of retail borrowing, that will have to remain on a bilateral over the counter basis. Whether this is done with a retail bank, or with an investment house, remains to be seen.

This leaves the question of what will happen to corporate banking, filling the intermediation requirements of large businesses. Two lessons from the recent crisis are that reliance on wholesale markets can be perilous and that such investment houses have been too big and interconnected to fail. This is, perhaps, where the developing form of financial regulation may make the greatest difference to future financial structure. One could envisage developments whereby large, corporate investment banking is done in specialised, (and perhaps small) investment houses, or in universal banks. It may well depend on the detail of access to central bank liquidity support and of the emerging form of CARs.

What is true is that the regulatory changes under consideration will affect ROE in financial intermediation, and that such shifting ROE will alter the structure of financial intermediation. Many now urge both tighter regulation and a return to traditional retail banking. But the former may lead to the demise of the latter, via its effect on ROE. Instead, we may get a mixture of money market mutual funds, a shift of retail lending into securitised markets, and specialised investment houses doing corporate finance. Are we about to slaughter traditional retail banking on the alter of enhanced regulation?

One accomplice to such murder will have been bank equity markets. 'Mr Market' has not been helpful to regulators. During booms, Mr Market systematically supports highly leveraged banks, while during financial crises it calls for ever higher core equity ratios. This is the opposite of sane counter-cyclical regulation. Indeed the most difficult task for regulators is to act as a counter-balance to the natural tendencies of markets. In so far as 'you cannot buck the market', the job of regulators becomes almost impossible.

EXECUTIVE REMUNERATION

Another right wing maxim is that 'guns do not kill people; people kill people'. Transformed into financial terms, this could be rephrased as 'excessive leverage does not kill banks; chief executives kill banks'. Decisions on how to run banks are generally made by a handful of top executives, with occasional input by large equity investors. The most important determinant of the risk profile of a bank is not, therefore, going to be the regulations on CARs, but the incentives facing top management.

Moral hazard arises when those taking decisions are insured against failure, since there will then be an incentive to gamble. The public fury against the rewards, bonuses and pensions to those in charge of failing banks is partly a witch-hunt, but it is also grounded in the perception that the expectation of such high returns, whatever the out-turn, was not only partly responsible for the genesis of this crisis, but will lead to the next one as well.

Perhaps the abolition of unlimited liability was premature. Could there be two classes of equity, with limited liability for all outside investors, and *unlimited* liability for senior executives, who are each forcibly vested with an unlimited liability share on reaching a top executive position, and have to continue holding it (non-transferable), until death or the termination of their bank? Sir Fred Goodwin and Dick Fuld, to name just two, would now be paupers. Might that make bank executives too cautious and risk averse?

Perhaps we should start from the other end. Exactly how risk averse do we want our banking CEOs to be? How might we start to think about this question? If we know how risk averse we want our bank executives to be, could we then engineer their remuneration package to achieve the desired level of risk aversion, always remembering that those who get to the top of the tree are likely to be supremely self-confident in the first place?

Regulators have hesitated to become involved in remuneration issues, for obvious reasons, but if this is where the fundamental moral hazard resides, perhaps they should overcome their cold feet.

NOTE

1. See the Turner Review, March 2009, Box 1C, p. 38, and Section 2.10 (ii), pp. 100–1.

REFERENCES

Brunnermeier, M.K., A. Crockett, C.A.E. Goodhart, A. Persaud and H.S. Shin (2009), 'The fundamental principles of financial regulation', Geneva Reports on the World Economy 11, Geneva: International Center for Monetary and Banking Studies and Centre for Economic Policy Research.

Buiter, W.H., and A.C. Silbert (2007), 'The central bank as market-maker of last resort 1', accessed at http://blogs.ft.com/maverecon/2007/08 the-central-banhtml/.

Demirgüç-Kunt, A. and E.J. Kane (2002), 'Deposit insurance around the globe: where does it work?', *Journal of Economic Perspectives*, **16**(2): 175–95.

Demirgüç-Kunt, A. and E. Detragiache (2002), 'Does deposit insurance increase banking system stability? An empirical investigation', *Journal of Monetary Economics*, **49**(7): 1373–406.

Demirgüç-Kunt, A. and H. Huizinga (2004), 'Market discipline and deposit insurance', *Journal of Monetary Economics*, **51**(2): 375–99.

Goodhart, C. (2009), *The Regulatory Response to the Financial Crisis*, Cheltenham, UK and Northampton, MA, USA: Edward Elgar.

House of Commons Treasury Committee (2008), 'The run on the Rock', Fifth Report of Session 2007–08 HC 56-I, Incorporating HC 999 i-iv, Session 2006–07.

Rae, G. (1885), *The Country Banker*, London: John Murray.

Turner Review (2009), *A Regulatory Response to the Global Banking Crisis*, Financial Services Authority, March.
Völtz, M. and M. Wedow (2009), 'Does banks' size distort market prices? Evidence for too-big-to-fail in the CDS market', Deutsche Bundesbank discussion paper series 2, no. 06/2009, March.

PART THREE

Macroprudential regulation

7. Implementing the macroprudential approach to financial regulation and supervision

Claudio Borio

INTRODUCTION[1]

Banking and regulatory issues have always been central to David Llewellyn's illustrious career as an academic, policy advisor and public servant. He has proved to be a particularly acute observer of trends in the banking industry (Llewellyn, 1999a). Above all, he always explored those trends not in the abstract, but with the objective of deriving implications for public policy. It is this natural inclination to pursue the public interest, I think, that explains his strong focus on regulation and supervision (Llewellyn, 1986, 1999b and Goodhart et al., 1998). In analysing these issues and in drawing policy prescriptions, Llewellyn's trademark has been a distinct and effortless mix of intellectual rigour and British pragmatism. We have all learnt a lot from him.

In what follows, I develop some reflections on a theme in regulation and supervision that has come to prominence in the wake of the recent financial crisis. Recent international reports have recommended that financial regulatory and supervisory frameworks strengthen their macroprudential orientation (G20, 2009 and de Larosière et al., 2009). The term has become so well accepted that, paraphrasing Milton Friedman, one could say that 'we are all macroprudentialists now'. And yet, a decade ago, the term was barely used and it would have been hard for supervisors to recognise that their tasks involved a significant macroprudential dimension, let alone that it would have been desirable to strengthen it.

In fact, the term is not new. At the Bank of International Settlements (BIS), its usage goes back to at least the late 1970s, to denote a systemic or system-wide orientation of regulatory and supervisory frameworks and the link to the macroeconomy, although public references are of more recent vintage (BIS, 1986). It was already recognised then that focusing exclusively on the financial strength of individual institutions could miss an important dimension of the task of securing financial stability. However, it was only at the beginning of the new century that efforts were made to define the term more precisely, so as to derive more specific implications for the architecture of prudential arrangements (Crockett, 2000, Borio, 2003). This was a phase during which its usage was already becoming more common (IMF, 2000). Subsequently, the macroprudential perspective slowly gained ground, until the current financial crisis gave it an extraordinary boost, as described in Knight (2006), White (2006), Borio (2008) and BIS (2009a).

At the same time, the usage of the term remains ambiguous. Sometimes it is used synonymously with prudential approaches designed to limit the pro-cyclicality of the financial system, seen as a key cause of financial instability. At other times it is still vaguely used to denote approaches designed to address systemic or system-wide risk more generally. What does macroprudential really mean? What are its implications for policy?

Drawing on the long BIS tradition, this chapter seeks to answer those two questions. It first summarises the specific definition and characterisation of the term macroprudential developed in the early 2000s at the BIS. It then considers the outline of policies that could strengthen the macroprudential orientation of regulatory and supervisory frameworks. In the process, it brings together what may appear as unrelated strands of analysis and policy initiatives.

THE MACROPRUDENTIAL APPROACH: DEFINITION, KEY FEATURES AND IMPLICATIONS

Definition and Key Features

It is useful to define macroprudential with the help of its antonym, microprudential, and to do so in an intentionally stylised way. So defined, by analogy with black and white, the macro and microprudential orientations would normally coexist in the more natural shades of grey of regulatory and supervisory arrangements.

As defined here, the three fundamental features that distinguish the macroprudential from the microprudential approach to regulation and supervision relate to objectives, focus and the characterisation of risk (see Table 7.1).

First, the proximate objective of a macroprudential approach is to limit the risk of episodes of system-wide financial distress so as to contain their cost for the macroeconomy. By contrast, the proximate objective of the microprudential approach is to limit the risk of failure of individual

Table 7.1 The macro and microprudential perspectives compared

	Macroprudential	Microprudential
Proximate objective	Limit financial system-wide distress	Limit distress of individual institutions
Ultimate objective	Avoid output (GDP) costs	Consumer (investor/ depositor) protection
Characterisation of risk	Seen as dependent on collective behaviour (endogenous)	Seen as independent of individual agents' behaviour (exogenous)
Correlations and common exposures across institutions	Important	Irrelevant
Calibration of prudential controls	In terms of system-wide risk; top-down	In terms of risks of individual institutions; bottom-up

Source: Borio (2003).

institutions, regardless of their impact on the overall economy. In turn, this is best rationalised in terms of consumer (depositor or investor) protection.[2]

Second, as a result, the focus of the macroprudential approach is the financial system as a whole; that of its microprudential counterpart is the individual institution. This distinguishing feature can best be illustrated with an analogy. One can think of the financial system as a portfolio of securities, with each security representing a financial institution. The microprudential approach would care equally about losses on each individual security; the macroprudential one would focus on the losses on the overall portfolio. What is crucial from a macroprudential perspective is the degree of diversification or concentration of risk not in individual institutions but in the overall system. Thus, what matters are the common (correlated) exposures across financial institutions, not so much those within the portfolios of individual institutions, which represent the main concern of the microprudential approach.

Finally, a macroprudential approach treats aggregate risk as dependent on the collective behaviour of institutions – in technical terms, as endogenous. This is because, collectively, institutions can affect the prices of financial assets, the quantities transacted (borrowed and lent) and hence the strength of the economy itself. This, in turn, has powerful feedback effects on the soundness of the institutions. By contrast, given its focus on individual institutions, a microprudential perspective ignores such feedbacks, treating risk as exogenous. Taken in isolation, individual institutions will generally have little impact on market prices or the economy as a whole. Indeed, this is very much how individual institutions treat risk: they regard asset prices, market/credit conditions and economic activity as unaffected by their decisions. For example, risk models and stress tests take as given the possible range of asset price movements, probabilities of default and the macroeconomy.[3]

Implications

The differences in focus and conception of risk have important implications for how the sources of financial distress are assessed in the two approaches.

From a macroprudential perspective, it is possible that individual institutions may seemingly appear to be safe, while the financial system as a whole is not.[4] This would occur, for instance, if greater diversification of risk in the portfolio of individual institutions was achieved by increasing its concentration in the overall financial system. Even as they disperse risk in their own balance sheets, institutions could be raising their exposure to common risk factors, such as through greater similarity in their portfolios. This would mean that negative shocks would affect more institutions simultaneously, that is that systematic, non-diversifiable risk in the system would increase.[5]

In addition, the endogeneity of risk highlights the possibility that actions that are optimal from the perspective of individual institutions may result in undesirable outcomes for the system as a whole, through adverse feedback effects. For example, retrenchment at times of financial strain is rational and almost irresistible for individual participants. If generalised, however, it could make everyone worse off, by inducing fire sales and tighter credit conditions. Such a possibility is ruled out by definition in the microprudential approach, as risk is treated as exogenous.

This sharp contrast between the two approaches is reflected in the fundamental disagreement over the validity of the microprudential dictum: 'for the financial system to be sound it is *necessary* and *sufficient* that each individual institution is sound'. From a macroprudential perspective, this condition is not necessary: the output costs of financial stress at individual institutions, or even groups of institutions, may not be large enough. More subtly, it is not sufficient either: by failing to take into account common exposures across financial institutions and the endogeneity of risk, a microprudential approach may not promote overall financial stability effectively.

The macroprudential approach to financial regulation and supervision is best thought of as consisting of two dimensions, which have different implications for the calibration of prudential tools. These dimensions are often not sufficiently distinguished in the common usage of the term. The first concerns how risk is distributed in the financial system *at a given point in time* – the cross-sectional dimension. The second concerns how aggregate risk evolves *over time* – the time dimension. The first is like taking a snapshot picture of the financial system; the second is like following its evolution in a movie.

The key issue in the cross-sectional dimension is the existence of common (correlated) exposures. These arise either because institutions are directly exposed to the same or similar asset classes or because of indirect exposures associated with linkages among them (such as counterparty relationships). Returning to the analogy with the portfolio of securities, the main distinction is between systematic or non-diversifiable risk across institutions, on the one hand, and idiosyncratic (or institution-specific) risk, on the other.

Correspondingly, the guiding principle for the calibration of prudential tools is to tailor them to the individual institutions' contribution to system-wide risk. Ideally, this would be done in a top-down way. One would start from a measure of system-wide tail risk, calculate the contribution of each institution to it and then adjust the tools (capital requirements, insurance premia, and so on) accordingly. This would imply having tighter standards for institutions whose contribution is larger. This contrasts sharply with the microprudential approach, which would have common standards for all institutions.

The key issue in the time dimension is how system-wide risk can be amplified by interactions within the financial system as well as between the financial system and the real economy. This is what pro-cyclicality is all about (BIS, 2001; Borio et al., 2001; Brunnermeier et al., 2009). Here feedback effects are of the essence. During expansions, the mutually reinforcing process between falling risk perceptions, rising risk tolerance, weakening financing constraints, rising leverage, higher market liquidity, booming asset prices and hence expenditures feeds onto itself, potentially leading to the overextension of balance sheets. This process, then, operates in reverse, and more abruptly, as financial strains emerge, amplifying financial distress. The main policy question, therefore, is how to dampen the inherent pro-cyclicality of the financial system.

The corresponding guiding principle is to calibrate policy tools so as to encourage the build-up of buffers in good times so that they can be used when strains materialise. This would help to limit the costs of incipient financial stress, by allowing the system to absorb the shock better. Moreover, the build-up of the buffers, to the extent that it acted as a kind of dragging anchor or soft speed limit, could also help to restrain the build-up of risk-taking during the expansion phase. As a result, it would also limit the risk of financial distress in the first place.

THE MACROPRUDENTIAL APPROACH: IMPLEMENTATION

The previous analysis highlights how the macro and microprudential perspectives inevitably coexist in current financial regulatory and supervisory frameworks. For example, tailoring the degree of prudential oversight to the systemic importance of institutions, or limiting risk concentration across the system, is consistent with a macroprudential perspective. By contrast, peer group analysis is micro: it seeks to identify outliers, without regard for whether average performance is appropriate. Importantly, micro is also the general practice of calibrating prudential tools uniformly with respect to the risk profile of individual institutions (for example, calibrating capital requirements so as to achieve a common probability of failure for all institutions). The key policy challenge, therefore, is how to strengthen the macroprudential orientation of current arrangements.

The urgency of this task has been highlighted by the current financial crisis (Borio, 2008). The crisis has put a premium on the need to assess risk from a system-wide perspective. It would have been impossible to detect the threat without considering the exposures held outside the banking system. In the run-up to the current crisis, it was erroneously felt that securitising mortgage portfolios, and slicing and dicing risk in the process, would make the overall system safer. Furthermore, the mistaken belief that the system was better diversified paradoxically encouraged each institution to take on more risk.[6] Moreover, the crisis has been a quintessential example of pro-cyclicality at work. Against the background of low interest rates and aggressive risk-taking, benign economic conditions masked the gradual overextension in private sector balance sheets. Traditional telltale signs of the build-up of risk included booming credit and asset prices, especially in the residential property sector, as well as unusually low volatilities and risk premia across a broad spectrum of asset classes. Once these financial imbalances finally unwound, the process went into reserve with a vengeance. It triggered and amplified financial distress and crippled the real economy.

In what follows I discuss, sequentially, the outline of the efforts needed to implement the guiding principles in the cross-sectional and time-dimensions respectively. I then consider briefly the implications for the institutional set-up.

THE CROSS-SECTIONAL DIMENSION: COMMON EXPOSURES

Current prudential frameworks to some extent already recognise the relevance of common exposures across financial institutions. Supervisors may, on a discretionary basis, constrain overall exposures to sectors that they regard as particularly risky at particular points in time (such as real estate and leveraged loans for example). More importantly, in several jurisdictions authorities have already sought to tailor the supervisory scrutiny of individual institutions to their systemic importance, devoting more resources to them. Steps in this direction have received greater attention since the recent financial strains. For example, a case in point is Switzerland, where the authorities have introduced tighter regulatory and supervisory requirements for the country's two large internationally active banks.

Strengthening further the macroprudential orientation would call for more systematic efforts to measure the contribution of individual institutions to system-wide risk from a top-down perspective. Such contributions would be determined by several characteristics of the institutions, notably their probability of default, relative size and their (direct and indirect) exposure to systematic risk, including that portion that reflects linkages among institutions, such as through counterparty relationships.

The main limitation here is that quantitative methodologies capable of informing such judgements are still in their infancy. Some tools, such as those for the estimation of domino effects through counterparty relationships, can provide a sense of the consequences of the failure of one or more institutions. However, they suffer from a number of drawbacks. They are exceedingly mechanical, eschewing behavioural responses; they call for information about such linkages that is generally not available, except perhaps for specific markets like organised exchanges; and they provide no information about the likelihood of a stress event (Upper, 2007). Other approaches, which generally rely on market prices (such as equities and credit spreads), can yield measures of system-wide tail risk, at least for groups of institutions. This is because they draw on the multivariate probability distribution that underlies asset price movements. Examples include measures of tail risk based on extreme value theory (Geluk et al., 2007) or quantile regressions (Adrian and Brunnermeier, 2008). However, it is either impossible to decompose and allocate these measures to individual institutions or, even if in principle feasible, the corresponding methodologies have not been explored much.

In research with colleagues at the BIS we are seeking to overcome these limitations (Tarashev et al., 2009, 2010). We have developed ways of decomposing aggregate measures of tail risk for groups of institutions, such as system-wide credit Value at Risk or expected shortfall, into additive contributions of the individual institutions. As other methodologies for measuring credit risk, this procedure relies on estimates of probabilities of default and exposure to systematic risk that can be based on market prices.[7] Moreover, the approach to decomposition is quite general and intuitive and can be applied to various metrics of system-wide risk. The approach can help to structure policymakers' thinking about the issues. In principle, tools of this kind could also be used to inform transparent adjustments to instruments such as capital requirements, the intensity of supervisory review or insurance premia.

From an operational perspective, three issues loom large when calibrating prudential tools with reference to the contribution to system-wide risk of individual institutions: the relationship between the cross-sectional and the time dimensions; the choice of portfolio of institutions; and, closely related, the scope of regulation (or its perimeter).

Approaches that estimate the marginal contribution of institutions based on market prices should take into account a fundamental limitation: these prices can be very deceptive measures of the time dimension of risk. This is, in fact, one of the key manifestations of pro-cyclicality. Market price measures of risk tend to be unusually low also when risks are building up, reflecting aggressive risk-taking in the system: risk premia, measured and implied volatilities, and correlations are unusually low. In other words, market prices behave more like thermometers of financial distress, measuring its temperature once it arises, than as barometers of distress, providing signals of its future materialisation (Borio and Drehmann, 2009a). Hence the paradox of financial instability: the system appears strongest precisely when it is most vulnerable. This can easily contaminate the point-in-time measures of system-wide risk and also individual institutions' contributions to it.[8]

One way of tackling this problem is to follow similar procedures to those adopted to adjust risk measures when addressing pro-cyclicality (see below). This means using stressed parameters (derived from periods of financial strains) or averages over long time periods. More generally, the objective would be to focus on the relative contribution of institutions to system-wide risk, rather than on their absolute one. And the risk of estimation error could be further reduced by dividing institutions into different categories, such as through a rating system.

The definition of the correct portfolio is not straightforward. Conceptually, how much of the financial system should be captured before the estimates can be regarded as reliable guides to system-wide risk? And should the portfolio relate to domestic financial systems or to those institutions that comprise the core of the global financial system? Moreover, the data needed for the calculations may not exist for significant parts of the financial sector (such as equities for savings or cooperative banks). A large dose of pragmatism is required. The correct portfolio will depend on priorities as well as the scope for effective international coordination. Practical limitations on the availability of the data may be addressed by using approximations or requiring firms to issue the instruments whose secondary market prices would be used in the estimation.

This also raises the question of the perimeter of regulation. A macroprudential framework would need to address the risks generated by all financial institutions that are capable on their own, as a group and through system interactions, to cause material system-wide damage. To the extent that an indirect approach based on restrictions on the regulated institutions proved insufficient, whether in terms of the ability to request information or take remedial action, the extension of the coverage of the prudential framework would need to be considered. To varying degrees, recent reports point in that direction (G20, 2009; de Larosière et al., 2009).

The analytical efforts to address the cross-sectional dimension of the macroprudential approach have so far been more directly applicable to instruments like capital or insurance schemes. Importantly, they have not targeted liquidity. To be sure, a number of suggestions have been made, including those in Brunnermeier et al. (2009) and Perotti and Suarez (2009). These have been portrayed as tackling pro-cyclicality, mainly by establishing speed limits during expansions or buffers that can cushion strains. However, all of these proposals are calibrated with respect to characteristics of the balance sheets of institutions on a stand alone basis. They fail to take into account common liquidity exposures across institutions. This is an area that deserves further attention.

THE TIME-DIMENSION: PRO-CYCLICALITY

In contrast to the scarcity of work considering the cross-sectional dimension, the time dimension has benefited from major analytical efforts in recent years. It has already given rise to a number of policy initiatives to dampen pro-cyclicality (G20, 2009; Financial Stability Forum, 2009; BIS, 2009b). The goal has been to limit the degree to which the prudential framework and accounting practices may contribute to the pro-cyclicality of the system and to introduce an element of counter-cyclicality in the arrangements. Rather than discussing that work in detail, what follows puts forward five general principles that could guide current efforts. In the process, it also highlights some thorny issues that deserve special attention.

First, a holistic approach is needed. A broad range of policies have an impact on the pro-cyclicality of the financial system. Thus, the required adjustments in the prudential framework will depend on the characteristics of other policies and on any adjustments made to them. For example, the current trend towards fair value accounting is likely to add to pro-cyclicality by making valuations more sensitive to the economic cycle: it embeds evolving estimates of future cash flows and risk premia in the accounting figures (Borio and Tsatsaronis, 2004; Goodhart, 2004; Adrian and Shin, 2008). Other obvious examples include the characteristics of deposit insurance schemes, of resolution procedures and of the monetary policy regime in place. Insurance schemes that are not pre-funded require institutions to pay precisely when the system is facing strains. Resolution procedures for individual institutions that do not take into account system-wide strains could force excessive liquidation.[9] Monetary policy regimes that do not restrain the build-up of financial imbalances, in the form of unusually rapid credit and asset price increases, when inflation is low and stable, may unwittingly accommodate their expansion (Borio et al., 2001; BIS, 2008).

Second, it is important to build on existing arrangements. In particular, Basel II represents a major improvement over Basel I. Through Pillar I, it has greatly improved the ability to discriminate across borrowers in the cross-section, by aligning capital charges much more closely with the relative riskiness of exposures. It has thereby greatly tightened the link between risk measures and minimum capital and reduced the scope for regulatory arbitrage. Through Pillar II, it has substantially enhanced the scope for supervisors to require levels of capital above the minima, thereby allowing them to tailor the capital cushion to the risk incurred by institutions (supervisory review). Through Pillar III, it has offered a tool to strengthen risk disclosures and market discipline. Above all, Basel II has helped to spread and hardwire best risk management practice within the banking industry. The challenge in this area is to reduce the pro-cyclical sensitivity of the framework without sacrificing its ability to differentiate across risks at a point in time, and to do so through simple and transparent adjustments.

Third, the spectrum of options for regulatory capital ranges from reducing its cyclical risk sensitivity to deliberately introducing elements of counter-cyclicality in the framework. There are various ways in which this can de done (Gordy and Howells, 2006; Borio and Drehmann, 2009a; BIS, 2009b; Financial Stability Forum, 2009). Examples include reducing the cyclical sensitivity of minimum requirements, by further smoothing the inputs (based on through-the-cycle or stressed parameters of probabilities of default) or the outputs, and adding transparent counter-cyclical adjustments that would allow the build-up and release of capital buffers. The adjustments could be hardwired to the minima (Pillar 1 in Basel II) or encouraged through the supervisory review process (Pillar II).

Fourth, while a lot of attention has been devoted to capital requirements, other prudential tools are also worth considering. As a preliminary step, prudential filters can be applied to accounting figures to offset undesirable features, such as loan provisioning rules that are not sufficiently forward-looking and prudent (see below). As the availability of funding liquidity is pro-cyclical, funding liquidity standards that rely on quantitative minimum requirements that are invariant to the state of the economy, risk exacerbating financial strains once they emerge. In other words, just like invariant capital requirements, they would act as shock amplifiers rather than shock absorbers (Goodhart, 2008 and Borio, 2010). Increasing variation margins when volatility spikes can have a similar effect. High loan-to-value ratios can add to pro-cyclicality by increasing the sensitivity of the supply of credit to the assets used as collateral (Borio et al., 2001). Arrangements could therefore be adjusted in all of these areas.

Fifth, the operational framework should rely as far as possible on built-in (automatic) stabilisers rather than discretion. This would help address the limitations in the measurement of aggregate risks in real time, which can make discretionary action error-prone. Admittedly, recent work at the BIS has confirmed that simple leading indicators of financial system distress can be developed and perform fairly well also out of sample. In particular, they provide warnings of the current crisis (Borio and Drehmann, 2009b). Even so, the margin of error remains significant. Moreover, relying on automatic stabilisers would limit the danger that, even when risks are correctly identified, action may not be taken at all. The fear of going against the manifest view of markets can have a powerful inhibiting effect. Once in place, automatic stabilisers can act as an effective pre-commitment device. They can help shift the burden of proof (Landau, 2009).

At the same time, automatic stabilisers and discretionary measures should not be seen as mutually exclusive. Discretionary measures could complement automatic stabilisers if the latter faced design limitations. Likewise, discretionary measures might be more easily tailored to the nature of the build-up in risk-taking and vulnerabilities as long as these are identifiable in real time. They may also be harder to arbitrage away, as circumvention becomes easier over time. The key issue would be how to constrain and discipline any such discretion.

There are a number of areas in which automatic stabilisers could be considered. As regards collateral practices, possibilities include seeking to implement through-the-cycle margining requirements (Geithner, 2006 and Financial Stability Forum, 2009) and enforcing maximum loan-to-value ratios that are low and/or based on valuations that are less sensitive to market prices. Similarly, supervisors may consider that accounting standards do not allow for sufficiently forward-looking or prudent provisions. One notable example includes obstacles to the adoption of through-the-cycle provisions for loans, sometimes known as dynamic provisions, based on average historical experience, in place until recently in Spain (Jiménez and Saurina, 2007). In that case, supervisors can add the difference between what they find appropriate and the accounting figures to minimum capital requirements. Importantly, adjustments to capital standards within the existing framework could be made based on specific rules rather than discretion.

It is not hard, however, to see how pure rule-based adjustments may be difficult in some cases. Consider the objective of establishing countercyclical regulatory capital buffers. It is not easy to devise rules that are equally effective during the expansion and contraction phases. For example, linking minimum requirements to credit growth, as suggested by Goodhart and Persaud (2008), could be effective during the expansion phase, but could fail to release buffers at the right time. As the current crisis has demonstrated again, the credit slowdown tends to lag the emergence of strains, not least owing to the drawdown of credit lines. Likewise, relating the minima to credit spreads may be an improvement from that perspective (Gordy, 2009), but their behaviour has not been uniform across stress periods. To be sure, these illustrations do not rule out the possibility of developing rules. They do highlight, however, that discretion and judgement may be necessary too (BIS, 2009a and Caruana, 2009).

Any efforts to build up and release buffers in a credible way will need to address head-on a major issue: as strains materialise, markets may prevent the drawdown from occurring. The recent experience has highlighted how at times of turbulence a sharp rise in the risk aversion and uncertainty of investors will require institutions to raise their capital cushions. There are ways in which this risk can be reduced. One is having buffers and minima that are sufficiently high, underpinned by a credible framework, so that the solvency of the institutions does not come into serious doubt. Another is communicating the rules of the game clearly, so that their application is not seen as a departure from standard practice, which could signal serious concern with the condition of the banks. Even so, it is hard to judge at this stage whether these steps would be sufficient to allow an effective operation of the buffers.

INSTITUTIONAL SET-UP

Two key issues that need to be addressed in the institutional set-up for the implementation of the framework are the needs to ensure accountability and to align objectives with the available know-how.

Accountability calls for a clear mandate, transparency and effective processes to hold policymakers responsible. Accountability is especially important to discipline any reliance on discretion that complements automatic stabilisers. It can generally be enhanced by making sure that the measures used are as simple and transparent as possible. One could imagine a set-up similar to the one now being employed for monetary policy. At the same time, given the lags involved and the inevitable fuzziness in definition and measurement, it would be unrealistic to expect that an equivalent degree of accountability and transparency is feasible (Borio and Drehmann, 2009a).

Addressing the imperfect alignment between goals, instruments and know-how in the institutional set-up is a difficult and controversial task. At a minimum, a financial stability framework with a macroprudential orientation requires close cooperation between a broad range of authorities with respect to both its development and implementation. After all, a wide range of policies under the responsibility of authorities with very different perspectives has a bearing on financial stability.

At the same time, a key ingredient of success is to leverage the comparative advantage of the various authorities involved. This is especially important for monetary and prudential authorities. Monetary authorities have an edge in understanding the nexus between the macroeconomy and the financial system and the functioning of financial markets. Prudential authorities have an edge in understanding the risk management practices of the regulated institutions. For instance, one could set up special committees involving these types of authority and charged with implementing macroprudential overlays in regulatory and supervisory tools that are executed on a discretionary basis. In all of this, it is critical to ensure a sufficient degree of operational independence from the political process. As in the case of monetary policy, this is essential to 'take away the punch-bowl when the party gets going'.

CONCLUSION

To use Llewellyn's expression, the recent crisis 'will be transformational', with deep and long-lasting implications for business models, the banking industry and regulation (Llewellyn, 2009). One implication that has already become apparent is the widespread recognition in the policy community of the need to strengthen the macroprudential orientation of financial regulatory and supervisory frameworks. This swell of support could not have been anticipated even as recently as a couple of years ago. The current financial crisis has been instrumental in underpinning it. So far, policy initiatives have largely focused on addressing pro-cyclicality – the time dimension of the macroprudential approach. Looking ahead, more attention will likely also be devoted to addressing common exposures within the financial system – the cross-sectional dimension. The task now is to examine concretely the spectrum of policy options, so as to evaluate their desirability and feasibility. The BIS is actively involved in this process.

NOTES

1. This chapter is a revised version of the one that appeared in a special issue of the Banque de France Financial Stability Review on 'the future of financial regulation', September 2009. The views expressed are those of the author and do not necessarily represent those of the Bank for International Settlements.
2. For a broader analysis of the justification for prudential regulation and supervision, one that covers the natural shades of grey of actual frameworks, see Llewellyn (1999b).
3. This also indicates that the previous analogy with the portfolio of securities is incomplete, since portfolio managers would also treat the underlying sources of risk as exogenous.
4. For an early academic contribution on this, see Hellwig (1995). See also Acharya (2001) for a perspective highlighting the importance of the cross-sectional dimension of a macroprudential approach, without using this specific terminology.
5. To return to the portfolio analogy, the total variance of a portfolio is equal to the sum of the variances of the returns on each security plus that of the covariances. The return on each security (read financial institution) may have a lower variance, but that of the portfolio as a whole may in fact be larger if the covariances increase by enough. The whole is not equal to the sum of its parts.
6. For an analysis that highlights the role of financial innovation in the recent crisis, see Llewellyn (2009).
7. While the specific implementation is based on market prices, the inputs could also be drawn from assessments of supervisors or combinations of such assessments and market prices.
8. Underlying this form of market failure are limitations in risk perceptions and incentives (Borio, 2003 and 2008; and BIS, 2009b). Llewellyn has always highlighted both, paying particular attention to the role of incentives, both within institutions and in markets more generally (Llewellyn, 1999b and 2008).
9. To this list, one should also add the role that prudential regulation can play in encouraging appropriate remuneration schemes, which can help to lengthen the effective horizon of private agents (Rajan, 2005 and BIS, 2009). This is another theme very close to Llewellyn's heart, given his strong focus on incentives (Llewellyn, 2008 and 2009).

REFERENCES

Acharya, V. (2001), 'A theory of systemic risk and design of prudential bank regulation', mimeo, London Business School.

Adrian, T. and H.S. Shin (2008), 'Liquidity and financial cycles', Bank for International Settlements working papers, no. 256, July.

Adrian, T. and M. Brunnermeier (2008), 'CoVar', Federal Reserve Bank of New York staff reports, no. 348.

Bank for International Settlements (BIS) (1986), 'Recent innovations in international banking', report prepared by a study group established by the central banks of the Group of Ten countries, April, Basel.
Bank for International Settlements (2001), *71st BIS Annual Report*, Basel: BIS.
Bank for International Settlements (2008), *78th BIS Annual Report*, Basel: BIS.
Bank for International Settlements (2009a), *79th BIS Annual Report*, Basel: BIS.
Bank for International Settlements (2009b), 'Addressing financial system procyclicality: a possible framework', note for the FSF working group on market and institutional resilience, April, accessed 5 October 2010 at http://www.financialstabilityboard.org/publications/r_0904e.pdf.
Borio, C. (2003), 'Towards a macroprudential framework for financial supervision and regulation?', *CESifo Economic Studies*, **49**(2): 181–216; also available as Bank for International Settlements working paper, no 128.
Borio, C. (2008), 'The financial turmoil of 2007–? A preliminary assessment and some policy considerations', in *Revista de Estabilidad Financiera*, Bank of Spain; also available as Bank for International Settlements working paper, no 251.
Borio, C. (2009), 'Ten propositions about liquidity crises', *CESifo Economic Studies*, **56**(1), 70–95.
Borio, C. and M. Drehmann (2009a), 'Towards an operational framework for financial stability: "fuzzy" measurement and its consequences', Bank for International Settlements working paper, no. 284, June; also in the conference proceedings of 12th Annual Conference of the Banco Central de Chile, 'Financial Stability, Monetary Policy and Central Banking', 6-7 November, Santiago.
Borio, C. and M. Drehmann (2009b), 'Assessing the risk of banking crises – revisited', *BIS Quarterly Review*, (March) 29–46.
Borio, C., C. Furfine and P. Lowe (2001), 'Pro-cyclicality of the financial system and financial stability: issues and policy options' in 'Marrying the macro- and micro-prudential dimensions of financial stability', *BIS Papers*, (1) (March) 1–57.
Borio, C. and K. Tsatsaronis (2004), 'Accounting and prudential regulation: from uncomfortable bedfellows to perfect partners?', *Journal of Financial Stability*, **1**(1): 111–35. A more extensive version is also available as 'Accounting, prudential regulation and financial stability: elements of a synthesis', Bank for International Settlements working paper, no. 180, September 2005.
Brunnermeier, M., A. Crockett, C.A.E. Goodhart, M. Hellwig, A. Persaud and H.S. Shin (2009), 'The fundamental principles of financial regulation', Geneva Reports on the World Economy 11, preliminary conference draft.
Caruana, J. (2009), 'The international policy response to financial crises: making the macroprudential approach operational', panel remarks at Financial Stability and Macroeconomic Policy Conference, 21-22 August, Jackson Hole, WY.
Crockett, A. (2000), 'Marrying the micro- and macroprudential dimensions of financial stability', speech to the Bank for International Settlements 11th International Conference of Banking Supervisors, 21 September, Basel.
de Larosière, J. et al. (2009), 'de Larosière report', various authors.
Geluk, J., L. De Haan and C. De Vries (2007), 'Weak and strong financial fragility', Tinbergen Institute discussion paper.
Financial Stability Forum (2009), 'Report of the Financial Stability Forum on addressing pro-cyclicality in the financial system', April, Basel.

Geithner, T. (2006), 'Hedge funds and derivatives and their implications for the financial system', remarks at the Distinguished Lecture 2006, sponsored by the Hong Kong Monetary Authority and Hong Kong Association of Banks, Hong Kong SAR.
Goodhart, C. (2004), 'Some new directions for financial stability?', The Per Jacobsson Lecture, 27 June, Zurich, Switzerland.
Goodhart, C. (2008), 'Liquidity risk management', Banque de France *Financial Stability Review* (February), 39–44.
Goodhart, C., P. Hartmann, D.T. Llewellyn, L. Rojas-Suarez and S. Weisbrod (1998), *Financial Regulation: Why, How and Where Now?*, London: Routledge.
Goodhart, C. and A. Persaud (2008), 'A party pooper's guide to financial stability', *Financial Times*, 4 June.
Gordy, M. (2009), 'First, do no harm – a hippocratic approach to pro-cyclicality in Basel II', Dutch National Central Bank Conference, February.
Gordy, M. and B. Howells (2006), 'Pro-cyclicality in Basel II: can we treat the disease without killing the patient?', *Journal of Financial Intermediation*, **15**(3): 395–417.
Group of Twenty (2009), 'Enhancing sound regulation and strengthening transparency', paper from G20 working group 1, 25 March.
Hellwig, M.F. (1995), 'Systemic aspects of risk management in banking and finance', *Swiss Journal of Economics and Statistics*, **131**: 723–37.
International Monetary Fund (IMF) (2000), 'Macroprudential indicators of financial system soundness', IMF occasional paper No. 192, April.
Jiménez, G. and J. Saurina (2006), 'Credit cycles, credit risk, and prudential regulation', *International Journal of Central Banking*, (June), 65–98.
Landau, J.P. (2009), 'Bubbles and macroprudential supervision', remarks at the conference on 'The future of financial regulation', Banque de France and Toulouse School of Economics, 28 January, Paris.
Llewellyn, D.T. (1986), *Regulation and Supervision of Financial Institutions*, London: Chartered Institute of Bankers.
Llewellyn, D.T. (1999a), 'The new economics of banking', SUERF Studies, no.5.
Llewellyn, D.T. (1999b), 'The economic rationale for financial regulation', Financial Services Authority Occasional Paper Series, no. 1, April.
Llewellyn, D.T. (2008), 'Key issues for regulators and supervisors', in D. Mayes, R. Pringle and M. Taylor (eds), *Towards a New Framework for Financial Stability*, Central Banking Publications.
Llewellyn, D.T. (2009), 'The banking crisis: how did we get here and where do we go from here?', lecture at PRMIA, Vienna Chapter Meeting, 9 November.
Perotti, E. and J. Suarez (2009), 'Liquidity insurance', *Vox*, 27 February.
Rajan, R.J. (2005), 'Financial markets, financial fragility, and central banking', paper presented at 'The Greenspan Era: Lessons for the Future' symposium sponsored by the Federal Reserve Bank of Kansas City, 25-27 August, Jackson Hole, WY.
Tarashev, N., C. Borio and K. Tsatsaronis (2009), 'The systemic importance of financial institutions', *BIS Quarterly Review* (September), 75–87.
Tarashev, N., C. Borio and K. Tsatsaronis (2010), 'Attributing risk to individual institutions', Bank for International Settlements working papers no. 308, March.
Upper, C. (2007), 'Using counterfactual simulations to assess the danger of

contagion in interbank markets', Bank for International Settlements working paper no. 234, August.
White, W. (2006), 'Pro-cyclicality in the financial system: do we need a new macrofinancial stabilisation framework?', Bank for International Settlements working papers no. 193, January.

8. Rules for money and rules for finance: a new relationship after the crisis?

Franco Bruni[1]

INTRODUCTION

Weaknesses in financial regulation and supervision are usually indicated as the most important cause of the global financial crisis. They are particularly harmful as financial innovation creates complex and opaque financial instruments. David Llewellyn's papers share this view, with which I agree as well.[2,3] However, monetary policy has serious responsibilities in causing the crisis. The abandonment of monetary discipline resulted in too low interest rates for too much time, nourishing asset price bubbles and financial instability. The consensus analysis of the crisis is in agreement with this idea but, when discussions look at the remedies to avoid future crises, monetary policy issues are left aside while re-regulation monopolises the discourse.

Proposals are put forward to organise new 'macroprudential controls', monitoring and checking systemic risks along the cycle and counteracting the pro-cyclicality of prudential regulations. Countercyclical macroprudential controls would work in parallel with monetary policies and could imply new responsibilities for central banks.

The next section recalls that monetary policies are among the causes of the crisis and amplify regulatory failures. The third section considers the complementary roles of monetary and prudential measures in crisis management and in improving the long run stability of the financial system. The fourth section discusses the past and future of the relationship between monetary and prudential policies, leading to the concept of macroprudential controls, which is developed in the fifth section. The conclusion points at the issues to be addressed for optimising the role of central banks as systemic regulators.

MONEY AS A CAUSE OF THE CRISIS AND AN AMPLIFIER OF REGULATORY FAILURES

The easiest way to accuse monetary expansion for inflating the bubble and, eventually, causing the crisis, is to look at central bank-controlled interest rates. A book by John Taylor discusses the deviations from the Taylor rule from 2002 to 2006.[4] The average (negative) deviation in the US has been around 3 per cent. The ECB's deviation has been smaller but consistent and persistent; it can be in part explained with an implicit exchange rate targeting, trying to limit the appreciation of the euro – under the pressure of European exporters and of their powerful political supporters – thus following the Fed's expansion. The latter is often explained in ways which give importance to the support of stock prices, generously offered by Alan Greenspan after the end of the tech-bubble.[5]

I think this standard way of discussing monetary indiscipline is inadequate. The problem is deeper and has its roots well before the excessive expansion of this decade. The failure of monetary policies came at the peak of what was considered a long lasting success, starting with the fight against the Great Inflation of the 1970s and reaching its triumph with the paeans to the Great Moderation, an oxymoronic background music to the euphoric growth boom of the late 1990s. In fact the pride of being 'greatly moderated' supported the idea of continuing to accelerate aggregate demand with monetary and fiscal policies, as followed the crash at the beginning of the 2000s. The success of monetary policy was thought to be grounded in some sort of orthodoxy developed as a reaction to the Great Inflation. The failure of monetary discipline in the new millennium casts doubts on this orthodoxy.

The orthodoxy was based on three ideas: high and variable inflation has high social costs; overabundant money and credit is a necessary condition for inflation; expectations and credibility are central in fighting inflation with monetary policy. Among the consequences of these ideas, orthodox monetary thinking included: considering price stability as the primary objective of central banks; defending central banks' independence of political powers; caring about the accountability and the transparency of monetary policy actions; using monetary rules to avoid the mystique of central bankers and the excesses of their discretion.[6] Manipulating short-term interest rates with flexible Taylor-type rules was the typical orthodox procedure, framed in central banks' strategies oriented towards expected inflation targeting.

The success of monetary orthodoxy turned out to be unsustainable. The reason can be traced to the weaknesses of orthodox thinking. First of all, strategies and institutional rules of central banks were far from complying with its principles. This was also the case for the primacy of price stability and for the independence and accountability of central banks, particularly in the US.

A second weakness was the bias of monetary policies towards fine tuning. Fine tuning was not excluded by orthodoxy, and Taylor-type rules were often interpreted as an encouragement to fine-tune the short-term behaviour of inflation and estimated output-gaps. Fine tuning is destabilising though, as indicators are faulty and monetary moves reach the economy with long and variable lags. Moreover, fine tuning offers frequent opportunities for political and market pressures to try and interfere with long term monetary strategies. The typical interference would be to underestimate the output gap and/or the inflation forecast implicit in an asset-price bubble, in order to obtain lower interest rates to benefit private and public debtors, short-sighted stockholders and speculators.

The process of globalisation put other weaknesses of the monetary orthodoxy in the spotlight, including its conception for a closed economy. The main problem with globalisation was the confusion it caused with the sources of inflation: US inflationary policies, for instance, tended to disperse their effects in the global economy while US domestic inflation was contained by low Chinese labour costs. Domestic product-price inflation indicators became less effective for inflation-targeting strategies. Insufficiently flexible exchange rates frustrated monetary policies aimed at national objectives.[7] Nevertheless international cooperation on monetary policies was nearly absent; from the late 1990s an evident dollar problem was left mounting for more than a decade, without even any summit-based cooperation in the style of the 1980s.

While monetary orthodoxy emphasised the independence of central banks from political powers, it was less concerned about pressures coming from the private sector. Monetary authorities risked being pliant when financial markets wanted cheap money for speculation and to boost the profitability of intermediaries funding their operations on the wholesale markets. Monetary orthodoxy also turned out to be unprepared for the intensity of financial innovations, which led to challenging changes in the transmission of monetary impulses and in the roles and meaning of liquidity.

In a world with an overabundant supply of liquidity and supply-driven low interest rates, the flow of credit is impetuous and disordered: regulatory failures become more probable and damaging. Inadequate prudential policies can therefore cause a crisis in ways connected with imprudent monetary policies. This was the case during the five years preceding the explosion of the crisis in 2007. Too low short-term risk-free interest rates distort the formation of risk premia: the possibility for opaque intermediaries to borrow liquid funds at nearly risk-free rates and invest them in risky projects, leads to smaller spreads as their borrowing costs decrease.[8] With undersized risk premia, prudential controls come under severe stress and can easily fail. Moreover, overabundant liquidity acts as an incentive for asset managers to over-compete in selling illiquidity, pretending to offer alpha extra performance while beta risky returns are engineered forgetting the fat tails of probability distributions.[9] Again, this over-competition puts dangerous stresses on prudential regulation and supervision.

There is also a pure macroeconomic effect of monetary expansion whereby financial instability is the consequence of price instability and of excesses in real investments and/or in consumption. Finally, monetary ease tends to take away pressure to reform inadequate regulations, as the low cost of borrowing acts as an (unsustainable) subsidy to compensate for the costs of mistaken and imprudent risk management.

MONEY VERSUS REGULATION AS CURES OF THE CRISIS

Monetary policies are among the causes of financial crises but are also crucial in curing them and in ensuring long-run stability. They must have the right relationship with prudential policies. Lending of last resort (LoLR) is the typical contribution of monetary policy to crisis management. LoLR can be more or less regulated with Bagehot-type rules that dictate conditions for a proper extension of central bank support to illiquid banks. The crisis has emphasized both the importance and the difficulty of distinguishing between illiquidity and insolvency. Central banks have played their role trying to exploit the vagueness of that distinction. They have offered increasing support to a failing interbank market, moving towards unlimited and unregulated LoLR. Risky securities have been accepted as collateral and no effort has been made to offer liquidity in return for transparency to strengthen the incentives for banks to reveal the location of toxic assets and rebuild informed trust on the money markets.

New thoughts on the rules for LoLR should result from the experience of the crisis. Bagehot's famous recipe suggested penalty rates for LoLR: a rule to be re-examined but too anxiously and opaquely wiped out during the crisis.[10] The idea of penalising the borrower with a requirement of increased transparency should also be discussed. *Lombard Street*'s modern aspects can be resuscitated: the book also implies an anti-cyclical rule for interest rate policy that would have prevented the boom that preceded the crisis.[11]

In managing the present crisis monetary policy looks to be a substitute rather than a complement of regulation. This also applies to the de-leveraging of banks. More than prescribing the extent and the timing for undoing the extra leverage, the authorities have subsidised banks' recapitalisation by enacting a zero-interest rate policy. Free liquidity is available for banks' high yielding and risky investments with an implicit guarantee of bailout. The resulting margins make up for the losses of the crisis and help de-leveraging. The access to central banks' money is also putting banks in a special position to exploit the steepness of the term structure and to help finance booming government deficits. In the meantime, a hardly effective moral suasion is exerted to push banks to pass on the low interest rates at which they are able to borrow plenty of liquidity, to crisis-stressed firms. In fact the aim of the monetary policy ease is more to support banks' capital accumulation than to stimulate lending to firms in the real economy.

Hopefully, the crisis will bring new policies to regulate banks' leverage and its profile during the cycle. Monetary policy cannot be a healthy solution for a lack of good rules to discipline the return of banks to sound levels of capitalisation. Moral hazard and the misuse of cheap liquidity could cause new dangers for financial stability.

Crisis management must become a better regulated affair, with less discretion for authorities to buy time with easy money, to exert forbearance and to postpone difficult real adjustments in the financial industry. Monetary and financial rules must therefore develop a more virtuous relationship in dealing with crises. This relationship has an even more important role in preventing crises and enhancing long-run systemic stability. To this end, what has been labelled monetary orthodoxy must be reconsidered, with an improved design of the role, the strategy and the institutional setting of central banking. New rules must be explicitly written in monetary constitutions to make them more clear, credible and strong.

The role of price-stability as a primary objective of monetary policy must be affirmed also in the US and reinforced. But, at the same time, the fact that price stability is a long-run goal must be taken more seriously. This requires the reconsideration of monetary policy rules, both by academics and policymakers, around three crucial issues.

The first is the role of asset-prices, which have been central in the subprime crisis. Certain economic conditions should require asset price dynamics to be considered in deciding countercyclical monetary policies. One example is when many asset prices are moving fast together and their movement has the same direction as that of large and sustained changes in monetary and credit aggregates. In these conditions, asset prices become good indicators of long-term potential consumer-price movements even when, for various reasons, short-term inflation indicators are silent.

The second issue is the role of monetary and credit aggregates as anticipators of price-dynamics and indicators of the aggregate risk exposure of financial intermediaries. Theoretical analysis, empirical research and central banks' experience must come together and provide a remedy to the current strange situation, where theoretical models of monetary policy do not even include money and banks, and where decisions on interest rates are taken disregarding the behaviour of any quantitative measure of liquidity.[12] Common sense and a long tradition of monetary studies, going back to the old debate between monetarists and Keynesians, must be able to generate a new attention to monetary aggregates.

The monetarist caution in manoeuvring the money stock to control the cycle, in view of the long and variable lags with which money affects the real economy, does not impede an intelligent use of monetary aggregates as indicators of portfolio disequilibria and of inflation tendencies. The Keynesian attention to the instability of the demand functions for financial assets and for the role of wildly changing expectations of financial speculators, the consideration for how financial innovation and the portfolio substitutability disrupt any simple relationship between financial aggregates and the real economy – all this does not impede a useful systematic reading of the messages conveyed to the interest rate setter by a well defined set of quantitative monetary indicators. A new 'Keynesian monetarism', aimed at the long-run stability of the economy, must reaffirm the importance of the quantities of money and credit even in the subtle complexity of modern financial sectors.

The information on systemic risks contained in the dynamics of credit aggregates must be carefully extracted. The third issue in re-appraising the role of monetary policy is the relationship between price and financial stability, where the former remains the target of monetary policy but cannot be the sole preoccupation of central banking. The role of central banks in maintaining sustainable financial stability must be redefined together with the policy tools required to cope with macro-systemic risks.

MONETARY POLICY AND FINANCIAL STABILITY

The relationship between the responsibilities and the policies aimed, respectively, at monetary and financial stability, has a long and noble history, and is an essential part of the history of central banking.

Central banking, in its oldest, archaic form, had nothing to do with financial stability nor with macro monetary policy: it was aimed at financing governments and sharing seigniorage in return for certain monopoly rights in note issuing.[13] Classical central banking during the gold standard, on the other hand, was very much about financial stability, as monetary policy was constrained by currency convertibility. After World War II, traditional central banking was ambitious in performing discretionary monetary management, while direct controls on financial markets and intermediaries imposed financial stability, paying high costs in terms of efficiency, helping the financing of governments' needs, and weakening the distinction between micro-supervision and financial dirigisme. In some countries a deliberate use of the inflation tax was facilitated by central banks' complicity with a regime of financial repression. The anti-inflation, pro-market reaction of the 1980s saw a rapid establishment, both in theory and in practice, of modern central banking, concentrated on pursuing price stability and refusing direct controls on markets and intermediaries.[14]

During these modern times, even if many central banks had both monetary and prudential responsibilities, a bias for separateness developed. Long years of absence of systemic crises produced an understatement of macro-stability issues, while caring for micro-stability – the stability of individual intermediaries – had an intrusive, politically-oriented flavour suggesting that it should be kept as separate as possible from independent monetary policies. Deregulation and global competition weakened the club-like behaviour of banks, making them more reluctant to help rescue a competitor with their own funds coordinated by central banks. Fiscal authorities were involved in emergency bailouts, thus claiming political control of financial supervision. Emphasis was placed on potential conflicts of interest arising when financial stability required cheap liquidity policies endangering monetary stability, and vice-versa.[15] In the 1990s this bias for separateness blocked the involvement of the newborn ECB in supervision and in 2000 produced the creation of the FSA in the UK.

We are now hopefully moving towards post-modern central banking. Deregulation, globalisation and financial innovation, starting from the late 1980s, have gradually increased the attention paid to financial fragilities which are also coherent with a world where technical progress and competition result in higher price flexibility, frequent productivity shocks and intensive international capital mobility. These developments echo certain aspects of classical times. Post-modern times might now meet classical times, with a return of central bank involvement in financial stability policies. After all, the preoccupation of classical central banks with currency convertibility and commercial banks' reserves was focused on indicators of macro-financial stability.

Financial macro-instability can have different origins. When it is caused by bad monetary policy, which is also endangering price stability, the task of preventing and curing instability is obviously with monetary policy itself. Traditional orthodoxy states that, from the point of view of monetary policy, financial stability is a by-product of price stability.[16] This is too simple an approach: when there are long and unpredictable delays between the dynamics of money and prices, monetary authorities must not wait for an alarm on the inflation front to start caring for indicators of financial instability, including the rates of growth of credit aggregates. On the contrary, these indicators must be highly influential on their countercyclical decisions on interest rates.

To the extent that macro-instability is instead a consequence of bad regulation and of inadequate supervision, monetary policy cannot be charged with the additional objective of preventing systemic risks. But even if monetary policy remains targeted to price stability, the responsibility for systemic financial stability can be kept under the same roof and assigned to central banks. By using two sets of instruments, the two types of targets can be pursued effectively. The term macroprudential controls is gradually becoming the official label to indicate the set of instruments devoted to macro financial stability, which is described below.[17]

The third possible origin of macro financial instability are non-monetary and non-financial real shocks, like negative macro-supply shocks, first causing direct troubles to the users of financial services and then resulting in systemic problems for financial markets and intermediaries. Central banking can hardly be involved in preventing these types of systemic shocks, and its role when they happen, is limited to help manage the crisis.

MACROPRUDENTIAL CONTROLS AND CENTRAL BANKING

The first tool for pursuing systemic financial stability is macro lending of last resort (LoLR). LoLR has been discussed above as the typical contribution of monetary policy to crisis management. Even if, in principle the assistance of central banks should be *erga omnes*, in practice micro LoLR reaches individual financial operators. As a tool for macro stability though, central banks' lending facilities and open market operations are targeted to the money market as an aggregate entity and are based on an evaluation of aggregate-systemic liquidity risks. In this perspective, LoLR appears less as an emergency action and more difficult to distinguish from the continuous flow of operations with which central banks maintain orderly markets for liquid funds, thus preventing macro instability. But the role of macro LoLR as an emergency tool can suddenly become very evident, as happened during the interbank market freeze that followed the explosion of the subprime crisis. On this occasion, so called quantitative easing and non-standard operations have also been used that cannot be easily distinguished from macro LoLR.

The second tool for macroprudential control is the collection of relevant information and the timely monitoring of indicators of systemic instability risks. The difficulty in defining and measuring systemic stability is sometimes cited as a serious problem in mandating its pursuit. But abstract definitions are academic curiosities while the real thing consists in selecting the statistical information to be regularly analysed as well as the critical values of alarm parameters. Recent experience has shown that certain sources of risk have been treated with insufficient care, like the intricacies of financial innovation, the indeterminacies of asset pricing and the risk of illiquidity. Effective approaches aimed at detecting the systemic nature of risks must be developed: this requires a well thought out equilibrium between an essentially macro view and a detailed set of micro information. The latter must not be simply aggregated but used smartly enough to understand how and when a micro problem could constitute a significant stress for the macro financial system. This understanding requires special attention to micro data on large and systemic intermediaries, independent from the fact that they are considered too large or too systemic to fail. If they are not allowed to fail, their surveillance must be special in order to avoid moral hazard and to be ready for micro-targeted LoLR; but even if allowed to fail, their systemic importance offers to the supervisors a special source of information to monitor the risks of macro instability.

The relationship between the institution responsible for macro stability and the micro supervisor must therefore be one of very intensive cooperation. A systemic approach to macro stability requires the availability of a third tool in the set of macroprudential controls: the coordination of micro stability policies and surveillance. The relationship between macro and micro stability authorities must be at least partially hierarchic, with macro authorities in a position not only to have full access to micro information but also to dictate and standardise the criteria for micro surveillance. Macro authorities must be able to judge when a micro episode has systemic importance, they must maximise the probability of detecting such episodes and they must have the powers to dictate micro interventions when required to preserve macro stability, as in the case of large, systemic institutions.

The fourth set of macroprudential controls is the newest one: its introduction is under discussion both in the EU and in the US. It consists in the countercyclical manoeuvring of regulated parameters such as capital ratios, dynamic provisioning, liquidity ratios, leverage ratios, and minimum trading margins. When endowed with this tool, the macro stability authority directly intervenes in piloting along the credit cycle the risk management of financial operators and intermediaries. This piloting does not aim at micromanaging individual institutions but influences macro stability mainly with regulatory moves implemented across the whole banking and financial system. It has a truly double nature of a monetary and prudential policy tool.

Monetary discipline and macroprudential controls have to be coordinated and the natural candidate to perform the role of macroprudential authority is the central bank. Only the central bank can extend micro and micro LoLR and a proper use of this instrument requires all the information that is needed to monitor systemic stability. Micro surveillance can be the task of a different agency, but the latter must follow the guidelines required for systemic purposes by the central bank, and the central bank must have complete and immediate access to the whole set of micro prudential data.

Under the roof of the central bank, monetary policy and macroprudential instruments can be optimally combined to target price and systemic financial stability. Any trade-offs between the two targets can be resolved with appropriate procedures inside the same institution. Moreover, the trade-offs cannot be very relevant to the extent that both policies are performed with a medium- to long-term horizon and in a countercyclical fashion, which must be very clearly stated in the mandate of the central bank. Conflicts of interest between the two policies requiring, for instance, higher interest rates for price stability and lower interest rates for financial stability, can arise only when at least one of the two policies has been wrongly phased in a pro-cyclical way, resulting in an inflationary (depressed) aggregate demand with too low (high) interest rates and too abundant (prudent) supply of credit.

Counter-cyclical coordinated monetary and macroprudential policies avoid these situations. During the rising part of the cycle, when insolvencies are rare, markets are very liquid and a brisk appetite for risk prevails, abundant credit flows are monitored and controlled with the joint use of monetary and systemic stability policies. Interest rates are raised in time, together with capital ratios of financial intermediaries, with higher provisioning for their future expected losses and higher precautionary balances of liquid funds. This combination of monetary and prudential restrictions checks the inflationary pressures that develop when the cycle reaches its highest phase and moderates the increase of the leverage of the intermediaries and of their clients and prevents bubbles in various asset prices inflated by injections of excessive credit. The timely and coordinated adoption of these policies decreases the probability that an excessive boom develops, followed by a crisis, and favours the setting aside of capital and liquidity to cope with the negative part of the cycle that follows, during which both monetary and prudential policies are gradually eased, allowing cheaper and easier credit to counteract the increase in the probability of losses and in the degree of risk aversion of intermediaries and investors. The profile of the cycle is thus stabilised and major crises avoided between booms and busts.

If central banks are also entrusted with the responsibility for systemic financial stability, the importance of their independence from political and market pressures, and of their accountability to democratically responsible powers, increase together with their powers.[18] While it is far from easy to guarantee the independence and accountability of a central bank, it might be easier to obtain them for a single agency than for two agencies, separately responsible for monetary and financial stability policies. On the other hand, the risk of having the two policies under the same roof is that a loss of independence and credibility of one infects the other.

The greater difficulty is with the independence of the financial stability authority: it is a serious, conceptual difficulty, arising from the role of public finance in the bailouts that can be needed when financial stability policies fail. The possibility of such failures can be used as an argument in favour of government interferences with financial surveillance. This problem has no simple solution as it creates a link between the rules for crisis management and the location of powers of financial surveillance in normal times.

CONCLUSIONS

Both monetary and prudential policies were responsible for the international financial crisis. Monetary mistakes have amplified prudential failures while weaknesses in monitoring financial stability have favoured monetary indiscipline. An important lesson to be drawn is that the two policies must develop a new relationship, with newly conceived macroprudential tools manoeuvred in coordination with revised orthodox interest rate-setting policies.

Detailed, concrete discussions of this coordination cannot abstract from the issue of the institutional architecture that locates the responsibilities for the two policies. Strong arguments seem to motivate their joint assignment to the central bank. The advantages of this solution look larger than the risks.

As a matter of fact, both in the US and in the EU, the crisis-induced reform proposals stress the importance of macroprudential controls and acknowledge the need to coordinate them with monetary policy. But the role of the central bank is controversial. In the EU the main problem is that, while monetary policy and the ECB are fully supranational, financial regulatory powers are still decentralised at the national level. This contrast is preventing the reform process, inspired by the de Larosière report, from seriously enhancing the ECB's powers in matters of systemic financial stability.[19] In the US, the tremendous political difficulties of simplifying the architecture of financial authorities have led the government to stop short of trying a radical reform while proposing a greater role for the central bank in systemic regulation and surveillance: but this proposed role is one of the main obstacles to the approval of the whole reform.[20]

Should the central bank be the systemic regulator? This problem delays the reforms dictated by the experience of the crisis. On both sides of the Atlantic, bureaucratic jealousies, nationalisms and political conservatisms, explain only part of this impasse as, on the issue, the opinions of prestigious academics as well as of experienced policymakers do not coincide either. Two types of old perplexities still play a role. One is best expressed by Andrew Crockett in saying that 'taking on supervision and regulation, central banks would thrust themselves into an inherently political role – that of telling businesses what they can and cannot do. It would be difficult for them to maintain the independence from the political process that they require to conduct monetary policy'.[21]

The other perplexity is the standard conflict of interest problem, already discussed above, that John Taylor described as follows in testifying to Congress: '. . . there will be a temptation to adjust the instruments of monetary policy to protect institutions by not increasing short-term interest rates even though such an increase would be warranted under the price stability goal. Or the Fed could mistakenly recommend an otherwise inappropriate start of the resolution regime for one or more [systemically important institutions] because that would make it easier to raise interest rates in order to achieve its price stability goals'.[22] Help to overcome these perplexities can come from a more transparent discussion of at least five aspects.

First is the exact specification of the systemic-prudential powers and responsibilities that can be handed to the central bank. Macroprudential tools, as described above in this chapter, are different, for instance, from the 'consolidated supervision and regulation of all large interconnected firms', as proposed in the US.

Second is the need for a binding mandate to manoeuvre monetary and prudential instruments in a transparently counter-cyclical manner. As argued above, this should avoid most of the risk of falling into a situation where monetary restriction (ease) is required together with a prudential ease (restriction). Stating the counter-cyclical rule in a very explicit way should also help the central bank to resist political and market pressures when, for instance, the time comes to start an unpopular restriction of both the money supply and the macroprudential tools in order to moderate, from its beginning, the expansionary phase of the credit cycle, thus avoiding asset prices deviating from fundamentals and starting a bubble.

A third aspect relates to the general issue of rules versus discretion. A powerful central bank, in charge of both monetary and prudential policies, can be perceived as dangerous if endowed with excessive discretion. Potential dangers consist, paradoxically, in the de facto weaknesses implied by discretion, as in the example just made of pressures to avoid stopping the beginning of a credit boom. But the opposite dangers can arise when discretion is used to arbitrarily manoeuvre the economy by a central banker that is effectively too powerful. Long-term stability-oriented rules should be specified in the mandate of the authority, including guidelines on the indicators to be used in deciding how and when to intervene. Appropriate accountability procedures should prevent any arbitrary use of the powers of the central bank and require corrections when the results are inadequate. Inserting the right amount of rules in the joint monetary and prudential mandates of central banks is also useful for international coordination purposes: similar and compatible rules adopted by the authorities of different countries would result in a higher degree of international monetary and financial stability.

Fourth, as 'he who pays the piper calls the tune',[23] preventive prudential responsibilities cannot be allocated independently of the rules and powers that govern crisis management, bankruptcy procedures, the issues of too big and too systemic to fail, LoLR versus bailouts and the national and international sharing of their burden.[24] This chapter does not discuss these topics, which require difficult political decisions for any effective re-regulation. The experience of the crisis shows too much opacity in its management, non-constructive ambiguity and a noise-producing confusion in both political and technical choices. This constitutes an obstacle in formulating credible prudential policies for future non-crisis times, as the impact of preventive rules depends on expectations on the *ex post* behaviour of authorities, when rules fail and crises erupt. In particular, the credibility of counter-cyclical macroprudential rules, governed by a politically independent central bank, needs explicit limits and rules for the socialisation of the costs of bubble bursting.

Finally, the discussions on extending the responsibilities of central banks to systemic stability must not be mixed up with quarrels on their past responsibilities. Removing the people and changing the governance that has allowed past mistakes at monetary and prudential institutions is not in contradiction with increasing their responsibilities in framing a new architecture of rules. The proposals to increase the future powers of central banks should not even be contrasted with the allegedly excessive, pervasive roles that they have assumed de facto in managing the crisis, after it exploded, with the large increases in their balance sheets and, seemingly, a weakening of their independence of political forces and large troubled banks. On the contrary, setting new and more precise rules for the future is the best way to end the distorting impact of emergency on the roles of the different institutions.

NOTES

1. This is a revised version of a paper presented at the conference on 'Financial Institutions, Systems and Markets: Structure, Performance and Regulation', Burleigh Court Loughborough University, 16 June 2009.
2. See, for instance, Llewellyn (2009a) and, on the UK case, Llewellyn (2009b).
3. Bruni (2009a).
4. Taylor (2009a), in particular Fig. 1, 2, 4, and 5.
5. Bruni (2009b), pp. 102–16.
6. In 2000 Mervyn King told a story of a dinner he had with Volcker in 1991, when he left the London School of Economics for the Bank of England. He asked Volcker if he had a word for a new central banker. The answer was literally a single whispered word: 'mystique'. King's story wanted to be a joke about the old views on central banking. But Volker's humour could have been overlooked by King, his whisper meaning that he was already critical about mystique ten years before his younger British colleague. In fact the preference of orthodox monetary thinking for rules and transparency started before the end of the 1980s.
7. China's exchange rate policy is the most cited example, but one can detect an implicit exchange rate target also where full flexibility is the official regime, as in the case of the euro area, allowing the US to 'export' part of the inflationary pressures they were creating.
8. Bruni (2009a), sec. 2.1.
9. Rajan (2006).
10. Castiglionesi and Wagner (2007) show that, when banks' efforts do not reduce sufficiently the probability of liquidity shocks, penalty rates cause moral hazard reducing banks' incentives to avoid insolvency.
11. O'Brien (2001).
12. For several years this has been the case also for the ECB, in spite of its official strategy that would have required to take into account the large deviations of the growth rate of M3 from a predetermined critical value.
13. Goodhart (1988), p. 20.
14. Bruni (2001).
15. A wide analysis, typical of the early 1990s, of the theoretical relationship between monetary policy, financial regulation and supervision, is in Bruni (1992). The issue of separateness was discussed by Goodhart and Shoenmaker (1995), where the 'conflict of interest' problem was suitably de-emphasized. A previous version of their famous paper was presented at a conference on prudential regulation and monetary policy organised by Bocconi University with proceedings published by the *Giornale degli Economisti* (1992). Inflationary consequences of central banks in charge of supervision were detected in the review article by Di Noia and Di Giorgio (1999).
16. See, for instance, Bordo, Dueker and Wheelock, 2000.

17. The most important contribution for designing macroprudential policies and their relationship with monetary policy has been given for many years by the Bank for International Settlements. Among the numerous papers available see, for instance, Borio (2007) and Borio and Shim (2007).
18. In fact, Goodhart and Shoenmaker (1995, p. 544) observe that 'there is a tendency for more dependent central banks to have combined [monetary and prudential] functions'.
19. de Larosière (2009), in particular section III and recommendations 16–18.
20. US Department of the Treasury (2009), in particular section I.
21. See IMF (2009).
22. Taylor (2009b), p. 2.
23. 'He who pays the piper calls the tune. As the rescues are increasingly being financed by the tax-payer, so the responsibility for supervision and regulation of the system – in order to avoid excessive calls on such tax-payers' funding – has been passing more and more from central banks to separate agencies established under the aegis of the authorities', Goodhart and Shoenmaker (1995), p. 544.
24. On international burden sharing see Goodhart and Shoenmaker (2006) and (2009).

REFERENCES

Bordo, M., M. Dueker and D. Wheelock (2000), 'Aggregate price shocks and financial instability: an historical analysis', National Bureau of Economic Affairs working paper 7652.

Borio, C. (2007), 'Monetary and prudential policies at a crossroads? New challenges in the new century', *Moneda y Crédito*, **224**: 63–101.

Borio, C. and I. Shim (2007), 'What can (macro-)prudential policy do to support monetary policy?', Bank for International Settlements working papers no. 242, December.

Bruni, F. (ed.) (1992), 'Prudential regulation, supervision and monetary policy: theory, international comparisons and the European system of central banks' role', proceedings of the conference, Giornale degli Economisti e Annali di Economia October–December.

Bruni, F. (1992), 'Sui rapporti fra politica monetaria, regolamentazione finanziaria e vigilanza', *Giornale degli Economisti e Annali di Economia*, (January–April), 27–75.

Bruni, F. (2001), 'Financial stability, regulation, supervision, and modern central banking', in A.M. Santomero, S. Viotti and A. Vredin (eds), *Challenges for Central Banking*, Boston: Kluwer Academic Publishers, pp. 19–37.

Bruni, F. (2009a), 'Do we understand it? Forbidden questions on the financial crisis', 'Paolo Baffi' Centre Research Paper Series No. 2009-36, accessed January 2010 at http://ssrn.com/abstract=1336406.

Bruni, F. (2009b), *L'acqua e la spugna: i guasti della troppa moneta*, Milano: Università Bocconi Editore.

Castiglionesi, F. and W. Wagner (2007), 'Turning Bagehot on his head: lending at penalty rates when banks can become insolvent', mimeo, October, University of Tilburg.

de Larosière, J. (2009), Report of the high-level group on financial supervision in the EU, 25 February, Brussels.

Di Noia, C. and G. Di Giorgio (1999), 'Should banking supervision and monetary policy tasks be given to different agencies?', *International Finance*, **2**(3), 361–78.

Goodhart, C.A.E. (1988), *The Evolution of Central Banks*, Cambridge, MA: MIT Press.

Goodhart, C.A.E. and D. Shoenmaker (1995), 'Should the functions of monetary policy and banking supervision be separated?', *Oxford Economic Papers*, **47**, 539–60.

Goodhart, C.A.E. and D. Shoenmaker (2006), 'Burden sharing in a banking crisis in Europe', *Sveriges Riksbank Economic Review*, **2**, 34–57.

Goodhart, C.A.E. and D. Shoenmaker (2009), 'Fiscal burden sharing in cross-border banking crises', *International Journal of Central Banking*, **5**(1), 141–65.

International Monetary Fund (IMF) (2009), 'How to ensure financial stability after the crisis', IMF online survey, 14 May.

King, M. (2000), Address to the joint luncheon of the AEA and the AFA, 7 January, Boston, MA.

Llewellyn, D.T. (2009a), 'The global financial crisis: the role of financial innovation', in P. Booth (ed.), *Verdict on the Crash: Causes and Policy Implications*, London: Institute of Economic Affairs.

Llewellyn, D.T. (2009b), 'The Northern Rock crisis: a multi-dimensional problem', in F. Bruni and D.T. Llewellyn (eds), *The Failure of Northern Rock: A Multi-dimensional Case Study*, Vienna: Suerf Studies.

O'Brien, D.P. (2001), 'Bagehot's *Lombard Street* and macroeconomic stabilisation', *Scottish Journal of Political Economy*, (September), 425–41.

Rajan, R.G. (2006), 'Monetary policy and incentives', address at the Bank of Spain conference on central banks in the twenty first century, June.

Taylor, J.B. (2009a), *Getting Off Track*, Stanford, CA: Hoover Institution Press.

Taylor, J.B. (2009b), 'Monetary policy and systemic risk regulation', testimony before the Subcommittee on Domestic Monetary Policy and Technology, Committee on Financial Services, US House of Representatives, July.

US Department of the Treasury (2009), *Financial Regulatory Reform – A New Foundation: Rebuilding Financial Supervision and Regulation*, Washington, DC.

9. Financial crises from 1803 to 2009: the crescendo of moral hazard

Forrest Capie and Geoffrey Wood[1]

INTRODUCTION

Since late 2007 the banking systems of the world have been in turmoil. Despite this, there has been little discussion of the classic Lender of Last Resort (LoLR), essentially no consideration of whether the use of that technique could have prevented these banking difficulties leading to the recent sharp economic slowdown and severe recession in many countries, both developed and developing. Our aim in this chapter is to consider why this was; to discuss whether LoLR operations could have prevented or at least mitigated the consequences of what has been often called a world-wide financial crisis; and, if the answer is negative, what this implies for both the LoLR and the range of policy tools which are currently available for the preservation of financial stability.

WHAT IS A FINANCIAL CRISIS?

An implicit definition of a financial crisis was developed in parallel with the policy for how to deal with such episodes. The policy was what has become known as a lender of last resort operation, and, very soon after Francis Baring's 1797 use of the term (in French) Henry Thornton (1802) provided a statement of what the LoLR was, why it was necessary, and how it should operate. This statement was an essentially complete description of the LoLR role as it worked up to the beginning of this century. His statement was made in a particular institutional context, and it is as well for the sake of subsequent clarity to set out what this context was.

There were many banks in England, all (except the Bank of England) constrained to being partnerships of six or fewer. The joint stock form was not generally allowed until 1826, and limited liability not until 1858. Even with the care that unlimited liability surely brought, failures were common. It is here that the Bank of England comes in.

> If any bank fails, a general run upon the neighbouring banks is apt to take place, which if not checked in the beginning by a pouring into the circulation of a very large quantity of gold, leads to very extensive mischief (Thornton, 1802, p. 182).

And who was to 'pour in' this gold? The Bank of England.

> . . . if the Bank of England, in future seasons of alarm, should be disposed to extend its discounts in a greater degree than heretofore, then the threatened calamity may be averted (Thornton, op. cit., p. 188).

This was not incompatible with allowing some individual institutions to fail.

> It is by no means intended to imply that it would become the Bank of England to relieve every distress which the rashness of country banks may bring upon them: the Bank by doing this, might encourage their improvidence. . . . The relief should neither be so prompt and liberal as to exempt those who misconduct their business from all the natural consequences of their fault, nor so scanty and slow as deeply to involve the general interests (Thornton, op. cit., p. 188).

Concern should be with the system as a whole. And the reason a 'pouring into the circulation' (to use Thornton's phrase) would stop a panic and thus protect the system was described with great clarity by Bagehot in 1873.

> What is wanted and what is necessary to stop a panic is to diffuse the impression that though money may be dear, still money is to be had. If people could really be convinced that they would have money. . . Most likely they would cease to run in such a herd-like way for money (1873, pp. 64–5).

In the kind of banking system which Britain had by the mid to late nineteenth century, a system based on gold but with the central bank the monopoly supplier of notes, the responsibility for diffusing '. . . the impression that . . . money is to be had' clearly rested with the central bank.

That summarises nineteenth century theory on the subject. Because the central bank was the main note issuer it was the ultimate source of cash.[2] If it does not by acting as LoLR supply cash in a panic, the panic will continue, get worse, and a widespread banking collapse ensue, bringing along with it a sharp monetary contraction.

The practice of that theory developed with remarkable rapidity. Sterling returned to its pre-war gold parity in 1821. The first subsequent occasion for emergency assistance from the Bank was in 1825. A stock market boom developed, particularly in Latin American stocks. There had been a substantial external drain of gold, and there was a shortage of currency. A panic developed, and there were runs on banks. The type of bills the Bank would normally discount soon ran out and the panic continued. If a wave of bank failures were to be prevented, the banks would have had to borrow on the security of other types of assets. On 14 December 1825 the Bank of England suddenly deviated from its normal practice, and made advances on government securities offered to it by the banks instead of limiting itself to discounting commercial bills. Of that change of policy Jeremiah Harman, a director of the Bank, spoke as follows when giving evidence before a Parliamentary Committee in 1832. The Bank had lent money '. . . by every possible means and in modes we had never adopted before; we took in stock on security, we purchased Exchequer bills, we made advances on Exchequer bills, we not only discounted outright but we made advances on the deposit of bills of exchange to an immense amount, in short by every means consistent with the safety of the Bank, and we were not on some occasions over nice'.

As Hawtrey (1932) wrote of these now famous remarks, 'In reality the advances he describes were of a highly conservative character'. (p. 122). But to continue that quotation from Hawtrey:

> The importance of the change in practice was that it admitted a class of borrowers on irreproachable security, who had nevertheless been barred by the previous limitations. The concession was a real one, and it stayed the panic.

Several steps followed in the next few decades. In the 1830s the usury laws were relaxed at least for the Bank. In the 1840s, following the tighter definition of the gold standard in 1844, there was the Chancellor's letter that relieved the Bank of the need to hold to the 1844 Act. That became understood in the 1850s to be a precedent. Interestingly, across these decades the general philosophy was laissez-faire and in banking we do indeed see a steady deregulation. The next step was taken in 1866, with the Overend, Gurney Crisis.

Overend, Gurney, and Co. originated with two eighteenth century firms, the Gurney Bank (of Norwich) and the London firm of Richardson, Overend and Company. By the 1850s the combined firm was very large; its annual turnover of bills of exchange was equal in value to about half the national debt, and its balance sheet was ten times the size of the next largest bank. It was floated during the stock market boom of 1865. By early 1866 the boom had ended. A good number of firms were failing. Bank rate had been raised from 3 per cent in July 1865 to 7 per cent in

January 1866. After February, bank rate started to ease, but on 11 May Gurney's was declared insolvent.

To quote the *Bankers' Magazine* for June 1866, 'a terror and anxiety took possession of men's minds for the remainder of that and the whole following day'. The Bank of England for a brief time made matters worse by hesitating to lend even on government debt. The Bank Charter Act (which, among other things, restricted the note issue to the extent of the gold reserve plus a small fiduciary issue) was then suspended, and the panic gradually subsided.

The failure in 1878 of the City of Glasgow Bank was much less dramatic. The bank had started respectably, was managed fraudulently, and failed. There was fear that the Bank Charter Act would have to be suspended again (see Pressnell, 1968), but no major problems appeared.

Then in 1890 came the (first) Baring Crisis. Barings was a large bank of great reputation; in 1877, when Treasury bills were introduced, Bagehot praised them as being 'as good as Barings'. It nevertheless became involved in a financial crisis in Argentina. The Argentinean government found difficulty in paying the interest on its debt in April 1890; then the national bank suspended interest payments on *its* debt. This precipitated a run on the Argentinean banking system. There was a revolution on 26 July. Barings had lent heavily to Argentina and on 8 November it revealed the resulting difficulties to the Bank of England. The Bank (and the government) were horrified, fearing a run on London should Barings default. A hurried inspection of Barings suggested that the situation could be saved, but that £10 million was needed to finance current and imminent obligations. A consortium was organised, initially with £17 million of capital. By 15 November the news had leaked, and there was some switching of bills of exchange into cash. But there was no major panic and no run on London or on sterling.

Why the great difference between the first, second, and third of these episodes? The Bank of England had both learnt to act as lender of last resort and it had become clear that it stood ready so to act. What the Bank had done wrong in 1866 was to lend '. . . hesitatingly, reluctantly, and with misgiving . . . (But) to make large advances in this faltering way is to incur the evil of making them without obtaining the advantage' (Bagehot, op. cit.). The Bank learned the appropriate action quickly; H.H. Gibb, governor of the Bank from 1875 to 1877 described the 1866 crisis as 'the Bank's only real blunder in his experience'; but he did not criticise the then governor, for '. . . the matter was not as well-understood then as it is now. . .'.

So by 1866 the lesson that was learned in Britain was that a banking crisis could be stopped by prompt LoLR action. One concern does however arise from drawing that conclusion solely on the basis of British nineteenth century experience, and it is a concern that, it will emerge, is of particular relevance to current difficulties. It is not quite so clear as Bagehot maintained that the Bank of England's taking on the LoLR role was what brought stability to Britain after 1866. For branch banking was starting to spread rapidly. By the fourth quarter of the nineteenth century, mergers among banks, leading to banks with wide geographical diversification and diversification by type of customer, were well advanced. Branched banks are more robust, at any rate to localised shocks, than unit banks; note that of the 9036 banks which failed in the US in the Great Depression, only ten were branched (Benston, 1990). (This may of course reflect not just the effect of branching, but also of other factors such as scale.) The British experience thus provides somewhat contaminated evidence of the success of LoLR action. A brief glance at some developments in France and in Italy, however, provides evidence free of such contamination.

The Banque de France can trace its origins to a bank founded in 1800 by a group of Parisian banks. Early in its history it was willing to discount commercial paper very freely in the face of liquidity crises. It did so in 1810, 1818 and 1826. But on other occasions it did not, and here the demonstration of the importance of LoLR is clear. In 1848 it allowed the failure of all provincial banks of issue. There is dispute over why it allowed these failures, but whatever the explanation the French experience supports the view that LoLR action contains a crisis, while absence of such action allows a localised panic to turn into a widespread banking crisis.

Italy confirms that lesson. The Kingdom of Italy was established in 1861. After the new state was founded the currency was unified, but there remained several banks of issue. In the 1880s there was a series of crises. Banks had rapidly expanded their loans to industry, and to real estate speculation. Following a rapid expansion in construction, prices collapsed and numerous real estate companies and banks failed. The banks of issue, themselves involved in this, were pressed by government to rescue other banks and in consequence got into severe problems. In 1893 the Banca d'Italia was founded and the number of banks of issue reduced from six to three. By 1907 the Banca d'Italia had adopted the Bagehot principle of lending freely in a crisis (it referred to Bagehot in its 1907 report and accounts), and in 1910 acted in accordance with his principles. In its report of that year, the Bank of Italy wrote:

> At that particular time, what was important to the Italian business community was not so much to obtain funds at reasonable conditions, but to know that credit was still available for good risk transactions. And the Bank did not fail to provide this type of credit.

In contrast to the 1880s, despite there still being a system of many banks each with at most a few branches, there was no crisis in the sense of a run on the banking system. Problems were contained by LoLR action. It thus seems reasonable to conclude that such action is sufficient to prevent localised panic leading to general crisis. This conclusion, based on nineteenth and early twentieth episodes, was re-emphasised recently, first in Argentina and more recently still in south east Asia. Argentina had adopted what was in all essential features a currency board, fixing the peso against the US dollar in April 1991. Inflation fell, fiscal discipline was restored, and private capital started to flow in. But there had been no reforms to the banking system. It was undercapitalised, and while the central bank had regulatory powers, because of the currency board arrangement it could act as LoLR to only a very modest extent. The banking system was thus both fragile and without access to abundant central bank liquidity provision in a panic.

Seeing the fall of the Mexican peso (in 1995) depositors at Argentinian banks had the similarities between Mexico's and Argentina's circumstances thrust before them. They withdrew pesos and converted them to US dollars. Inevitably in the absence of a LoLR, there was a sharp monetary contraction. GDP fell by over 5 per cent in 1995, and unemployment rose from 10 per cent to 17 per cent. The still more recent south east Asian experience is similar. In the wake of the collapse of the Thai baht, attention turned to Indonesia, Malaysia and the Philippines. Banks had been lending extensively in domestic currency while borrowing in foreign currency. When depositors started to withdraw their funds, no liquidity could be provided by the central bank. Again consequent upon lack – indeed impossibility – of LoLR action, severe problems followed.

A brief summary of the evidence, up to the early twentieth century, on the effectiveness of LoLR action in the traditional sense would be that whenever it was used in a banking crisis the crisis ended, and wherever in such times of crisis it was not used, the crisis continued and got worse, usually with serious consequences for the economy affected. This conclusion was reinforced by a very brief glance at the experience of some developing countries late in the twentieth century.

How did the LoLR perform – indeed, was it called on – in Britain, the country of its birth, in the twentieth century?

BRITISH BANKING IN THE TWENTIETH CENTURY

The first problem to hit British banking (and much else besides) in the twentieth century was the outbreak of the First World War. Just like the outbreak of the Napoleonic Wars in 1793, the first economic impact was felt through failure, and the expectation of failure, of remittance from abroad.

The Balkan Wars had left a legacy of political tension in Europe, and there was a widespread belief that problems were not over. Nevertheless the tension was chronic rather than acute until the assassination of the heir to the throne of Austria on 29 June 1914. Even then there was a temporary calm until 24 July, when Austria sent its ultimatum to Serbia. This ultimatum, together with the fear that hostilities would encompass all Europe, created a financial panic.

On the London Stock Exchange in the last two weeks of July there was a rush to sell, and it started to be feared that foreign borrowers would not be able to remit payment to the accepting houses.[3] When war broke out between Austria and Serbia on 28 July there was an immediate scramble for liquidity. The banks called in loans from the stock exchange and the discount market, leading to further falls on the former and forcing the latter to borrow from the Bank of England. Bank rate was raised from 3 per cent to 4 per cent on 30 July. On 31 July the stock exchange closed to trading and bank rate was raised to 8 per cent. The next day bank rate was raised again to 10 per cent. The panic had by this time spread to the general public, and the banks, fearing a drain of gold, refused to pay out gold coin to their customers.

On 2 August there came the formal declaration of war between Russia and Germany. The next day, a Monday, was a bank holiday in Britain, and to provide thinking time the closure of the banks was extended for three days. In addition, to protect the accepting houses from their immediate difficulties a moratorium on bills of exchange was declared. By 6 August the main measures to deal with the crisis had been decided. (Meanwhile Britain had declared war on Germany on 5 August; in those days the British government could walk and chew gum at the same time).

A general moratorium was then declared, the 1844 Bank Act was suspended, and bank rate started to be reduced. Meanwhile, as there were fears of an internal currency drain, plans were made to print Treasury notes. However, when the banks opened again on 7 August this fear turned out to be unfounded, and Bank rate was reduced again the next day to 5 per cent. There remained problems in the bill market, and these were dealt with by direct government assistance, plans for which were announced on 13 August and 5 September. Describing the crisis, Hartley Withers (1915) wrote, '. . . it came upon us like a thunderbolt from a clear sky . . . no credit system could have stood up to the events'; this reflected the view of most contemporary financiers and journalists.

The unexpected and total failure of remittance had placed stockbrokers in difficulties, as they had borrowed to finance the purchase of stock for clients. These securities were often given as collateral for the loan, and as their prices fell so did the value of them as collateral. The resulting forced sales drove prices down further. Had the banks not called in their loans or demanded increased collateral, the secondary selling would not have taken place; it is on those grounds that Keynes and some other contemporaries criticised the actions of the banks.

The banks also came under attack over their money market operations. At the end of July 1914 there were some £350 million of bills outstanding in the London market. Of these, about £3 million fell due each day. The failure of remittance meant that a good proportion of this – that corresponding to loans to foreigners – was irrecoverable for the foreseeable future. The accepting houses, who were liable to meet them on maturity, were immediately in difficulties. They had not expected such a sudden and large increase in defaults. The banks were concerned about the effect on their liquidity position that defaults on these bills would cause, so started to call in funds from the discount market. This in turn forced the discount market into the Bank.

The banks' behaviour was in fact perfectly comprehensible from their point of view. As Withers (1915, op. cit.), Morgan (1952) and Sayers (1976) have all pointed out, taking the liquidity position of the banks into account shows that they had good reason to call in loans from the stock market and the discount market and, to withdraw gold deposited at the Bank of England, another action they were criticised for at the time. For the banks were expecting heavy withdrawals by their depositors and, in addition, a good proportion of their assets had become illiquid or of uncertain value. The failure of international remittance had rendered one of their most liquid assets, the bill of exchange (then some 9 per cent of total assets) illiquid. In addition, they had themselves accepted some £69 million of such bills, and were liable to meet them on maturity. Stockbrokers were in no position to repay many of their loans from the banks, and the banks themselves had their security holdings locked up when the stock exchange closed. All in all it was neither surprising nor unreasonable, despite criticism at the time and occasionally subsequently (for example, de Cecco, 1974) that the banks sought liquidity wherever they could find it.

As is clear, the system coped well after a brief period of panic. A traditional LoLR operation, the provision of funds to the discount market, maintained liquidity in the system. That of course was insufficient, for problems of solvency loomed. Indeed, it was fear over solvency that led to the scramble for liquidity (just as in the case of Northern Rock). A large amount of debt had suddenly, to use a modern term useful in pointing up parallels, become toxic. Looking to precedent, the Bank in 1914 could have recollected the example of Barings in 1890. When that bank had been at risk of insolvency, a lifeboat (another modern term used to help point parallels) was launched and capital provided. But the scale of the 1914 problem was much greater. The Bank did not have a big enough balance sheet to help. The banks were themselves threatened. The government did not have funds immediately available, and a gilts issue was obviously impracticable. Further, supposing anyone had time to think of it as events progressed, there need be no concern over moral hazard and therefore no need to discriminate between the deserving and the undeserving. It was a common shock, one which could not have been insured against except by stopping doing business before the shock had hit the system. The moratorium dealt with the immediate consequences of this shock, and assistance to the bill markets tidied things up subsequently. Suspension of the 1844 Bank Act had always been possible in a crisis, and the issue of Treasury notes turned out to be unnecessary.

Thus the nature of the crisis influenced the solution. It was not a pure liquidity crisis, so other measures were needed. But there was a liquidity crisis, so the LoLR was not redundant, although it had to be supplemented by other policy tools.[4] Certainly at the beginning of the twentieth century, the LoLR played a crucial role in Britain. Did it continue to do so in later British episodes?

PEACE THEN WAR AGAIN

In the interwar years, although economic performance was mixed the banking system remained essentially robust. Even in 1931, which is sometimes misleadingly referred to as a financial crisis, the banks performed moderately well. Their profits were down a bit (the full extent was disguised at the time) but there were no grounds for concern about them. There was a currency crisis and the mistake of 1925 had to be corrected but apart from that the system was undisturbed. The Bank had imperceptibly become an overseer of the banking system. When a bank got into difficulty the Bank would suggest to another bank that it might take it over and might indeed itself provide that bank with an indemnity against loss in the process.

Although there was an immediate rise in bank rate when war broke out in 1939, in fact there was no need for it and there was no drama. After the Second World War the banking system continued to remain strong and anyone talking about financial stability in Britain would have been regarded as strange. Financial stability was taken for granted. But then as is frequently the case, after a period of increased competition in 1971–73 and of expansionary monetary policy, there was a huge growth of the fringe banking sector. This sector lay outside the banks subject to credit controls (and in many ways was a consequence of avoiding the controls) and its business model was to borrow in the short-term money markets (the interbank market) and lend on property. A great property boom developed, with all the accompanying dodgy practices that are expected. When the monetary authorities then tightened policy in the face of spiralling inflation, the market turned down, the euphoria turned to gloom, property companies failed and then too the fringe banks seemed in danger.

There were then fears that the difficulties might spread to other parts of the banking system and the Bank launched a rescue operation that came to be called the lifeboat. This should properly be called crisis management of the kind that was organised for Barings in 1891. The question that arises is: why not rely on that former stabiliser, the LoLR, if indeed it were needed? Any bank in difficulty that held good assets could have gone to the Bank and got the necessary liquidity. If they did not hold the appropriate assets then that might be considered poor management and they could be left to fail. If they were thought of as sufficiently good risks then a clearing bank might well have thought it worth while rescuing them.

Instead of which the Bank became involved in a long process (many years in some cases) of propping up or winding down a large number of institutions at considerable cost in terms of resources devoted and in some cases in substantial losses. That seems to have been the Bank's approach thereafter: quietly to bail out or otherwise arrange the affairs of banks in trouble no matter how small and insignificant they were. In the mini-crises of the early 1980s and 1990s, and from year to year across the last third of the century, that was the practice. How much moral hazard was being stoked up is hard to say.

THE FRINGE BANKS AND DIVERSIFICATION

The fringe banks got into difficulties for two reasons. They were undiversified, primarily lending on commercial property, and they relied on short-term money to finance long-term lending (just as did Northern Rock). The dangers of lack of diversified lending are highlighted by evidence from past rescues. In the course of the Great Depression over 9000 banks (roughly one-third of all banks) failed in the US. During the same period, in adjacent Canada there were no overt bank failures, although one bank, supposedly the weakest in the Canadian system, merged with another. In Britain there were no bank failures. Even after allowing for the different economic sizes of these countries (and in those days the US was not so large relative to Britain as it is now) there is still a striking discrepancy that requires explanation. It is also worth observing that in any year in the period 1950 to 2000, one could say that more banks had failed in the US in the previous year than had failed in Britain in the previous century. In good times and in bad, banks in the US seemed to be more fragile than those in the UK. Why is that the case?

SYSTEM STRUCTURE

In the US there are many small banks. There were in the 1930s, and indeed still are, unit banks – banks with only one office, concentrated in one area and doing retail banking only. These banks are very exposed to the problems of their local area – a shock, such as a major firm being in difficulties there, and the bank may well fail. These banks were the ones that predominantly suffered as a consequence of the Federal Reserve's mistakes in the 1930s, and these were the banks that so regularly failed over the past century in the US.

In the Great Depression, banks which had diversified geographically to the extent US law at that time allowed, and which had gone into investment as well as retail banking, were more robust than their unbranched retail fellows. And in the UK and Canada, banks were allowed to diversify and had branched not only across the country but, particularly in the UK case, across the world.

Not surprisingly, diversification brought stability. If one line of business or activity in one geographical area of operation did not do well, another did, or at least sufficiently so to keep the bank afloat. The main cause of the wave of bank failures, and subsequent severe monetary contraction in the US, was the behaviour of the Fed but in the banking sector the burden of the Fed's failure fell predominantly on the small undiversified retail banks. Does that mean that despite the current enthusiasm for separating 'utility banks' (retail) from 'casino banks' (investment), banks should actually be allowed to remain as they currently are, not even nudged to do something else?

The answer is not a simple yes or no. The implications of the above outline of the experiences of bank stability in different countries, and the relationship of bank stability to bank structure, are several. First, investment banking is not necessarily undesirable as an adjunct to commercial banking. It does provide a diversified income stream. But it can also be a more volatile investment stream, so there may well need to be capital requirement differences between banks which carry out investment banking as well as retail banking, and those which are purely retail

Second, and very important, one should look below the simplistic label 'diversification'. Banks can diversify their businesses and remain different from each other. This, for example, is what British banks did in the late nineteenth and early twentieth centuries, when there was the amalgamations movement and banks diversified across Britain, thus becoming exposed to more varied industries.[5] They also diversified overseas but, quite interestingly, to somewhat different places. There were overlaps between Barclays DCO, Lloyds, Standard Chartered, and the Hong Kong and Shang Hai Banking Corporation (as it then was), but they were far from complete overlaps.

In other words, so long as banks can diversify and remain different from each other both the individual banks and the system gain resilience to shocks. But if they diversify and in doing so become more like each other, each individual bank may think itself more robust, and rightly so, and the regulators may agree, and rightly so, but the system has become more fragile; for since all banks are now alike, a shock to one is a shock to all. Every individual shock is also a common shock.

There can thus be bad diversification as well as good diversification. The first leads to homogeneity, the second does not. This simple observation has a policy implication of considerable importance. The FSA is committed to moving away from an almost mechanical checking of processes to an examination of banks' strategies (Lord Turner, Oral Evidence, Treasury Select Committee, 25 February, 2009). That is sensible from the point of view of ensuring that each individual bank is stable, but it does not tell anything about system stability until these individual strategies are compared. If on doing so they are different, then system stability has been promoted by diversification. But if they are the same, then it has not.

Two questions of considerable difficulty then follow for the regulator. More straightforward, how will similarity be measured? And much more difficult, if similarity is found, what will be done about it? Will one bank be told to do something about it, even if the management thinks it would be to the detriment of their shareholders? These issues seem to us to be rather complex, but as they do not arise from policies which we have proposed we set them aside for others to address. We turn next to some straightforward lessons from our present troubles.

LESSONS FROM 2007–2009

The regulation of banks has failed; it must be tougher; and it will be more expensive. Everyone is agreed on these propositions. Such universal agreement is unusual, and is actually easily explained. The first two statements have many possible meanings, and the third is an inevitable part of almost any government's response to a problem – more must be spent.

What should be meant by the first two remarks? What is the kind of regulation to which they lead? First, though, we define what is meant by a bank in the present context. It is a business which takes retail and wholesale deposits and makes loans. By creating deposits it contributes to the money stock, and is part of the payments system. Investment banks, whether of the traditional advisory sort or the modern type which keeps loans on its own books, are for present purposes set aside, with the remark only that when they fail it must be orderly, with due regard for the numerous types of contract and counterparty that they have.[6] When a bank which does both kinds of business fails, the traditional banking part should be handled as described below, and the investment banking part closed in an orderly manner and any remaining value used to protect the 'traditional banking' part.

Why are traditional banks regulated? All firms are regulated, but banks are regulated in a way different from any non-financial firm. There is regulation of how much capital they have, and regular testing to see if it is adequate to withstand a range of possible shocks. What is the point of this? It is undoubtedly troublesome if a bank fails; there is disruption to the businesses and lives of its customers in ways and to an extent that is not true of the failure of most kinds of firm. This does not, however, require extensive regulation, but rather a legal framework so that a bank can 'fail' while continuing to operate. That is to say, as in the US, it should be possible to take a bank away from its shareholders and management while it is still solvent, and keep it running so that all who transact with it can continue doing so. The bank can then be sold on, in an orderly way, in whole or in parts, to buyers who will keep it running and restore it to financial health. The proceeds from the sale can be used to settle the bank's debts, and anything left should go to the shareholders. For banks for which that can be done, the choice of capital ratio could be left to the management of the institutions concerned; they would simply be told that if it went below some fairly arbitrary number their assets would be expropriated. Such a facility exists in the US, was proposed in the UK by the Treasury Select Committee of the House of Commons, and is now embodied in the 2009 Banking Act. With that in place, why is any regulation different from that of non-financial firms necessary?

The answer to that question is in two parts. First, if banks are to be capable of being closed while still solvent, their capital must be monitored, and not just by their management – for in distress there would be a desire to be optimistic at the very least. Second, some banks are so big that taking them over and running them would present enormous problems. It is preferable that such large banks do not fail. In the remainder of these remarks we focus on that second reason for regulation, on the grounds that smaller banks are adequately dealt with by monitoring and prompt closure when necessary.[7] How should 'large' banks be regulated?

A digression on liquidity is necessary at this point, for a liquidity shortage can quickly turn into a capital shortage if it forces asset sales at distressed prices. Banks must hold assets which can be readily turned into cash. These must of course include government paper, but they can extend beyond that, for in a time of general shortage of liquidity the central bank should accept a wide range of securities in exchange for cash. In doing so the central bank would be following the precedent set by the Bank of England, to such stabilising effect, in the nineteenth century, when it started to implement the concept of LoLR. Of course, that action is intended to relieve only a general shortage of liquidity. If an institution cannot get liquidity from financial markets when these markets are not paralysed by panic then that is an institution which has run out of generally acceptable collateral, would start undertaking distress sales, and would soon collapse into the insolvency regime. These points on liquidity apply to small and to large banks alike.

And that brings us back to banks which are too big for the special insolvency regime – not too big to fail, but so big that managing an orderly failure in the sense in which small banks can fail in an orderly fashion would be hard. Such banks raise two problems. The first is how to diminish the risks of their failure, and the second is what to do about them in the long term.

Such large banks should require higher capital ratios than small banks. This is counterintuitive at first glance, because size usually brings diversification, and diversification brings stability. But that is to neglect the problems caused by the failure of such institutions. Second, the capital requirement must, for the same reason, be modelled under extreme assumptions. Extreme outcomes do sometimes occur. Hence, capital ratios should be high. What is high? A way of thinking about this would be to look back and see what capital ratios were required over a period of years, good and bad, for such banks to have the same return on equity as other types of large firms in industries where competition, in the sense of freedom of entry and exit, prevailed. We consider that would be a good starting point because it would mean that at least by that measure banks would be no more risky users of capital than other firms. But it is not a good finishing point. The reason is that it neglects incentives.[8]

There is much concern about the bonuses bankers have received. This concern is largely on their size, and therefore manages to miss not one point but several. The first point is that there is nothing wrong with bonuses, but they must be framed so as to ensure that in a business where continuity is important, they reward not the signing of a deal but its successful conclusion. Second, there should be attention to incentive structures from top to bottom of the firm, and all the way down the firm these structures should, as at the top, encourage efforts to maintain profits rather than simply reward individual deals. Transactions-oriented reward structures should be eschewed for chief executives and loan officers alike. An illustration of the importance of this is given by the much more rapid deterioration of the mortgage books of those firms which relied on independent financial advisors for mortgage business rather than getting it through their own staff dealing, either online or in person, with the mortgagor. Bonuses, whoever they go to, should be paid on the final completion of a deal, not on its successful initiation. That would have an additional benefit – it would inevitably ensure that deals were monitored throughout their life, and perhaps even encourage banks to keep a small stake in every transaction they initiated (as was customary for them to do, as a sign of good faith, until quite recently). At the least banks would not be able to pursue a policy of 'originate and forget'. Third, management should be required to hold shares in their company. This is not foolproof – there was extensive such holding of Lehman's shares, and Andy Hornby, chief executive of HBOS when it fell, had invested all his bonuses in HBOS shares – but it should help to ensure caution, especially if the shares could not be sold until some years (five is a nice round number) after retirement or otherwise leaving the firm.[9] Who imposes these rules is considered immediately below.

Now we come to the firms' owners, the shareholders. In the UK bank shareholders appear sometimes to be a rather strange group. They are strange in that they sometimes behave differently to the banks they own than they do to other types of firm they own. With banks, they can be passive, accepting what the management does to them. With other firms they are much more active in their monitoring. This does not happen all the time, but the takeover by RBS of a foreign bank at the very peak of an asset price boom is a truly striking example of shareholder passivity.[10] It might be helpful if shareholders became at least as active with banks as they are with their other investments.[11] If they do not do so, and fail to pay adequate attention to the incentive structures in the firms they own, should regulators do it for them? That would be extraordinarily intrusive upon rights of ownership; and worse, it might not be effective. The same incentive structure is unlikely to be appropriate across all banks; the managers and owners have information about their own firms that no outsider can possibly have, and they are therefore far and away the best able to devise a sensible incentive structure. There can be no harm in regulators setting out what they see as a set of principles to guide incentive structures, but these should be for discussion, comment, and if shareholders wish rejection. The consequences of getting it wrong fall primarily on them.

But with all that done, there is yet more. Regulators should prepare for the failure of banks. They should do that because it is almost certain that something will go wrong at some time, and because the consequence of lack of preparedness when Northern Rock got into difficulties was a nearly disastrous bank run. This preparation should have two parts. The regulators should regularly plan what they are going to do in the event of a big bank needing help, and, because each bank will be somewhat different, there should be a plan for every bank, and these plans should be regularly updated. The regulators should also plan, and announce that they have planned to sell off in parts, not as a whole, any big bank that they have to take over. This would have three benefits. It would reduce competition problems arising from the existence of large banks capable perhaps of setting up barriers to entry. While this may not be a problem worldwide, it is surely possible that it becomes so in the UK following the Lloyds Bank takeover of HBOS; after all, competition rules had formally to be waived to allow the takeover to be approved by the competition authorities. Second, it would further encourage management to be cautious. And perhaps most important, it would if carried out get rid of one of these troublesome big banks, and give us a few more that would not be 'too big to fail easily'.

WHY NOT JUST LoLR?

Why, having started this chapter by showing the effectiveness of classic LoLR in preserving financial stability, have we added some suggestions for bank regulation? Do not our prior arguments and evidence make such regulation unnecessary? In fact our regulatory proposal derives, as does our defence of LoLR, from examination of the Bank of England's behaviour in the nineteenth century. That examination shows that the Bank's approach to financial stability had more than one aspect.

First it developed and practised LoLR. Second, with Barings in 1890, it refined its objective of systemic stability and became concerned to ensure that any closure of a bank did not threaten the system as a whole, through reputational channels in the Barings case but disorderly closure would also have been a source of difficulty. It therefore became concerned with individual institutions. Note, though, that the owners of Barings saw their investment in it wiped out, and the management of the institution was replaced from top to bottom.

Such drastic penalties were, very reasonably, not imposed in 1914. Perhaps with the passage of time and no longer remembering how special the crisis of 1914 was, the Bank continued to look after troubled institutions. It did not always do so; but at a minimum it always ensured such institutions a tidy end.[12] This may lie at the root of our present troubles. The idea got about that individual banks, unless actively criminal like the Bank of Credit and Commerce International (BCCI), would always be looked after by the authorities. Thus bank managements and shareholders may have become a little less cautious in both their own lending and borrowing, and in their monitoring of that of others.

Our regulatory proposal is designed to deal with this attitude. We need not go all the way back to 1866 to find an appropriate rule of conduct for the Bank.[13] The Bank should maintain its role in producing a tidy resolution, rapid or slow according to circumstances, of an individual bank problem. But it should be explicit in advance over the fates in such cases of management, shareholders, and bondholders.

The lessons the Bank had learned by 1866 are not sufficient to guide it in the twenty-first century. But the lessons it had learned by 1890, and put into practice with the failure of Barings in that year, are. Tidy failure is necessary: but the price of that tidy failure should fall as fully today on bankers and those who provide them with capital as it did in the 1890 Barings failure.

NOTES

1. Written for the conference and volume in honour of David Llewellyn on the occasion of his retirement.
2. After 1844 it gradually became the only note issuer, as other banks which before that date had been banks of issue lost that right as they amalgamated or were taken over.
3. Accepting Houses guaranteed bills of exchange; discount houses lent on such bills, using both their own capital and funds borrowed from clearing banks; and clearing banks also lent on them, using their own and depositors' funds.
4. This seems to us an early example of policy assignment, a practice that the Bank of England seems to have followed from 1866.
5. See Capie and Rodrik-Bali (1982).
6. The problem of Lehman Brothers was not that it was closed. Inside the US problems were caused by the inconsistency of treatment as compared to, for example, Bear Sterns; and outside the US problems resulted from, *inter alia*, the fact that normal bankruptcy procedures are intrinsically slow, so many contracts remained open much longer than expected. Indeed, many still are open at the time of writing (June 2009). In addition, only when the bank was closed did regulators discover that it had been the custom always to sweep all cash back to head office overnight.
7. They would therefore be essentially unregulated apart from the monitoring of their capital.
8. Professor Shelagh Heffernan's chapter in this volume discusses in some detail the importance of these.
9. Death would also trigger the right to sell.
10. This comment does not apply to all shareholders. Many individual shareholders objected, as did some investment trusts and the Legal and General Insurance Company. So far as one can tell from the published correspondence, these objections received only

a polite brush off (at best). This episode did also reveal a problem not noticed before. Legal and General even if it had wanted to sell its shares could not do so, as it was running index-tracking funds. How to tackle this issue is of course aside from the theme of the present paper.

11. One has to say 'might' because one active major shareholder in a bank targeted very aggressively HSBC, a bank which seemed to be in better shape than most.
12 The closure of BCCI may seem an exception to this rule, but in that case the law forced the Bank's hand.
13. At this point we use Bank as a form of shorthand, to avoid discussion of which of Britain's Tripartite Authorities should have this responsibility. We are concerned in this chapter only to establish that there is such a responsibility.

REFERENCES

Bagehot, W. (1873), *Lombard Street*, London: Henry King.

Benston, G.J. (1990), *The Separation of Commercial and Investment Banking. The Glass-Steagall Act Revisited and Reconsidered*, New York: Macmillan.

Capie, F. and G. Rodrik-Bali (1982), 'Concentration in British banking 1870-1920', *Business History*, **6**, 107–25.

De Cecco, M. (1974), *Money and Empire: The International Gold Standard*, Oxford: Basil Blackwell.

Hawtrey, R.G. (1932), *The Art of Central Banking*, London: Longmans, Green & Co.

Morgan, E.V. (1952), *Studies in British Financial Policy 1914–1925*, London: Macmillan.

Pressnel, L. (1968), 'Gold flows, banking reserves and the Baring crisis of 1890', in C.R Whittlesey and J.S.G. Wilson (eds), *Essays in Money and Banking in Honour of R.S. Sayers*, Oxford: Oxford University Press.

Sayers, R. (1976), *The Bank of England 1891–1944*, Cambridge: Cambridge University Press.

Thornton, H. (1802), *An Enquiry in to the Effects of the Paper Credit of Great Britain*, reprinted 1978 with an introduction by F.A. Hayek, Fairfield, NJ: Augustus Kelly.

Withers, H. (1915), *War and Lombard Street* London: J. Murray.

PART FOUR

Regulation of financial firms

10. Early intervention and prompt corrective action in Europe

David G. Mayes

INTRODUCTION

The recent crisis has taught us (at least) five main lessons, all of which were known beforehand but not appreciated so graphically:

1. Banks can get into trouble extremely rapidly. The authorities therefore need to have extensive 'pre-positioning' if they are to handle the difficulty efficiently.
2. Depositors need to be guaranteed almost uninterrupted access to their funds and full insurance of most deposits if bank runs are to be avoided.
3. The whole system of prompt corrective action (PCA) needs to start early, before the capital triggers are reached, and hence requires a basis in risk assessment and market signals.
4. It is necessary to be able to step into a bank and take it over before its capital is entirely depleted.
5. If these were not enough, acting on cross-border banks is much more difficult as the tools and responsibilities are national, hence the chances of a disorderly failure are much greater.

It is easy to extend the list.

The major problems have largely occurred in 'national' banks yet the authorities had problems coping. When they reached cross-border banks the authorities often could not manage unless the home country was to assume responsibility and get on with the job, and their interests were in line with those of the other countries involved, or where the bank could be readily split into its national components as in the case of Dexia and Fortis. In the case of Lehman Brothers it was a case of 'too complex to save'. Neither the authorities nor the private sector could put together a rescue plan fast enough because of the difficulty of assessing the potential losses, assisted by the natural reluctance of the existing management to accept a low value deal. In the case of the three main Icelandic banks it was a case of 'too big to save', a problem clearly identified by Sigurðsson (2003) well before the event. Where a bank is too large relative to its home country the authorities cannot afford either rescue or the payout of all insured depositors. Since this had been clearly recognized and put into the legislative framework by the Swiss authorities (Hüpkes, 2003) it is strange that this untenable situation could persist elsewhere. It presumably reflects the belief that, whatever is said, such banks cannot fail.[1]

The main lesson from this experience is that if a similar problem is to be avoided with any of the larger cross-border banks, the individual authorities need to have similar powers and compulsions and be able to take into account problems in the rest of the financial group when taking action. Even in Europe regulatory systems differ considerably. However, large cross-border banks are not simply European and having to co-ordinate more widely, particularly with the US, widens the problem further.[2] There are already many suggestions available for future action. The recommendations of the de Larosière Group (2009) set up by the European Commission were among the more influential but they did not address the hardest issues directly – how can authorities manage to act promptly together in their joint interest? How could joint resolution of groups that are not readily divisible be organized?[3]

This is a huge agenda even at a national level. Experience suggests that it could easily take six years or so to implement the changes after the decision to go ahead is made. Taking the decisions themselves is a different issue. On the whole it is easier to take them quickly while the problems are obvious and decision-makers are still concerned by the problems they found themselves in. Postponing until there is adequate time for reflection can mean that the issue goes right down the order of priority and the political window of opportunity is lost. On the other hand rapid legislation can sometimes offer new problems of its own as illustrated by Sarbanes-Oxley. In the aftermath of the difficulties that have assailed the world there is now an opportunity for change before the problem strikes – waiting until the next crisis happens with cross-border banks and extra losses are incurred because systems have not been adequately revised would be, to use the word of Padoa-Schioppa (2007), 'irresponsible'.

This chapter sets out some suggestions about helpful changes that could be made in the current environment but it also admits that some of the changes required need very fundamental reviews about how cross-border problems should be tackled, particularly within Europe. The focus is on how problems in banks can be identified early and dealt with quickly.

THE TASK AHEAD FOR EUROPE

Outside the US and market transition countries, the financial safety net had been largely untested until the recent crisis. It could cope with small problems such as failures of fringe banks but its ability to handle larger problems had in many cases been only theoretical, despite simulation exercises. The problems in the UK prompted the authorities to embark on a wholesale reform, revising deposit insurance, instituting a special resolution regime, ensuring earlier action and reorganizing the structure of responsibility to give a leading role to the central bank. The question at issue is what should be done more broadly in Europe, particularly for financial institutions whose activities run across borders?

In many respects the need for action is driven by moral hazard. If the state has been prepared to step in on this occasion then it can be expected to do the same in the future. This may exacerbate the under-pricing of risk and encourage excessive risk-taking in the future. A more prosaic reason for action is that the political windows for such change tend not to be open for long.

However, unlike the UK, many smaller European countries do not have largely national banks; their banks are largely cross-border, headquartered in other member states. Unilateral action might be either confusing or ineffective. Indeed, attempts to put greater constraints on banks than in partner countries might simply drive the rest of the banking system into other jurisdictions.

The issue of incentive is a potential way to deal with one large problem facing a special resolution regime for banks. Currently, as a result of the Pafitis case, it may well be difficult to impose a special resolution regime on banks for fear of violating the human rights of shareholders, although the Roskilde example in Denmark suggests that there may be ways round this.[4] This argues for a package approach to change. If the benefits are dispensed before the costs, the banks may be able to lobby successfully against the imposition of the costs. Nevertheless, under the great pressure of the crisis, shareholders in two of the main commercial banks in the UK have been prepared to accept a considerable dilution of their rights in return for major investments by the government.

The most serious lesson has come from the failure of the three main Icelandic banks, Landsbanki, Glitnir and Kaupthing. This has shown that the European approach to cross-border failure and crisis resolution has some major flaws – as pointed out well in advance by Mayes and Vesala (2000) *inter alia*. If any solution other than keeping the banking group afloat through the actions of the home country supervisor is to be followed, then the authorities in other countries need to be able to intervene in the entities within their boundaries. Where there are subsidiaries that are separable units this may well be possible, provided that the authorities are jointly willing to act in complementary manner. Where there are branches there is no such elegant option and closure is likely to be the only viable option, unless it is possible to carve out the activities of the branch if they are sufficiently acceptable given the agreement of the home country supervisor.

This point is addressed by the Turner Review in the UK (Turner, 2009) in reaction to the adverse experience over the Icelandic banks but without suggesting a clear way of resolving the problem. Outside the EU, New Zealand has effectively solved the issue by insisting that all significant banks must not merely be subsidiaries but subsidiaries that can operate independently within the value day.[5] No such compulsion can at present be applied in the EU as a result of the 'passport principle' and indeed were it to exist it would have the consequence of severely restricting the concept of cross-border banks to something fairly close to a holding company with largely autonomous subsidiaries. Clearly, cross-border (and other large complex financial institutions) must have a structure such that the authorities can handle them swiftly and efficiently without recourse to a bailout. In part this can be addressed by changing the structure of banks and the market (as argued by Stern and Feldman (2004) *inter alia*) but also by changing the tools and legal framework in which the authorities can operate.

This chapter focuses on just one aspect – Structured Early Intervention and Resolution (SEIR), or Prompt Corrective Action (PCA) as it tends to be labeled in the US – although it only makes sense as part of an integrated safety net. The reasons for this focus are simple.

First, SEIR has proved credible in the US. It is readily possible to see how it was implemented in practice and there is experience with its drawbacks. Although a European version would undoubtedly be different in detail there is a working template to follow and such a system would find it relatively easy to gain credibility in Europe as well.

Second, it deals with several of the key points of the safety net. It is designed to cut in early. It offers strong incentives for the private sector to solve the problems first. It gives some certainty as to how problems will be resolved and it makes it clear that not only is there a timetable for solution but that should all the early stages fail, the problem can be brought to a conclusion in a manner that will avoid a financial crisis, avoid any bailout of the shareholders, avoid exposing the taxpayer to direct losses, and leave the creditors better off than they would be in a traditional insolvency.

Third, SEIR can be introduced in Europe within the current supervisory structures. It does not require the creation of a grand European institution nor, with one exception, does it require any extensive new legislation that might be difficult to agree across the member states.[6] (The exception is the closure rule.) Its existence will make it easier for the present authorities to work together and achieve a coordinated solution.

Fourth, it does not impose any substantial new regulatory burden on banks and through harmonization will make it easier for them to operate across borders. Fifth, use of SEIR substantially reduces the chance that there will be an awkward problem of burden sharing among the countries involved in supervising a problem bank.

But it is not a panacea. As in the US, operating a complex network of supervisors is not the efficient solution for the cross-border institutions that the EU is encouraging. It is a pragmatic step forward. Ultimately, offering a European level regulatory environment for European level financial institutions sounds more promising and would reflect the US experience with the Federal Reserve, the Comptroller of the Currency and the Federal Deposit Insurance Corporation (FDIC).

A LITTLE BACKGROUND ON SEIR[7]

SEIR was first laid out by Benston and Kaufman (1988) as a means of minimizing deposit insurance losses by requiring a series of mandatory supervisory interventions as a bank's regulatory capital ratio falls.[8] They proposed that banks be placed in one of four categories:

1. No problem
2. Potential problems that would be subject to more intensive supervision and regulation
3. Problem intensive that would face even more intensive supervision and regulation with mandatory suspension of dividends
4. Reorganization mandatory, with ownership of these banks automatically transferred to the deposit insurer.[9]

Although the deposit insurer would assume control of the bank, Benston and Kaufman (1988, p. 68) ordinarily would have the bank continue in operation under the temporary control of the relevant deposit insurer, the FDIC, or be sold to another bank, with liquidation only as a last resort. The deposit insurer would remain at risk under SEIR, but only to the extent of covering losses to insured depositors. However, Benston and Kaufman did not expect such a takeover to be necessary, except when a bank's capital was depleted before the supervisors could act, perhaps as a result of a massive undetected fraud. Because the bank's owners would realize that the supervisors were mandated to take over a bank while it was solvent (3 per cent market value of capital-to-asset ratio, in their proposal),

Table 10.1 The US framework for Prompt Corrective Action

			Capital ratios		
			Risk-based capital		Leverage
Category	Mandatory provisions	Discretionary provisions	Total	Tier 1	Ratio
Well capitalized	1. No capital distribution or payment of management fees that would cause the bank to become undercapitalized		>10%	>6%	>5%
Adequately capitalized	1. Same as well capitalized		>8%	>4%	>4%
Undercapitalized	1. Capital distributions and management fees suspended 2. Capital restoration plan 3. Asset growth restricted 4. Prior approval for branching, acquisitions, and new lines of business 5. No brokered deposits	1. Require recapitalization by issuing capital or selling to another firm 2. Restricting transactions with affiliates 3. Restricting rates on new deposits 4. Restricting asset growth 5. Restricting activities 6. Improving management by replacing directors or managers 7. Prohibit deposits from correspondent banks	<8%	<4%	<4%

		8. Requiring prior approval for capital distribution by bank holding company 9. Requiring divestiture			
Significantly undercapitalized	1. Same as undercapitalized 2. At least one of the nine discretionary provisions under undercapitalized. Presumption in favour of (1) (required capital issuance only), (2), and (3) 3. Senior officer compensation restricted		<6%	<3%	<3%
Critically undercapitalized	1. Any action authorized for significantly undercapitalized banks 2. Payments on subordinated debt prohibited[1] 3. Conservatorship or receivership within 90 days[1]				<2%[2]

Notes:
1. Not required if certain conditions are met.
2. Tangible equity only.
3. Note, this is a general summary of PCA only. Other parts of the U.S. code may also impose limits based on a bank's capital category.

Source: Federal Deposit Insurance Corporation.

the owners had strong incentives to recapitalize, sell, or liquidate the bank rather than put it to the FDIC.

A version of SEIR was adopted under the title prompt corrective action (PCA) with the 1991 passage of the Federal Deposit Insurance Corporation Improvement Act (FDICIA). PCA deals with prudential supervisors' agency problem by first allowing and then requiring specific intervention by the supervisory authorities on a timely basis. It is worth recalling that FDICIA was enacted in the light of the savings and loans problems in the US and reflected dissatisfaction with the previous regime.

Whereas SEIR sketches out how supervisors would respond to a drop in capital adequacy, PCA provides a list of actions the supervisors may take and another set of actions the supervisor must take to further the goals of PCA (minimizing losses to the FDIC). While PCA reduces supervisory discretion as a bank's capital level falls, supervisors retain substantial discretion over almost all banks. Even the mandatory provisions often include a significant element of discretion. For example, while an undercapitalized bank must submit a capital restoration plan, the supervisors have discretion over whether to approve it.

PCA may appear to be simply a set of supervisory corrective measures that should be taken as a bank's capital declines that any country could easily adopt. However, PCA is unlikely to work as intended if a country has not accepted PCA's underlying philosophy, or lacks the necessary institutional prerequisites. The adoption of a version of PCA would provide the EU with a set of minimum supervisory responses to violations of the Capital Requirement Directive (CRD). However, as the present crisis has revealed, these interventions are needed in response to other weaknesses in the banks' prudential management well in advance of any threat to required capital ratios. Nevertheless, the same principles would need to apply – that early intervention is mandatory and that the form of that intervention should become progressively harsher as the violation of prudential standards increases (Nieto and Wall, 2006).

The focus on PCA reflects four things. First that the key concern is to deal with problems expeditiously. Hence, the focus for harmonization should be on the actions that can be taken by the various authorities and on the thresholds that trigger them. While considerable harmonization may be required for authorities in one jurisdiction to be satisfied that all that is necessary is being done to ensure prudent operation in normal times, it is not necessary to eradicate all the national discrepancies to achieve this. Second, the national authorities must be capable of taking actions that are in the interests of the other countries involved in a cross-border banking group and not just their own. This is a very substantial requirement. It may be necessary to impose constraints on a healthy subsidiary in one country in order to assist a troubled subsidiary in another country where it otherwise threatens to cause financial instability. Third, there must be adequate and timely information, both for the different supervisors to be able to compile an adequate picture of a cross-border bank, and for a national supervisor to be able to assess the financial stability in his country where many of the banks are cross-border. Fourth, there must be adequate resolution procedures for handling cross-border banks.

A PROBLEM OF TRIGGERS

The US version of PCA is based on a set of capital triggers. However, intervention has tended to occur before the capital triggers are breached (Peek and Rosengren, 1997). It is information obtained as part of the normal regular assessment and in the compilation of CAMELS ratings that triggers the move from the first category.[10] As in Benston and Kaufman (1988), the first category for PCA should be the onset of suspicion that something is wrong. Apparently, in practice the move from the well-capitalized category to adequately capitalized is done on this basis by the FDIC (Lane, 2008).

As mentioned, one of the main lessons we have relearnt in the current crisis is the need to act very early. The literature on early warning indicators is quite well developed (Davis and Dilruba, 2008). We have a fairly good idea of the sorts of macroeconomic indicators that will tell us something about the general economic cycle, and CAMELS-style sets of indicators for the individual institution seem to work reasonably well. The problem normally is that the indications are only completely clear with the benefit of hindsight. Some banks will evade detection, while others will trigger closer investigation unnecessarily. This is a standard type I and type II error problem and deciding on the particular dividing line will depend on the preferences for making the two types of mistake.

In implementing PCA in a European environment it would be helpful to acknowledge explicitly that other triggers will cut in earlier than capital triggers. The most useful additional triggers would be related to the existing supervisory process. For example, both the risk assessment under Pillar 2 of Basel II and the disclosures under Pillar 3 are of value. Of course one other feature of the present crisis has been that supervisors and the banks themselves have recognized that many of their stress-testing procedures are inadequate. Once these are refined, detection should be somewhat easier. Pillar 3 disclosures give a better opportunity for market discipline to operate. Poor performance is likely to be reflected in the share price and substantial falls in short periods of time should trigger action.

In Norway, for example, if the share price of a bank falls by more than 25 per cent between AGMs the authorities can require an extraordinary meeting of shareholders to be called to discuss how the bank might reverse the decline. (If the share price falls by 75 per cent a second meeting can be required, where this time the question is whether the bank should continue trading. The implication is that it should be closed in an orderly manner unless any capital injection can be obtained).

Supervisors have been reluctant to use market signals to determine the capital category of banks operating under PCA. A less controversial and perhaps easier approach to implement would be to use market-risk measures as triggers for closer supervisory scrutiny of a bank. These measures could include subordinated debt spreads and other measures such as the pricing of credit derivatives, or equity-based measures, such as Moody's KMV Expected Default Frequency. Market-risk measures could be used to trigger a mandatory meeting of the college of supervisors to review the group's condition and, when appropriate, a coordinated special examination of the group.

However, the current crisis shows some of the limitations of market signals, as such crises only occur when the market as a whole misprices risk. In the main their use is in more normal times in the relative pricing of securities. Nevertheless, while they may form the only signal on occasion, they are only an indicator and may well not pick up an impending problem or indicate incorrectly. The present crisis emphasizes all too clearly that the nature of the shocks to which institutions can be exposed lies outside those commonly considered. While liquidity requirements might have eased the problem, the shocks lay outside the boundary of any stress tests that organizations or their supervisors are likely to have made.

The Committee of European Banking Supervisors (CEBS, 2009) completed a major survey of the Member States including a mapping of their early intervention measures. It appears that there is wide variation in powers. Even when powers and procedures are similar in character there are extensive differences in the detail. Only the Czech Republic, Hungary and Slovakia have any automatic triggers for action and most countries can exercise forbearance. The task for harmonization is thus huge, as recognized by the de Larosière Report.

INFORMATION

In order for bank supervisors to use their powers effectively, they must have an accurate understanding of the bank's and banking group's financial condition. A potential problem for a prudential supervisor of a cross-border banking group is that of determining the status of those parts of the group outside its supervisory control.

While the information sharing mandated by the CRD should provide national supervisors with the information they need, ad hoc sharing on a banking group-by-banking group basis is likely to be inefficient and leave room for gaps in information sharing. The enhanced sharing of information among supervisors is aimed at reducing the incentives of supervisors of the subsidiaries, or parent bank, to exploit the information to their advantage; and it is a precondition for the effective implementation of PCA as a mechanism aimed at resolving the cross-border agency problems that arise in supervising and resolving cross-border banking groups. Mayes (2006) and Vesala (2005) advocate a policy of information sharing via the establishment of a common database. At a minimum this database should contain quarterly consolidated financial statements from all insured banks and their non-bank corporate parents (when one exists) that is available to all bank supervisors. Ideally these financial statements would also be publicly available. Additionally, there would be some merit in establishing a database with confidential supervisory information, and analysis would also be available to the appropriate national supervisory agencies to assist all prudential supervisors in understanding the condition of the group as a whole and its relationship to the bank they each supervise. The ECB or the European Banking Authority could harbour that database.

INSTITUTIONS

Memoranda of Understanding (MoUs) are important tools in establishing contact networks and a common language, which would be helpful in a crisis. However, because of their lack of binding legal status they are hardly sufficient for further development of the handling of cross-border banking. Furthermore, practical issues do not speak for MoUs as an optimal long run solution – for example, in the extreme, there may be up to 81 separate entities involved in agreeing a joint assessment. Instead, they should be considered as a first step, and later as a complement, in facilitating international monitoring and supervision. While the CRD provides for a general mechanism of coordination and cooperation among supervisors, it also envisages a stronger arrangement, in that the host supervisor of a subsidiary may delegate its responsibility to the home country prudential supervisor of the subsidiary's parent.

The primary problem with using the authority provided by the CRD is that delegating supervisory responsibility to the home country supervisor of the parent bank is likely to worsen the principal–agent conflict between the parent's supervisor as agent, and the subsidiary's country's taxpayers and voters, as principal. The parent's supervisor would be responsible for the impact of its supervisory action on the deposit insurance fund and possibly the financial stability of the host country of the subsidiary, but the parent's supervisor would not be directly accountable to the host country government and the taxpayers.

The mechanism for coordinating discretionary PCA actions is likely to be through the 'college' of the prudential supervisors of the banks in the group. Short of having a European level supervisor that replaces the current arrangements, this is the obvious way to proceed. However, there is more than one view of what constitutes a college. A college could encompass the cooperation of the consolidating supervisor with the competent authorities of the subsidiaries, which is the route advocated by de Larosière.[11] The coordination mechanisms could be merely advisory, leaving the final decision up to the national supervisors of each bank, or it could be binding upon the members. However, leaving the final decision in the hands of each bank's national supervisor is not likely to result in effective coordination to the extent that different supervisors reach different conclusions about the appropriate actions, either because they have different incentives or because they have reached different judgements. Thus, for an effective implementation of a PCA policy as a coordination mechanism between supervisors, a better solution would be to give prudential supervisors in the college the authority to take discretionary actions that would also be binding on then all. The idea behind such a grouping is that the supervisors can become in some sense jointly responsible for the actions the group takes. In such a case it may then be easier to agree to remedial actions. A problem arises if the resolution authority and the supervisory authority are not one and the same.

The formation of the college does not mean that decisions will always be made in a timely and harmonious fashion. Even the best of colleges is likely to be an inefficient mechanism for addressing most issues that require consultation or negotiation with the banking group. For example, if a cross-border banking group with capital below the minimum capital requirements is required to develop a capital restoration plan that is acceptable to its supervisors, having the bank negotiate the plan with each of the college members would be slow and inefficient. A better alternative would be for the committee to select one supervisor as the primary contact with the bank. The role of the college would then be to review and approve the contact supervisor's agreement with the bank. In both the de Larosière proposals and the suggestions of the Financial Stability Forum for colleges that extend beyond the EU/European Economic Area, (EEA) it is not clear if the role of the lead supervisor would extend that far.

One way of forcing timely action would be for PCA to establish a presumption that a certain action will automatically be effective, say 30 days after a bank violates one of the PCA triggers, unless the college determines that taking the action will not further the purposes of PCA. This would prevent a subset of the college from using committee deliberations to stall effective action. Additionally, the colleges may somewhat reduce the scope for relatively unimportant disagreements to stall decision-making by specifying in advance that the college will follow decision rules that give greater weight to the judgements of supervisors of the larger banks in the group and the supervisors from countries where the banking group is systemically important. De Larosière proposes that a new European Banking Authority would resolve such disputes. The question is whether this would be able to operate effectively in the early stages of the 'amber' phase when the hope is that PCA will return the institution to green status rather than permit the problems to continue or, worse, sink into the 'red' zone.

Although a college provides a mechanism for all affected countries to have a voice in the decision about corrective measures taken under PCA, the college does not solve the agency problem caused by the mismatch between supervisory powers and supervisory accountability to voters. Giving each country's supervisor a say in a coordinating college is not equivalent to the power that the supervisor would have to protect its country's interests as it could with a purely domestic bank. However, the inability of supervisors in each country to have the same control as they would over a purely domestic group is an unavoidable consequence of groups operating as integrated entities in more than one member state. Corrective measures taken (or left untaken) will have sometimes different consequences for different countries. The best that can be said is that a college structure will typically provide better representation of each of the affected countries than would a system that gives all of the power to a single supervisor.

Views have changed in the EU and it is no longer the presupposition that the safety net can be maintained adequately even for cross-border banks while using the existing national institutions. The de Laroisère proposals have largely been adopted by the European Commission. Unlike some previous proposals they did not assign the ECB some supervisory responsibility, as is possible under the Lisbon Treaty,[12] but they suggest that it was necessary to create a new institution, the European System of Financial Supervision. Like the earlier proposals for a European System of Financial Supervisors (matching the European System of Central Banks) advocated by Schoenmaker and Oosterloo (2006) and a European Organisation for Financial Supervision as suggested by Ingves (2006) and Persson (2009), the framework is designed to coordinate existing supervisors for significant cross-border banks while permitting existing national supervisory arrangements for the remainder. They suggested turning the three 'level 3' committees (CEBS, Committee of European Insurance and Occupational Pensions Supervisors and Committee of European Securities Regulators) into authorities (European Banking Authority, European Insurance Authority, European Securities Authority), which would be responsible *inter alia* for: legally binding mediation between national supervisors; oversight and coordination of colleges of supervisors; licensing and supervision of specific EU-wide institutions (such as credit rating agencies and post-trading infrastructure); and playing a strong coordinating role in crisis situations.

The Turner Report, while having a rather different approach to the detail, with lesser powers over national authorities, also saw the level 3 committees as lying at the heart of the way forward, although it opts for an integrated authority covering all three committees on the grounds that large complex organizations, especially those running across borders, need to be treated as single entities.

Thus neither report took a strong stand on trying to have an EU-level of supervision for significant entities that run across borders, although the de Larosière proposals would go a lot further forward towards harmonization of the tools that can be used both in supervision and in the resolution of problems. What might prove rather easier would be to follow the suggestion of Čihák and Decressin (2007) and introduce a separate European level of supervision for which banks could opt if they chose to use the European Company Statute as their form of incorporation. As suggested by Eisenbeis and Kaufman (2007), there could be some financial incentive for them to adopt this, say in the form of a reduced deposit insurance premium as the risks involved are lower. As this regime would be new it could incorporate a PCA approach and the ability to close banks while they still had positive capital, as in the US system. This would not involve taking any rights away from existing shareholders, and would also make it easier for the authorities to decide on the acceptable structure of the banking group.

If one followed the US example more closely, then in many respects it is a version of the FDIC, perhaps labeled a European Deposit Insurance Corporation (EDIC), that would be the most important institution to create. Thus colleges of supervisors could cover the group in normal times but as soon as any problem was thought imminent a single authority would take over to ensure the necessary speedy action. This would then provide a European level equivalent to the UK approach, where the FSA remains responsible in the 'amber' phase but the Bank of England is alerted and begins preparations in case the 'red' phase is necessary and the authorities need to step in to organize a resolution.

One of the major objections raised to EU-level organizations having an operational role is that they do not have access to any 'federal' funds. They would have to rely on deposit insurers and other national instruments. Countries are unwilling to subscribe in advance to participating in bailouts or other resolution costs for a number of reasons: first because of the moral hazard it might impose on other authorities seeking to shift the cost, and second because the willingness to bail out depends on countries' views of who was responsible for the problem in the first place.

PRE-POSITIONING

Probably the most important element of being able to act rapidly and avoid getting into a serious crisis is being fully prepared beforehand. With large and complex financial institutions running across borders this is no mean task, although not necessarily a particularly costly one. The FDIC has realized that its existing powers and provisions are insufficient and has set out proposals as to how it should proceed (FDIC, 2008). The primary ingredient is that it needs extensive understanding of the bank's computer systems and the detailed structure of its deposits, so if something went wrong it could act rapidly, either to transfer the insured deposits to a bridge bank or to another institution.

If depositors are to remain assured that they will not suffer a material break in access to their funds, the practical ability of the authorities to ensure this must be obvious. In most European countries the practical implication is that no such assurance can be made. Therefore, if a bank gets in difficulty it will be rational for there to be a run and the authorities will be precipitated into drastic action such as a blanket guarantee. This in turn destroys the ability of the safety net to head off severe problems. While it is normally problems with wholesale financing that will project banks into the arms of the authorities, because those lenders are better informed, it is usually a retail run that will end the viability of a bank. Wholesale failures can usually be countered by emergency collateralized lending by the central bank on previously laid down terms (at a margin over the market rate and with haircuts sufficient to avoid loss).

However, such pre-positioning needs to be much more extensive than simply being able to organize deposit insurance. LaBrosse and Walker (2007) point out that the deposit insurer itself needs to be carefully structured to ensure that it can cope with a rapid resolution. This not only entails a range of procedures that need to be in place but also access to funding, appropriate skilled staff and access to specialist advice.

The most comprehensive version of pre-positioning in place is probably that of New Zealand. Here the onus is primarily on the bank itself. Because the four largest banks are foreign-owned (Australian), this arrangement is highly relevant for cross-border concerns in Europe. These banks all have to be locally incorporated and be capable of being free-standing within the value day (Reserve Bank of New Zealand, 2006).

In Europe there is no requirement that banks operating in host countries have any self-sustainable structure whether they are locally incorporated subsidiaries or just branches. Indeed the logic of European integration suggests that they should not be free-standing so that the group can reap the efficiencies of economies of scale and pooling reserves. While initially cross-border arrangements may have taken the form of a holding company with separately operating subsidiaries in other countries, this is becoming increasingly less the pattern.

This idea of being free-standing means that the bank can keep vital functions going in the event of the failure of any of its important suppliers and counterparties. This includes the parent. Thus if the Australian parent were to fail the New Zealand authorities need to be able to step in to the New Zealand subsidiary, ring fence and ensure that it is adequately capitalized in a manner that it can continue operating without any loss of confidence (or indeed downrating). Doing this requires considerable pre-positioning, as the statutory manager appointed by the courts on the advice of the supervisor – the Reserve Bank of New Zealand (RBNZ) – has to be able to identify the claims on the bank, value them sufficiently accurately that they can be written down, and the bank reopen without any material break. This requires substantial prior information. Normally in the event of bank failure it is not a complete surprise and there would be some time to activate the systems and cooperation with the RBNZ before the drastic need for action arose. In the event of an earthquake or similar natural disaster there is likely to be no warning at all, so the recovery systems have to be able to operate immediately and rapidly. Such pre-positioning is not normal practice in Europe.

CONCLUDING REMARKS

PCA was designed to improve the prudential supervision of banks in the US, most of which operate in a single market. An EU version of PCA could also improve the prudential supervision of banks operating in more than one member state. However, to be as effective as possible, the EU version should address a number of cross-border issues that are incompatible with the existing decentralized structure of the EU safety net and indeed with that proposed in the de Larosière Report.

The form of PCA proposed here facilitates the resolution of conflicts among supervisors of different countries so that the cost of reconciling the conflicts is less than the cost of going it alone. Bank supervisors need to understand the overall financial condition of a banking group and its various individual banks if they are to anticipate problems and take appropriate corrective measures. The effectiveness of PCA as a mechanism to reduce agency problems among supervisors would rely on the availability of information to prudential supervisors as well as supervisors use of market information. Availability could be improved by reducing information asymmetries among supervisors on an individual bank's financial condition. The use of market-based risk measures could be mandated in the supervisory process. At a minimum, this would include requiring additional examinations of banking groups whose reported capital exceeds minimum required levels but which are identified as high risk by financial markets; and mandating that the relevant banking supervisors meet to share their evaluations of the group.

PCA reduces supervisors' ability to exercise forbearance, but it by no means eliminates supervisory discretion. Supervisors retain substantial discretion in their implementation of PCA so long as a bank's regulatory capital exceeds the critical level at which it is forced into resolution. If the consequences of bank supervision in one country can have large consequences for the group's banks in other countries, then deciding how best to exercise this discretion should be decided by the supervisors of all of the significant banks in a collegial format. However, even if a satisfactory means of deciding what to do can be implemented, the actual powers of supervisors in the EU are not identical. Some may not be able to implement the actions others wish to vote for. Hence, effective implementation would require as a precondition that prudential supervisors be given the same and comprehensive authority to take the corrective measures in PCA.

The recent financial instability makes it clear that a European version of PCA would need to incorporate new triggers for early intervention relating to risk assessment and market information, in addition to those on capital adequacy, if intervention is to start early enough. The rapidity with which problems have emerged suggests that the time constraints under which PCA operates would need to be shorter. Furthermore for PCA to operate in a complex cross-border institution, there would need to be considerable pre-positioning by the supervisory/resolution authority to ensure that claims, especially insured deposits, could be identified rapidly so that the resolution procedures are credible and depositors do not expect there to be any material break in access to their funds.

All this could be achieved within existing supervisory and resolution structures, especially as enhanced by the de Larosière proposals, although some changes will be necessary in some countries to ensure that banks can be reorganized before they run out of capital. However, US experience suggests that in due course it will be found necessary to have a European-level institution. There is probably a greater need to have a European resolution agency than a European supervisor but if a new single regime for cross-border banks were implemented, this might provide an easier solution than inter-agency cooperation.[13] There is a strong, understandable dislike of making *ex ante* commitments to burden sharing. And if problems can be addressed early and acted upon rapidly then there may be little burden to share even if the institution actually fails. Nevertheless when there is a need for action, having a single unified agency greatly eases the task. In the US such an agency is involved with supervision but in the new arrangements in the UK it is not. Nevertheless, looking to the relatively loose coordination among national supervisors sounds relatively less plausible than having a single main agency with the power and resources to act.

NOTES

1. Given the willingness that authorities have shown for rescuing national banks in the present crisis, this belief is clearly generally justified. Much of the major impact of the failure of Lehman Brothers was because it was unexpected despite its problems. Given the saving of Bear Stearns many investors could be forgiven for expecting a similar rescue despite any assertions to the contrary.
2. In the event of a cross-border failure, disputes among the different jurisdictions trying to protect their own stakeholders is inevitable. The dispute over the location of assets within a week of the collapse of Lehman Brothers was a good illustration, as those trying to realize parts of the group as going concerns sought to get rapid deals. (*Financial Times*, 20/21 September, p. 1).
3. It identifies the problem in paragraph 201 but does not offer a way forward.
4. There also appear to be unusual features in the treatment of Tier 2 capital in Denmark, which enable rapid resolutions. For debt to be acceptable as Tier 2 capital in Denmark it has to have provision for writing down and for deferring interest. Clearly if other countries were to switch to this requirement it might increase the cost of subordinated debt slightly, but then this position effectively applies in the US, Canada and other countries with a special resolution regime already, so it is clearly not something prohibitive.
5. Outside the EU, other countries such as the US and Canada have imposed conditions of registration even for branches that give the host authorities supervisory rights and the ability to intervene in the event of difficulty.
6. It would, however, require considerable regulatory convergence at the detailed level but no greater than that envisaged in the de Larosière Report, for example.
7. This section draws on Mayes, Nieto and Wall (2008).
8. For a discussion of the intellectual history of PCA, see Benston and Kaufman (1994).
9. The US scheme as implemented has five zones (as set out in Table 10.1), whereas the UK has decided to have only three zones where the second and third categories in the

Benston and Kaufman list are combined. The principle is the same but the advantage of having the second and third zones is that they distinguish heightened concern from the definite requirement to take action.

10. CAMELS: Capital adequacy, Asset quality, Management, Earnings, Liquidity and Sensitivity to market risk.
11. L 177/48, *Official Journal of the European Union*, 30 June 2006.
12. Article 127§6, Consolidated Version of the Treaty on the Functioning of the European Union (Lisbon Treaty) 2008.
13. Since this chapter was written there have been major changes in the global regulatory framework including the agreement on Basel 3. One facet of this discussed only in part is that capital offers could be made much more efficient if they permit contingent capital that can be converted from debt to equity in the event of a problem. In such a case it would become much easier to handle cross-border banks without the need to involve taxpayer funding.

REFERENCES

Benston, G.J. and G. Kaufman (1988), *Risk and Solvency Regulation of Depositor Institutions: Past Policies and Current Options*, New York: Salomon Brothers Center, Graduate School of Business, New York University.

Benston, G.J. and G. Kaufman (1994), 'The Intellectual History of the Federal Deposit Insurance Corporation Improvement Act of 1991', in G.G. Kaufman (ed.), *Reforming Financial Institutions and Markets in the United States*, Boston: Kluwer, pp. 1–17.

Committee of European Banking Supervisors (CEBS) (2009), 'Mapping of supervisory objectives and powers, including early intervention measures and sanctioning powers', CEBS paper 47, March, London.

Čihák, M. and J. Decressin (2007), 'The case for a European Banking License', International Monetary Fund working paper/07/73.

Davis, E.P. and K. Dilruba (2008), 'Comparing early warning systems for banking crises', *Journal of Financial Stability*, **4**(2), 89–120.

de Larosière, J. (with L. Balcerowicz, O. Issing, R. Masera, C. McCarthy, L. Nyberg, J. Pérez and O. Ruding) (2009), *Report of the High-Level Expert Group on Financial Supervision in the EU*, Brussels: European Commission.

Eisenbeis, R.A. and G.G. Kaufman (2007), 'Cross-border banking: challenges for deposit insurance and financial stability in the European Union', in D. Evanoff and G.G. Kaufman (eds), *Challenges for Deposit Insurance and Financial Stability in Cross-Border Banking Environments with Emphasis on the European Union*, Singapore: World Scientific.

FDIC (2008) 'Processing deposit accounts in a bank failure; modernizing large-bank insurance determinations notice of proposed rulemaking', January, accessed 5 October 2010 at www.fdic.gov/news/news/financial/2008/fil08002.html#body.

Hüpkes, E. (2003), 'Bank insolvency regulation in Switzerland', in D.G. Mayes and A. Liuksila, *Who Pays for Bank Insolvency?*, Basingstoke: Palgrave-Macmillan.

Ingves, S. (2006), 'Cross-border banking regulation – a way forward: the European case', presented at the Conference on International Financial Instability: Cross-Border Banking and National Regulation, October, accessed 5 October 2010 at www.riksbank.com/templates/Page.aspx?id=22795.

LaBrosse, R. and D. Walker (2007), 'Contingency planning: a practitioners guide drawing from lessons learned from dealing with bank failures', in A. Campbell, R. Labrosse, D.G. Mayes. and D. Singh (eds), *Deposit Insurance*, Basingstoke: Palgrave-Macmillan.

Lane, J. (2008), 'A view from the FDIC', Norges Bank Workshop on Prompt Corrective Action, March.

Mayes, D.G. (2006), 'Financial stability in a world of cross-border banking: Nordic and antipodean solutions to the problem of responsibility without power', *Journal of Banking Regulation*, **8**(1), 20–39.

Mayes, D.G., M. Nieto and L. Wall (2008), 'Multiple safety net regulators and agency problems in the EU: is Prompt Corrective Action partly the solution?, *Journal of Financial Stability*, **4**, 232–57.

Mayes, D.G. and J. Vesala, (2000), 'On the problems of home country control', *Current Economics and Politics of Europe*, **10**(1), 1–25.

Nieto, M.J. and L.D. Wall (2006), 'Preconditions for a successful implementation of supervisors' Prompt Corrective Action: is there a case for a banking standard in the EU?', London School of Economics Financial Markets Group special paper series, no. 165, March.

Padoa-Schioppa, T. (2007), 'Europe needs a single financial rule book', *Financial Times*, 10 December.

Peek, J. and E. Rosengren (1997), 'Will legislated early intervention prevent the next banking crisis?', *Southern Economic Journal*, **64**(1), 268–80.

Persson, M. (2009), 'Achieving financial stability with cross-border banking in an EU perspective', in D.G. Mayes and G.E. Wood (eds), *Designing Central Banks*, Abingdon: Routledge, chapter 9.

Reserve Bank of New Zealand (2006), Outsourcing Policy, Document BS11, January.

Schoenmaker, D. and S. Oosterloo (2007), 'Cross-border issues in European financial supervision', in D. Mayes and G. Wood (eds), *The Structure of Financial Regulation*, Abingdon: Routledge, pp. 264–91.

Sigurðsson, J. (2003), 'Small countries, large multi-country banks: a challenge to supervisors', in D.G. Mayes and A. Liuksila (eds), *Who Pays for Bank Insolvency?*, Basingstoke: Palgrave-Macmillan.

Stern, G. and R. Feldman (2004), *Too Big to Fail: The Hazards of Big Bank Bailouts*, Washington, DC: Brookings Institution.

Turner, A. (2009), *A Regulatory Response to the Global Banking Crisis*, London: Financial Services Authority.

Vesala, J. (2005), *Prudential Supervision and Deposit Insurance Issues Raised by the European Company Statute*, Frankfurt: European Central Bank.

11. The world of unintended consequences: a post-mortem on Regulation Q and prologue for the future

Robert A. Eisenbeis and George G. Kaufman

INTRODUCTION

The US and world financial systems are in the midst of what is widely perceived as the worst financial crisis since the Great Depression of the 1930s. Like other financial crises, it has ignited an adverse feedback loop to the real economy, causing serious declines in real income and employment.[1] Because of their great costs, major financial crises tend to be quickly followed by proposals to reform the financial system to ensure that whatever happened 'never happens again'. The current crisis is no exception. It has exposed widespread breakdowns in corporate governance of financial institutions, managerial failures in financial institutions, and supervisory failures by the responsible banking and financial institution regulatory agencies. As a result, the focus of much of the immediate regulatory reform proposals is likely to be on 'fixing' how institutions and the regulatory agencies conduct their business once the crisis has passed. In addition, there are likely to be efforts to expand the types of financial institutions that will be subject to government regulation and supervision, and to regulate both the types of financial products and the terms under which they are offered to the public.

Experience has shown, however, that the middle of a crisis or immediately afterwards are the worst times to attempt to address financial and regulatory reform issues efficiently. The true causes of the crisis are likely to be not yet well understood. As a result, the reforms enacted are usually poorly motivated and not necessarily targeted to the real underlying problems. The regulations adopted often suffer from time inconsistency problems, where the cost of the unintended consequences may over time exceed the cost of the problems they were intended to address and may lead to even greater problems in the future. It may take years both to recognize these costs and to unwind what turn out to be misguided regulatory responses to perceived problems that may or may not have been real.

One classic example of just such a regulatory response to a crisis was the imposition in 1933 of ceilings on interest rates that commercial banks (and later thrift institutions) in the US may pay on time deposits. These ceilings were referred to as Regulation Q, or Reg. Q ceilings, named after the Federal Reserve regulation that implemented the ceilings for member banks. It took over 50 years for sufficient market pressures to develop for its removal and it is now nearly 25 years after its complete demise in 1986. It is thus fitting and proper that we focus on this now old regulation in honour of David Llewellyn's impending retirement and the more than 25 years that he has devoted to the study of banking and banking regulation.

Deposit rate ceilings were introduced on commercial banks at the national level in the US in the Banking (Glass-Steagall) Act of 1933 and were phased out in the Depository Institutions Deregulation and Monetary Control Act (DIDMCA) of 1980 effective 1986.[2] Reg. Q was extended to thrift institutions in 1966. Although it represents price regulation, Reg. Q is different from the regulation of other prices in that it limits expenses rather than revenues. This form of price regulation is rare and, unlike most forms of price controls, was supported by the majority of the affected industry.

The long run implications of Reg. Q in terms of the avoidance-innovations and resource misallocations it spawned are similar to those of other types of price or rate regulation. When proposed, there appears to have been little if any consideration of long-term consequences for either the banking or thrift industry. The focus was all on defusing the problem of that day – the failure of nearly 10 000 banks since 1929 and the almost complete breakdown of the banking system. Unfortunately, over the longer-term, Reg. Q contributed to major distortions in both credit flows and real resource allocation and did not ultimately benefit either the industry or consumers. In particular, it contributed substantially to the start and high cost of the thrift crisis of the 1980s, which led to the subsequent virtual demise of the industry in the US. It also led to the growth of non-bank competitors, not subject to the regulation, such as money market funds.

HISTORY

Reg. Q was adopted in response to a perfect financial storm that caused the worst economic depression and the largest number of bank failures in

US history. Unemployment reached more than 25 per cent in 1933 and real GDP declined by nearly 50 per cent from 1929. The public demanded quick action from its elected officials to do something, anything that sounds good. In light of the large number of bank failures, the numerous provisions in the Banking Act of 1933 focused on ensuring their safety. Besides Reg. Q, the Act prohibited interest payments on demand deposits, introduced federal deposit insurance by the FDIC, separated deposit banking from private securities underwriting and trading (Glass-Steagall), imposed margin requirements on security purchases financed by loans, restricted new national bank charters, and permitted national banks to branch equal to that permitted state banks in each state. The enactment of these provisions reflected large-scale horse-trading among the affected parties. For example, small banks were generally willing to support or at least not to oppose the prohibition of interest payments on demand deposits and the limited expanded branching authority, both of which were favored by the large banks, in order to obtain Q protections and deposit insurance.

The stated major objectives in imposing Reg. Q included:

- reducing bank risk and probability of bank failure by reducing interest costs so as to reduce bank incentives to invest in high yielding, high risk loans
- reducing bank failures by limiting what was believed to be ruinous inter-bank deposit rate competition among banks
- reducing loan rates by reducing the cost of funds to banks
- reducing unfair fund flows from small and rural banks to large and city banks
- helping banks to offset the premium cost of the newly adopted deposit insurance (Gilbert 1986).

Some or all of these reasons were rooted in the belief that competition for deposits was associated with banking failures. Subsequent research, however, has shown that many of these beliefs were not supported by the empirical evidence.[3]

Because market rates were below ceiling rates in the early days after enactment, there was little opposition to Reg. Q. It was rarely binding and when it was the regulators increased the ceiling rate to reduce outflows or disintermediation from the banks to other non-covered institutions or markets. Reg. Q became briefly binding in 1953, 1955 and 1958, when market interest rates rose more swiftly above the Q ceilings, and minor disintermediation from banks resulted. It became seriously binding in the mid-1960s, when regulators did not raise Q ceilings in response to sharply rising market rates from sharply higher inflationary expectations and disintermediation from covered institutions jumped sharply.

With support from the thrift industry, regulators and legislators responded to the higher rates by extending the Q ceilings to savings and loan associations in 1966, but at a slightly higher level.[4] This gave savings and loans associates a competitive advantage over commercial banks. The primary objectives of the extension to savings and loans associates were to:

- protect against thrift insolvency by tying their cost of funds closer to revenues from their long-term, low rate, fixed rate mortgages issued earlier in lower rate environments
- encourage flow of low cost funds into the mortgage market to support residential housing
- reduce credit extension by banks to large corporations, which were viewed as important contributors to inflation, by inducing savers to shift funds from banks to thrift institutions.

But, the short-term consequences turned out to be quite different:

- Large banks innovated ways to avoid the restrictions through developing sources of funds not subject to Q ceilings, such as Eurodollar deposits at banks outside the US and commercial paper issued by the banks' parent holding companies, both of which could be recycled to Q-affected banks.
- Banks offered small time depositors gifts such as radios, TV sets, various electric appliances, and other forms of implicit interest. On the one hand, these were less valued by savers and, on the other hand, they upset the regulators, who viewed them as circumventing the regulation. In response, they developed numerous very detailed rules on what value gifts could be offered for what size deposits.
- Substantial disintermediation from both banks and thrifts occurred as interest rates continued to climb and accelerated the growth of competitors, particularly money market funds that were not subject to Q ceilings and did not often exist in any major form before 1974, Disintermediation reduced the flow of funds to mortgages but did not reduce mortgage interest rates
- Rates paid to small savers on deposits were held below market interest rates
- Although not strictly the result of Reg. Q, state chartered thrifts in New England, which were not subject to federal regulation at the time, innovated NOW (Negotiable Order of Withdrawal) accounts which enabled them to offer a transaction account that paid explicit interest.

The regulators, in turn, in a game of point and counterpoint, responded to each regulatory avoidance action on the part of financial institutions by:

- progressively lifting Q ceilings off large time deposits in excess of $100 000, first for short-term deposits at the time of the Penn Central Railroad bankruptcy commercial paper crisis in 1970, and then off all such large deposits in 1973. This effectively removed the largest banks from Reg. Q as they were financed heavily by large time deposits
- introducing new types of small (under $100 000) time deposits that were exempt from Q with differing terms to maturity and minimum denominations. For example both a no rate ceiling, no minimum denomination, but a minimum three and a half year maturity savings certificate, and a higher ceiling, floating rate, $7500 minimum, 91-day maturity certificate were introduced in 1982. In all, there were some 20 specific targeted piecemeal deregulation actions affecting deposits below $100 000 between 1978 and 1986, the final date of termination. Depositing funds at banks became a difficult task for many households
- Having the US Treasury raise the minimum denomination of Treasury bills from $1000 to $10 000 to discourage disintermediation by small savers into this market.

REPEAL

The above series of events, coupled with the increase in interest rates that resulted from the rapid rise in inflation during that era of the 1970s, greatly reduced the effectiveness of Reg. Q and made *de jure* repeal eventually inevitable. Its objectives were not achieved, rather a number of unintended consequences developed:

- many thrifts redirected their risk-taking from growing rapidly by outbidding their competitors for funds to taking greater risks with the funds available, particularly if the institutions were insolvent or near-insolvent, to ‘gamble for resurrection’
- thrift failures were not prevented
- aggregate mortgage funds were both reduced and became more volatile
- small banks and thrifts were not helped through time.

In addition, the deadweight costs associated with avoidance and evasion of Q were high, growing and became progressively more transparent. Almost all parties participating in financial markets became dissatisfied and disillusioned with it and began to express their sentiments more vocally.

Perhaps most visible and disconcerting to Congress were groups of senior citizens, calling themselves the Gray Panthers, who filled the halls of the Congressional office buildings and spilled over into the hearing rooms to complain loudly that Reg. Q was preventing them, who were primarily savers and on fixed incomes, from obtaining a market interest rate on their savings, and was transferring the benefits to mortgage borrowers, who were younger and less on fixed-incomes. By the time of the repeal of Q in DIDMCA in 1980, Congress had concluded in its opening set of findings justifying the Act that,

> Limitations on the interest rates which are payable on deposits . . . discourage persons from saving money, create inequities for depositors, impede the ability of depository institutions to compete for funds, and have not achieved their purpose of providing an even flow of funds for home mortgages.

Since repeal, there has been far less volatility in bank and thrift credit and little, if any, disintermediation from depository institutions. This has been true for banks even during the current crisis. Through 2007, before the onset of the financial meltdown, flows of funds to the mortgage market had been at record levels and at relatively low interest rates. Indeed, public policy concern was frequently about the large volume of mortgage loans rather than an insufficient flow. Small savers have been paid at nearer to market rates on larger units of funds. Both banks and thrifts are more competitive.

Few of the problems experienced by the banks in the early 2000s and the current crisis can be attributed to excessive interest payments on time deposits. Both the industry and consumers appear to have been better off since the repeal of Q than during its lifetime. This satisfaction is reflected in the total absence of any outcry from any party for the return of Q since its demise, even during the depth of the financial crisis in 2008. It remains buried with few visitors to its gravesite.

The lessons from the Reg. Q reforms should serve as a caution to reformers as they consider responses to the current financial crisis. Policymakers responded immediately to the current ongoing financial turmoil with a number of ad hoc emergency measures, such as the nationalization of Freddie and Fannie, the extension of government guarantees to bank debt issuance, the raising of deposit insurance limits, and the effective imposition of limits on executive compensation for institutions receiving government financial support. But, unless terminated in a timely manner once the crisis has abated, or simply not enacted after closer examination, emergency regulations like Reg. Q before them, promise to have longer-term implications that will be quite different from either the intended short-term or long-term effects.

PROPOSED CURRENT REGULATORY 'REFORMS'

The Obama Administration and congressional leaders have already begun consideration of potentially far-reaching modifications of government regulation of financial institutions and markets, in addition to the ad hoc changes already in place. We examine three of these likely reforms – authorizing the Federal Reserve (or some other body) to act as the regulator of systemic risk, extending the bank insolvency resolution regime to a broader range of institutions, and extending restrictions on executive compensation imposed during the crisis. Two of these would be new initiatives while the last would continue and perhaps even extend what was a short-term response to a perceived emergency.

Federal Reserve as a Primary Regulator of Systemic Risk

The 2007–09 financial crisis is widely considered to be a systemic crisis. In parallel, many large institutions are being referred to as systemically important institutions. This is because the crisis has adversely affected almost every large commercial bank and many so-called shadow banks (investment banks, hedge funds, insurance companies) in both the US and most other industrial countries. These two uses of the term systemic, however, differ in meaning. The first refers to the size of the event and implies the existence of a large shock that directly impacts many institutions simultaneously. The second focuses on the strong interrelationships between a (systemic) institution and other important financial institutions, such that its collapse would endanger those other institutions. The different definitions demonstrate that there is no single, standard definition of systemic risk or a systemic shock in the literature.

Kaufman and Scott (2003) discuss three possible definitions of systemic shocks or risk. The first is a very big exogenous shock that impacts all or nearly all financial institutions, seriously damaging their ability to conduct their business activities efficiently. An example of this would be the bursting of a nationwide bubble in house prices in the US.

The second focuses on a shock that affects only some institutions, but where the market is temporarily uncertain about both which institutions are exposed and the extent of that exposure, and thus are unsure about its damage. An example here would be a micro information shock, as in the classic bank run, in which adverse news about the financial condition of one or a small number of banks creates uncertainty about the financial condition of a large number of banks. Another example would be a macro shock that affects some but not all players, such as the Asian financial crisis of the late 1990s, in which the prices of all developing country debt declined temporarily as a result of the economic outlook for the region, irrespective of the true financial condition of individual countries. In either of these cases, financial markets need time to separate the sick from the healthy parties, be they institutions or countries. In the meantime, market participants will avoid conducting business with all institutions until they discover the extent of each institution's exposure. They will then conduct transactions only with those that are not seriously harmed.

The third definition of systemic risk focuses on interrelationships between an impacted institution and other institutions through inter-institution lending, deposits, or other counterparty relationships. Thus, if one impacted institution fails, the shock travels among the interrelationship chain impacting the other institutions in sequence, as in a series of falling dominos. This would occur if banks held significant interbank deposits and a large bank in this chain became insolvent spreading losses to their counterparty banks that drove them into insolvency, and so on down the chain.

Recently a number of federal banking regulators and the US Treasury have argued strongly for the establishment of a systemic risk regulator. Views have ebbed and flowed as to whether this responsibility would be vested in the Fed, the US Treasury, a college or committee of banking regulators, or a new institution. At a minimum, the systemic risk regulator's responsibilities would include monitoring developments across financial markets, identifying trends and interconnections among institutions, and focusing on potential macro imbalances that might pose systemic risks to the financial system or economy. But some see a much broader role for the systemic risk regulator to include the identification of systemically important institutions, the regulation and prudential supervision of such institutions, and the ability to require the responsible agency to address any problems or imbalances that may possibly have systemic consequences.

However, the case for a new systemic risk regulator is not all that obvious. As Wallison (2009) points out, the Fed, like most other central banks around the world, has been functioning de facto as a systemic risk authority, either alone or in cooperation with the US Treasury and FDIC for many years. In 1984, the Fed and FDIC provided support for Continental Illinois National Bank, both the bank and its parent holding company. The institution was subsequently reorganized and continued operations. In 1995, the US Treasury, Fed, other central banks and IMF provided support to Mexico when it experienced a currency crisis and debt default, to help prevent the systemic risks that might have infected the world financial system.

However, the Fed has often been conflicted, encouraging financial institutions to assume greater risks while at the same time being concerned about their safety. For example, before the Mexican crisis, the Fed encouraged US banks not only to assume risks by lending to Mexico, but also informed the banks that this lending would not be held against them when it came to regulatory risk assessments. Similarly, in 1998, the Fed also served as a catalyst in encouraging market participants to provide loans and other support in order to prevent the collapse of the large hedge fund Long Term Capital Management. Finally, in 2008, the Fed invoked the rarely used emergency lending powers granted to it under section 13 of the Federal Reserve Act, permitting it to lend to any party in exigent circumstances. These emergency powers enabled the Fed to provide financial support to both banks and non-banking institutions with direct loans and through security purchases.

The function of a systemic risk regulator should be to minimize the probability of a systemic event occurring, however defined, and to contain the resulting damage. This involves combining information about the financial condition of individual financial institutions (micro) that are perceived as sufficiently important or systemic (whether commercial banks, insurance companies, investment banks and so on), with information about the state of the economy (macro), and analysing the interrelationship for the financial system as a whole (horizontal analysis). This task is more difficult to achieve if there is no agreement on the definition of systemic risk or what costs and losses are to be contained. Under such circumstances it is difficult to specify the authorities, powers or resources to grant to the systemic risk regulator, or to decide how to respond, control or regulate a problem that cannot be defined in the same way by all the responsible parties. As a consequence, this ambiguity is also likely to result in substantial discretion by the appointed regulator in ways that may generate large costs to the taxpayer.

As mentioned previously, some have suggested that the Fed be appointed as the systemic risk regulator. As a routine part of its monetary policy responsibilities, the Fed already has responsibility for managing both macroeconomic conditions (monetary stability), through its monetary policy functions, and financial stability – as well as individual bank (financial) holding companies. Likewise, the Fed also follows developments in capital, equity and financial markets, and its payments and settlement services are a major part of the financial infrastructure that enables US financial markets to function efficiently. Thus, it has ongoing access to both macro and micro data and the ability to impose its policies. It has a large staff of respected economists and supervisors with the capacity to perform the monitoring function required. Finally, it has the resources to counter financial crises as they arise without the need to request additional appropriations from Congress.

The Fed has also demonstrated the capacity to address potentially systemically important concerns and shocks without an additional Congressional mandate to do so. Three recent examples – Y2K in the 1990s, the 9/11 terrorist attack in New York City in 2001, and Hurricane Katrina in 2005 – demonstrate the Fed's broad interpretation of its responsibilities for financial stability.

In advance of the turn of the twenty-first century, many financial experts were concerned that a programming flaw in many legacy financial service processing and record keeping software would trigger a widespread halt in banking and financial service operations. The Fed assumed leadership in anticipation of this problem in the early 1990s. It required, in cooperation with other banking agencies, that banks reprogram their systems to correct the problem rather than waiting to see whether it proved to have the feared consequences. The result was a massive reinvestment in software and related technology that most likely would never have been undertaken otherwise. No important Y2K problems occurred when 1999 turned into the year 2000, and the potential breakdown in transactions and financial service processing was averted.

When the 9/11 terrorist attack essentially closed down US financial markets in 2001, the Fed injected liquidity into the market place, cobbled together alternative transportation systems to ensure that checks were cleared and payments made, and provided loans to counterparties that failed to collect funds owned, and even guaranteed payment of funds for key institutions. In the wake of Hurricane Katrina in 2005, the Fed trucked currency to troubled communities along the Gulf Coast and worked to ensure that banks would continue operating. It had the necessary resources to do so.

This wide variety of experiences demonstrates that systemic risk management and response capabilities were not only in place but operated quite effectively in the face of a wide variety of different threats to financial stability without the presence of an officially designated systemic regulator. But choosing the Fed as the systemic risk regulatory and supervisory authority can also pose conflicts of goals for it (or for that matter, any other existing regulator should it be granted that responsibility) (Eisenbeis and Wall, 1999 and Wallison, 2009). Achieving financial stability and minimizing the probability of, and damage from systemic risk may conflict with the Fed's responsibility for achieving monetary stability. Specifically, Calomiris and Litan (2000) suggest that a conflict may arise if there is the need to offset systemic shocks that threaten some large bank or other financial institution (through providing additional liquidity), at a time that the rate of inflation exceeds the target for price stability (when macro-liquidity should be reduced). More broadly, a central bank with systemic risk mitigation responsibility might find it advantageous to pursue a more lax monetary policy to cushion a weakness in the financial system. This might impart tolerance of a higher rate of inflation than might otherwise be desirable.

Bernanke (2001) turns this argument on its head when he suggests that because the economy and banking system are strongly influenced by central bank interest rate policy, monetary policy formulation requires the central bank to be aware of the financial condition of banks. Similarly, he argues that because the discount window plays a role in affecting the money supply and interest rates, evaluation of a bank's need to use the discount window can only be acquired if the central bank is engaged in banking supervision.

At the same time, Bernanke recognizes the conflicts that may exist among competing regulatory and monetary policy objectives. He has noted that,

> To the extent that the Fed has institutional objectives other than maximizing social welfare, giving the central bank too broad a range of powers may invite abuse. For example, if the Fed were anxious to conceal the insolvency of some part of the banking system (an impulse we have seen at times in other supervisory agencies), it might be tempted to distort interest rate policies in a way that increase bank profits or asset values at the expense of macroeconomic objectives.[5]

There may also be temptations to use supervisory power to encourage bank lending in a downturn during a so-called credit crunch in order to jump-start the economy. Other goal conflicts may also present themselves to the systemic risk supervisor. A conflict may arise between the Fed's objective of financial stability and pursuing efficiency in the banking system through encouraging greater competition. The more intense the competition, the greater is the likelihood of bank failures and financial instability.

During times of financial distress, conflicts may also arise between the interests of shareholders and investors and the interests of those responsible for financial stability. For example, while the complete story is yet to be told, it does appear that pressure was brought to bear on Bank of America (BoA) CEO Kenneth Lewis to complete BoA's acquisition of the severely troubled investment bank Merrill Lynch by Secretary of the Treasury Paulson and Fed Chairman Bernanke. They apparently made it clear that they didn't want information on the true financial condition of Merrill Lynch to become public information before the acquisition. This put Lewis potentially in the position of having to trade off the interests of his company's shareholders for the greater good of avoiding a systemic risk problem for the US financial system.

Whether, as a matter of public policy, it is desirable to combine regulatory, monetary policy and systemic risk responsibilities in a single agency or in multiple agencies, it is important to recognize the potential for goal conflicts, especially during crisis periods. Allowing a single agency to decide the trade offs among competing goals rather than externalizing the conflicts by lodging them in separate agencies depends not only on the nature and potential seriousness of the conflicts but also on the primacy that the responsible agency gives to its objectives and congressional mandate. For example, typically the FDIC is more likely to give primacy to protecting the insurance fund as opposed to interest of creditors or bank shareholders, whereas the Fed is more likely to give primacy to its monetary policy objectives. But when there are many objectives, it not only becomes more difficult to ascertain how goal conflicts might be resolved but it also opens up the door for political interference as potentially adversely affected parties resort to lobbying their congressional representatives to protect their interests.

Extending the Bank Resolution Regime to Other 'Systemic' Financial Institutions and Bank Holding Companies

In the US, insolvent banks are resolved differently than insolvent non-bank firms, primarily because delays that typically occur in the bankruptcy resolution of non-bank entities, and uncertainties in transferring funds with the insolvent bank's counterparties, would have severe adverse effects on the economy in the market area that the bank serves. The specifics of the resolution process for banks are incorporated in the Federal Deposit Insurance Act (FDIA), rather than the federal bankruptcy code. The Act assigns the responsibility for initiating legal closure of a bank to bank regulators rather than to large unpaid creditors or the firm itself, according to a number of criteria enumerated in the FDIA, including having insufficient though possibly positive capital. The Act also:

- mandates that the insolvent bank be put in receivership and that its charter be cancelled;
- appoints the FDIC as receiver and provides it with significant flexibility as to the type and speed of the resolution process, and whether the bank is merged or liquidated

- allows the immediate sale of the institution's assets and liabilities in part or total to another bank or, particularly for larger banks, to a newly chartered, temporary FDIC-owned and operated bridge bank, while the bank is being wound down in an orderly fashion
- prohibits *ex ante* appeals to the regulators' actions
- applies absolute priorities in settling claims
- prohibits most stays
- requires the resolution to be at least cost to the FDIC (Bliss and Kaufman, 2007).

The Act does, however, permit some exceptions to these provisions, including least cost resolution and absolute priority, if applying these provisions may destabilize the financial system. The bank resolution process is a regulatory rather than judicial process. On the whole, it also is a more certain and lower cost process than the process for resolving non-banks.

In its dual capacity as deposit insurer and receiver, the FDIC operates so that depositors incur no loss on insured deposits and are generally provided full access to these funds the next business day. They experience neither a credit nor a liquidity loss. On the other hand, uninsured depositors may suffer both. They receive receivership certificates for the amount of their uninsured deposits, which are paid as the FDIC (as receiver) collects the proceeds from the sale of the bank's assets. These are likely to be less than the par value of deposits and other liabilities so that these depositors and creditors suffer credit losses. They are likely also to suffer liquidity losses if all the bank's assets are not sold immediately. But more recently, the FDIC has on occasion paid advance dividends to uninsured depositors and some other counterparties the next business day equal to a conservative estimate of the recovery value. However, because the FDIC is currently required to achieve the least-cost resolution for itself, it has no obligation to protect the value of unsecured non-depositor claims, which have lower absolute priority.

But there are disadvantages and drawbacks to the current bank resolution process. There is no provision for rehabilitation as in Chapter 11 of the federal bankruptcy code. Once put into receivership by the relevant regulator, the bank under that charter is dead and its equity holders are wiped out, except to the extent that there may be some residual value after resolution. Among other reasons, banks may be put in receivership by the regulators for breeching a low but positive capital ratio as specified in the FDICIA of 1991. Currently this minimum tangible equity to total asset ratio is 2 per cent. As long as capital is greater than zero, this may be viewed as a taking of private property that would be particularly unfair in light of the inability to be given a chance to rehabilitate, and may lead to inefficient outcomes. Nor does the FDICIA process end 'too-big-to-fail', as a systemic risk exemption provides for potential support to the *de jure* uninsured depositors and creditors. Indeed, the application of too-big-to-fail to protect creditors has been more frequent for banks than for non-banks.

It is important to note that the FDICIA resolution process applies only to banks and not to bank holding companies, whose resolution processes are governed by the general corporate bankruptcy code. Thus, resolution of the failure of a large US bank holding company would most likely not be quite as smooth as for the bank alone since most of these holding companies have not only substantial holdings of foreign bank subsidiaries chartered in many countries throughout the world, but also often many non-bank subsidiaries and affiliates. While these affiliates and subsidiaries are legally separate entities, and hence subject to the bankruptcy and resolution policies in the countries in which they are chartered, they are often operationally so interconnected that it would be virtually impossible to extract them from the consolidated entity. This was one of the complexities that prompted the US government's rescue of Bear Stearns and AIG. The following quote from William C. Dudley (2009), current president of the Federal Reserve Bank of New York illustrates this clearly:

> The Federal Reserve made its decision to lend based on a judgment that a failure of AIG would cause dramatically negative consequences for the financial system and the economy – consequences worse than what occurred in the aftermath of the failure of Lehman Brothers. We stand by that judgment today. In the case of Lehman, some of the most severe repercussions related to the difficulties in coordinating cross-border insolvency regimes and in coordinating the insolvency regimes among different types of institutions within the organization's corporate structure. In light of AIG's unparalleled global footprint – operating in more than 130 countries around the globe – and the multiplicity of different types of financial services entities within its structure – including insurance providers, foreign banks, consumer lending companies and OTC derivatives affiliates – the factors that proved unmanageable in the Lehman insolvency threatened to be much more severe in AIG's case. The fact that no effective emergency resolution procedures exist under US law to reconcile these difficulties heightened the need for quick, effective action by the Federal Reserve, in consultation with and supported by the US Treasury.

It follows that extending the current FDIA to non-banks and bank holding companies is likely to involve numerous issues, besides the obvious one of concentrating greater power in the bank regulators. Some of these are clearly evident while others are not. Thus, in drafting new legislation, policy-makers need be careful to avoid serious unintended consequences.

Limitations on Executive Compensation in Banking

Annual compensation for executives in banking and other financial firms, especially in investment banks, is generally higher than compensation for comparable executives in non-financial firms. It has been structured in recent years so that a larger proportion of the total compensation package is in the form of bonuses, generally tied to the performance of the executive, or his/her division or employer as a whole. Recently, the large bonuses paid to executives at insolvent or government-assisted financial firms have drawn widespread public criticism.

The bonuses were typically based on a single year's performance. Thus, longer-term ramifications of the employee's short-term actions, particularly negative implications, were not considered and clawbacks were not provided for in the contracts. This structure introduced moral hazard risk-taking incentives that encouraged maximizing current gains at the expense of larger losses in the future. Indeed, such a structuring of compensation has often been cited as an important cause of the ongoing financial crisis. Numerous observers have proposed limiting the size of bonuses or eliminating bonuses altogether.

However, placing severe restrictions on compensation is likely to have broad consequences, including contributing to the loss of the bank's most productive employees to firms not covered by the restrictions. Restrictions can usually also be easily circumvented. This is not the first time that restrictions on executive compensation have been proposed in the US. Restrictions were even enacted by Congress in 1993, limiting the maximum cash compensation that business firms can expense for corporate income tax purposes for executive pay to $1 million per top executive. But exceptions are permitted when bonus payments are (a) geared to performance based upon objective standards (b) approved by a compensation committee who have reviewed the performance goals and determined that the goals have been met and (c) have received shareholder approval of such performance-based plans. The Internal Revenue Service (IRS) treats stock option plans as a form of performance-based compensation when they have been approved by stockholders and reviewed by the incentive compensation committee like other performance-based compensation.[6] Firms quickly avoided this limitation by increasing sharply the compensation paid in performance-based stock or stock options. However, over time, public dissatisfaction with the pay-for-performance format introduced by many firms has also increased as the size of the bonuses has increased rapidly and the tie with performance has become increasingly less visible.

Recently, both financial and non-financial firms that received government financial assistance were queried by the government about their executive compensation practices and encouraged to review and modify them if they resulted in perceived excessive rewards for the performance achieved. In June of 2009, the Obama administration appointed a pay czar who would oversee, and have the power to rule on and restrict, the pay of top executives receiving governmental support.[7]

One unintended consequence of the federal government's intervention in the executive compensation restrictions is that it is providing an incentive for healthy financial institutions to back out of the government assistance programme. The original term of the government's preferred stock injections was three years. But many institutions are lobbying to accelerate the timetable for repayment. Government officials are attempting to decide what criteria will be employed for repayment, including the price at which the associated warrants will be repurchased. The original intent of the programme was to inject capital into both healthy and distressed institutions to avoid stigmatizing those institutions receiving government help. However, interference with compensation practices is providing incentives for healthier institutions to exit the programme sooner and thereby potentially creating a separating equilibrium: only distressed institutions would remain in the programme. This would conflict with concerns about potential systemic risk.

SUMMARY AND CONCLUSION

One of the worst times for governments to consider financial regulatory reforms is in the midst of a crisis. Typically the reforms enacted treat symptoms of the crisis rather than root causes in a rush to demonstrate to constituents that something is being done. One consequence is that the reforms passed tend to be both ill conceived and ill designed, resulting in distortions to the functioning of financial markets and large and lasting unintended consequences that may take decades to unwind. This was the case in the US with Regulation Q, enacted in 1933 during the crisis of the Great Depression and extended in the 1960s to limit the interest rates that banks and thrifts could pay on time deposits. Before its expiration in 1986, this restriction turned out to be one of the root causes of the costly thrift crisis of the late 1980s and early 1990s, and failed to achieve its initial objectives of strengthening the safety of the banking system and benefiting consumers through lower borrowing rates.

Similar risks exist today that regulatory changes will be enacted hastily to curb perceived current abuses or to rectify problems perceived to have been at the heart of the current financial crisis. While it is difficult to forecast at this time which of the many proposed changes or reforms currently being floated will prove to have political legs and be enacted, this chapter has identified and considered the risks that would be associated with three possibilities: (1) creating a systemic risk regulator; (2) extending bank-like resolution processes to non-bank financial institutions; and (3) imposing restrictions on executive compensation. If not carefully crafted, all these changes promise to have unintended consequences (like Reg. Q) long after the initial reasons for enactment have been forgotten.

NOTES

1. Reinhart and Rogoff (2008), Caprio and Klingebiel (2003), Caprio, Klingebiel, Laeven and Noguera (2005).
2. Another provision in the Banking Act prohibited cash interest payments on bank demand deposits. That statutory prohibition is still in effect.
3. Benston (1964).
4. Initially the differential was 25 basis points in 1966 but it was later raised to 50 basis points.
5. Bernanke (2001).
6. Internal Revenue Service Code Section 162 (m).
7. Beyond this, it also announced the intention to seek legislation: to require that compensation committees (for more than just banking companies) be independent of management and answerable only to independent advisors; to empower the SEC to strengthen compensation committee independence; and to empower the SEC to require 'say-on-pay' votes by shareholders.

REFERENCES

Benston, G.J. (1964), 'Interest payments on demand deposits and bank investment behavior', *Journal of Political Economy*, (October), 431–49.

Bernanke, B. (2001), 'Comment on synergies between bank supervision and monetary policy: implications for design of bank regulatory structure', in F.S. Mishkin (ed.), *Prudential Supervision: What Works and What Doesn't*, Chicago: National Bureau of Economic Research, and University of Chicago Press.

Bliss, R.R. and G.G. Kaufman (2007), 'US corporate and bank insolvency regimes: a comparison and evaluation', *Virginia Law and Business Review*, **2**(1), 144–77.

Calomiris, C.W. and R.E. Litan (2000), 'Financial regulation in a global marketplace', in A.M. Santomero and R.E. Litan (eds), *Brookings-Wharton Papers on Financial Services*, Washington, DC: Brookings Institution Press, p. 292.

Caprio, G. Jr. and D. Klingebiel (2003), 'Episodes of systemic and borderline financial crises', accessed January 2010 at http://go.worldbank.org/5DYGICS7B0 (Dataset 1).

Caprio, G. Jr., D. Klingebiel, L. Laeven and G. Noguera (2005), 'Banking crisis database,' in P. Honohan and L. Laeven (eds), *Systemic Financial Crises*, Cambridge: Cambridge University Press.

Eisenbeis, R.A. and L.D. Wall (1999), 'Financial regulatory structure and the resolution of conflicting goals', *Journal of Financial Services Research*, **16**(2/3), 223–45.

Gilbert, A. (1986), 'Requiem for Regulation Q: what did it do and why did it pass away?', *Federal Reserve Bank of St Louis. Review*, February.
Kaufman, G.G. and K.E. Scott (2003), 'What is systemic risk?', *Independent Review*, (Winter), 371–92.
Reinhart, C.M. and K.S. Rogoff (2008), 'Banking crises: an equal opportunity menace', National Bureau of Economic Affairs working paper, no. 14587, December.
Wallison, P.J. (2009), 'Risky business,' Financial Services Outlook series, Washington, DC: American Enterprise Institute, February.

12. UK financial reform post crisis: is more regulation the answer?

Shelagh Heffernan[1]

INTRODUCTION

I am delighted to be invited to contribute to this volume in honour of David Llewellyn. His contribution in the field of banking, finance and money is legendary, especially his ability to combine theory with practice. My choice of topic is one Llewellyn has discussed in papers published over many years.[2] In a key speech in January 2009, Lord Turner, chairman of the FSA, made it clear that the days of light regulation were over:

> The changes which we need to make to create a sounder system for the future will be profound. . . . The response needs to be multifaceted. . . . These include actions relating to remuneration and incentives, to rating agencies, to counterparty risk in derivatives. They also involve consideration of the appropriate balance between mark to market and accrual accounting principles in published accounts. And, very importantly, we need to address issues relating to the regulation of large cross-border financial institutions, the realistic scope for global supervisory coordination, appropriate structures for local operations (subsidiaries or branches) and the appropriate balance of responsibility between home and host supervisors.[3]

In a March 2009 discussion paper, he goes further, calling for an EU super-regulatory structure:

> It is essential that the European Union now considers the appropriate way forward. The FSA Discussion Paper therefore proposes for debate a number of options, expressing a current preference for the creation of a new European Union institutional structure, which would replace the Lamfalussy committees. This body would be an independent authority with regulatory powers, a standard setter and overseer in the area of supervision (Turner, 2009b, p. 102).

In the sections below, events since the autumn of 2007 are reviewed to illustrate that the existing UK regulatory system had the authority to stop the British banking crisis but failed to exercise it. The so called light touch regulation is not the source of the ongoing crisis, making radical reforms unnecessary. Rather, the authorities, especially the FSA should exercise their existing powers to supervise banks more effectively, free from political meddling. Regulation of shadow banks need not be altered. The tripartite arrangement and future moral hazard remain sources of concern.

THE UK FINANCIAL SERVICES AUTHORITY

The Financial Services and Markets Act was passed in 2000, though the FSA had acted in a regulatory capacity after the Securities and Investment Board became the FSA in late 1997. The Act formalised its statutory obligations, namely to:

- instil confidence in the UK financial system by promoting financial stability, to be achieved through a memorandum of understanding, now known as the 'tripartite agreement' which makes the Bank of England (BoE), the Treasury (HMT) and the FSA jointly responsible for financial stability
- educate the public, for example on the risks of investing in different types of financial instruments
- protect consumers, but encourage them to take greater responsibility
- reduce financial crime.

Compared to other countries with single financial regulators, this range of objectives is very broad. In addition, the FSA was and is expected to be cost effective. All new regulations are subject to cost-benefit analysis. Since the banks are central to the crisis, the extent of FSA authority is important. Early on the FSA adopted a risk based approach to regulation.[4] All FSA regulated firms, from banks to financial advisors, are assigned a score based on 'risk to our objectives' (RTO):

Impact Score = [*Impact of the problem*] X [*probability of problem arising*]

RTO refers to all four of the FSA's statutory objectives rather than financial/systemic risk *per se*. Scores range from A (very high impact) to D (low risk). Category A includes major banks (such as Northern Rock), large insurance firms and pension funds, stock exchanges, and big broker-dealers. These high scoring firms receive more regulatory attention. For banks, an extensive list of requirements ensure they conform to certain prudential norms and do not undermine the FSA's RTO. The key ones are:

- banks must be licensed by the FSA
- key management must meet fit and proper criteria
- compliance with the Basel I and II Accords, all bank-related EU directives, and international accounting rules
- satisfy FSA imposed bank-specific risk weighted capital ratios.
- banks in the high impact category are subject to internal/external audits and on site FSA examinations
- monitor banks' overseas activities
- major Financial Groups Division, responsible for approximately 50 of the most complex financial firms headquartered in the UK, chosen according to size, systemic importance, and complexity of business. Each conglomerate is assigned a micro-regulator who coordinates communication between the different divisions and supervisors within the FSA, assessing overall management and risk exposure.

Banks are subject to the Advanced Risk Responsive Operating framework (ARROW). It uses peer group analysis to identify unmanaged or unacceptable risks by assessing each bank's:[5]

1. exposure to environmental risks
2. business model and any prudential issues arising from it
3. prudential, financial, operating, customer, product, and market controls
4. governance, with an emphasis on top management being aware of risk exposure and risk management models
5. other variables such as capital and liquidity ratios.

WHERE DID THE FSA GO WRONG?

Based on ARROW and RTO, the FSA has the power to stop any activity it considers excessively risky. So what went wrong? To answer this question, it is instructive to review the problem banks that contributed to the crisis.

Northern Rock and Bradford and Bingley

Northern Rock had a business plan which consisted of growing its assets book at 25 per cent per annum, concentrating on one market – mortgages. By the time of its demise in September 2007, the bank had captured 20 per cent of the UK mortgage market, using several tactics. The first way was by securitisation – Northern Rock moved mortgages off balance sheet by creating mortgage-backed securities and selling them to investors via a special purpose vehicle (SPV) and an investment bank. This meant Northern Rock could engage in more mortgage lending. Though the quality of its mortgage book was thought to be reasonably good prior to nationalisation, by the second quarter of 2008 the newly nationalised bank announced losses of more than half a billion pounds, largely caused by growing mortgage arrears.

Second, Northern Rock attracted new mortgagees by allowing high loan to value ratios (up to 125 per cent) and high loan to income ratios, which rose from under two in the 1970s to over three by the early twenty-first century.[6] Careless scrutiny of applicants through self-certification (borrowers report their income without having to supply supporting evidence) or other forms of liars loans were an invitation to adverse selection.[7] The FSA admits that in 2007 up to 45 per cent of UK mortgages were granted without income being checked.[8] Third, 'borrow short, lend long' is the traditional mantra of most commercial banks and NR was no exception. However, Northern Rock became increasingly dependent on the interbank markets for funding rather than more traditional and relatively stable retail deposits. By 2007, at least 75 per cent of its loans were funded through the wholesale market with a mere 25 per cent from deposits.

Northern Rock failed its ARROW, which identifies unmanaged or unacceptable risks in a bank, in 2006. The FSA expressed concern that its business model was 'at the extreme end of the spectrum'. The FSA did not prescribe a risk mitigation programme even though it is considered crucial to stopping a bank failure, because the bank receives some direction on how to address the problem. But FSA staff did not appear to know how to implement a risk mitigation programme . In its place was hands on, continuous supervision consisting of numerous phone calls and eight meetings, most of them held on the same day. This suggests that the way the FSA goes about dealing with banks identified as risky must be improved. In its March 2008 internal audit report[9] on Northern Rock, the FSA admitted to failing to exercise its powers (there have been no further reports on other bank failures and the FSA's role).

Even though the FSA had branded the Northern Rock model unacceptable in 2006, Bradford and Bingley (B&B) and other banks adopted similar business models, with some variations. B&B targeted the buy to let market (more than 80 per cent of its mortgages) and championed self-certification mortgages, funded by the interbank markets. Attempts to raise new capital through a £300 million rights issue in early summer 2008 proved a dismal failure. By the time it was nationalised (29 September 2008) B&B's

mortgage portfolio stood at £40 billion, with mortgage arrears that were double the national average; the government also picked up the rest of its loan portfolio. Its deposits and branches were sold to Santander, which had purchased another troubled former mutual, Alliance and Leicester, in July.

B&B should have been on the FSA's radar screen: in 2004 it fined the bank £650000 for mis-selling precipice and with-profits bonds. B&B also agreed to pay £6 million to compensate 6800 customers. In a statement 2004 the FSA said:

> The firm did not make suitable recommendations to customers, did not maintain adequate records of sales and did not have in place adequate systems and controls to prevent and ultimately address these failures.

The same report notes that the bank had been warned of the poor quality of its customer record keeping as early as 1998.

The Icelandic Banks

The failure of the UK subsidiaries of Icelandic banks was due to the collapse of their parents.[10] According to Buiter and Sibert (2008), about two thirds of their funding came from the interbank market; the rest came from deposits, though in the case of Kaupthing (the parent to Kaupthing, Singer and Friedlander Bank-KSF), interbank funding was high as 75 per cent. These banks were truly global, with about half of Landsbanki's assets located outside Iceland, rising to two thirds for Kaupthing. The principal cause of their demise was the absence of willing interbank lenders, despite these banks' respectable financial ratios. Though the FSA could not be expected to interfere with the business model of foreign parents, it did not attempt to rein in the subsidiaries' activities, nor did it warn depositors to be wary of banks offering excessively high interest rates. The diplomatic repercussions might have been considerable (though less dramatic than the use of anti-terrorist legislation to freeze the assets of Icelandic bank subsidiaries by Chancellor Darling in October 2008) but this is not the FSA's concern.[11]

HBOS and Lloyds

HBOS's downfall was largely due to three factors. First, there was a rapid build up of bad debt. In two months (October to December 2008) its retail bad debt increased to just under £3 billion (from £1 billion) but it was in corporate lending where billions worth of loans turned out to be duds.

Most of the losses were in commercial property, amounting to just under £7 billion in 2007.[12] Second, there was excessive dependence on wholesale funding which by early 2008 amounted to just over 50 per cent; the rest came from retail deposits. Third, the group's risk management practices were problematic – as early as 2002, the FSA's ARROW on HBOS called for improved risk management procedures. After a follow up assessment in 2004, the FSA concluded progress had been made but there was room for improvement. In June 2006, the FSA wrote to HBOS saying there were still issues of control and the bank's growth strategy needed to be better managed and mitigated – both threatened the group as a whole.[13] Yet the FSA was, apparently, content to let advances and loans to corporates rise by 22 per cent in 2007 compared to just 8 per cent in 2006.

In March 2008, due to false rumours that HBOS approached the Bank of England for emergency funding, its share price fell by 17 per cent. In April, it announced a rights issue at 275p (a 50 per cent discount to the current market price) to raise £4 billion. But it flopped – just 8 per cent of the shares were taken up, leaving underwriters holding £3.8 billion worth of shares. The writing was on the wall. Despite reassurances by the FSA, its share price fluctuated wildly on 17 September 2008 (immediately after Lehman Brothers collapsed), hitting a low of 88p. Later that day HBOS confirmed BBC reports that it was in advanced takeover talks with Lloyds TSB. The next day, the price was set at 0.83 Lloyds shares for each HBOS share, equivalent to 232p per share. Just over a month later this price was renegotiated down to 0.605, and both banks announced they would participate in the government's recapitalisation scheme. In exchange for shares, the two banks accepted injections totalling £17 billion, which resulted in the government owning 43 per cent of the newly merged bank.[14]

The chairman of Lloyds TSB (Sir Victor Blank), a personal friend of the Prime Minister Gordon Brown, is believed to have been persuaded by him to take over HBOS. Normal competition rules were waived, creating the country's biggest mortgage and savings bank. The acquisition was completed in record time on 19 January 2009. On 13 February, Lloyds Banking Group revealed that the losses at HBOS were greater than anticipated, at around £10 billion. Its share price plunged by 32 per cent on the London Stock Exchange, carrying other bank shares with it.

Royal Bank of Scotland

On 19 January 2009 the Royal Bank of Scotland (RBS) announced the largest losses in UK corporate history, amounting to £24 billion – £8 billion from trading losses and another £16 billion of write-downs on assets, primarily arising from the takeover of Dutch bank ABN Amro.

RBS carried out due diligence on ABN Amro in May 2007 – six months before the takeover was completed. Despite the unprecedented global banking crisis which began late that summer, RBS was content to rely on statements from ABN Amro that the credit quality of its assets had not been unduly affected by these events.

The announcement reflected continuing problems at RBS which had effectively forced the bank to accept a state capital injection in October 2008, consisting of £5 billion in preference shares and £15 billion in ordinary shares. Only a tiny percentage (0.24 per cent) of the latter was taken up (in a rights issue) by investors, leaving government owning 58 per cent of RBS. In January 2009, this rose to 68 per cent when the preference shares were swapped for equity.

Building Societies

The FSA had been ordered by the Chancellor of the Exchequer to report on why Dunfermline Building Society failed. Dunfermline got into trouble after it built up a toxic commercial property loan book and UK subprime MBS of £800 million. On 30 March 2009, in a deal brokered by the Treasury, Nationwide took over Dunfermline's deposits, residential mortgages and branches. Nationwide was also paid £1.6 billion by the government because it had assumed all of Dunfermline's liabilities but not all its assets.[15]

In addition, four rescue mergers took place between building societies in December 2008.[16] According to the CEO of Nationwide, Graham Beale, the other building societies got into trouble because they were inexperienced in the new risks taken on.[17] Building societies' funding from wholesale markets cannot exceed 50 per cent (in 2007 the ceiling rose from half to three quarters, subject to a resolution being passed by members) and average around 30 per cent.[18] Up to 20 per cent of their funds are kept liquid.

It is worth summarising the FSA's oversights in the troubled UK banking sector.

- In 2002, the FSA threatened to ban self-certification but the mortgage industry dissuaded them from taking any action. In 2003, the BBC's *Money Programme* showed not only that self-certification was endemic at HBOS, but fraud was being committed. Mortgage brokers advised undercover applicants (BBC researchers) to lie on self-certification applications from HBOS group subsidiaries (The Mortgage Business and Birmingham Midshires) and The Bank of Scotland. Brokers, sometimes without the applicant's knowledge, used HBOS's fast track processing systems to enter false details. But the FSA failed to act.

- Bradford and Bingley was fined as early as 2004 after being found to be mis-selling, and with inadequate records. The incident should have resulted in the bank being closely monitored but it was not.
- With the Icelandic banks, the FSA failed to warn depositors of the possible dangers of banks offering excessively high deposit rates. The FSA did not use its authority to investigate if these rates were sustainable.
- After Northern Rock failed its ARROW in 2006, there was virtually no follow-up to ensure the problems were addressed.
- From the HBOS 2002 ARROW the FSA was aware of questionable risk management practices. Follow-up assessments appear to have proved ineffective. In 2006, questions about the bank's growth strategy were raised but not addressed.
- The FSA overlooked the failure of RBS to engage in timely due diligence during its takeover of ABN Amro. It apparently ignored the fact that Lloyds undertook just a third of its normal due diligence in its takeover of HBOS.
- The FSA has not questioned the long-term competition implications of the creation of the Lloyds Bank group.
- Dunfermline increased its commercial property lending and invested in UK sub-prime securities, as did some other building societies. Yet the FSA, apparently, did not act upon the change in these risk profiles.
- Rapidly expanding mortgages and loans against real estate, leading to jumps in arrears when these markets turn down, are a recurrent element in this catalogue of misfortunes. The years 1973–6 and 1990–92 had displayed large real-terms declines in UK commercial property and house prices. In the boom years of 2003–07, did the institutions and the FSA really believe that history could not repeat itself?

Had the FSA intervened forcefully to resolve such problems, bankers and politicians would have complained (more loudly than they did) that the FSA was stifling banks' innovative activities. For example, some claim the banks encouraged more home ownership by seeking out the cheapest rates on the wholesale funding markets.[19] But these are profit maximising banks, not instruments of social engineering. Nonetheless, Prime Minister Blair (2005) described the FSA's rules as 'hugely inhibiting of efficient business' illustrating the sort of pressure the FSA was under. In an interview, Lord Turner said:

> If a year and a half ago, the FSA had wanted higher capital adequacy, more information on liquidity – had said it was worried about the business models at Bradford & Bingley and Northern Rock – and had wanted to ask questions about remuneration . . . we would have been strongly criticised for harming the competitiveness of the City of London, for red tape and for over-regulation (Interview with *The Guardian*, 17 October 2008).

It is also suggested that because the FSA is financed by the firms it supervises, it succumbed to pressure for less onerous regulation. The Centre for the Study of Financial Innovation (CSFI, 2005, 2006) twice surveyed over 600 bankers and related experts in 2005 and 2006 on the risks facing the sector. Excessive regulation (cost of compliance, too many new micro regulations, and interference) was identified as the greatest risk, up from sixth place in 2004. Though there is nothing in the FSA's statutory objectives requiring it to kowtow to politicians or to the firms it supervises, political reality makes them susceptible to pressure.

Prior to the euro (and its predecessor, the exchange rate mechanism) the Bundesbank illustrated the importance of earning a reputation for credibility and independence. With the exception of allowing the ostmark and deutschmark to be converted at par in 1990 it steadfastly ignored periodic calls by German politicians to change monetary policy and focused on its key objective: a low inflation rate. Credibility in prudential regulation is equally important. The FSA should continue to be funded through levies on the financial institutions it regulates, but with constitutionally enshrined independence from undue lobbying and/or political pressure.

It is also argued that improved training is essential so that FSA regulators, at all levels, have the skill set needed to supervise the complex activities banks engage in. A myriad of initiatives have been announced. The status of FSA supervisory teams is to be upgraded/enhanced, and the budget has increased by £15 million to attract those with extensive City experience to join the FSA. In June 2009, the FSA announced that charges to firms it regulates would increase by 38 per cent.[20] It might also benefit from secondments to and from banks. However, it is worth stressing that the FSA had spotted many of the difficulties early on – the problem was inaction.

The FSA has also been criticised for not focusing on macroprudential regulation – ensuring the whole system is stable in addition to the individual parts. To meet this objective, the FSA must use its existing toolkit to supervise banks and get away from a silo-like mentality encouraged by its organisational structure. But the FSA should only shoulder part of the blame. Senior bank management made a catalogue of errors, as revealed in the case review of the most problematic banks.

Digging below the surface of these disasters, what is found? A fundamental failure to properly assess credit risk, from the smallest building societies to the largest global financial conglomerates – hardly a first in economic history. Instruments such as structured credit, securitisation, derivatives, structured investment vehicles, and so on helped to obscure credit risk issues and shift bad credit risk around. But in all of these cases, high risk debtors were given loans or mortgages. The strong message for senior management is to understand where the credit risk is being shifted, and more fundamentally to assess the credit risk accurately.

Nevertheless, data deficiencies constitute a major challenge. With every passing year there is some improvement in data: the trend is for them to become more frequent, more timely, more disaggregated, and more dependable. However, whether it is market participants attempting to determine covariances between different financial instruments, risk managers applying Value at Risk techniques, or regulators/credit rating agencies/econometricians trying to uncover statistical relationships and glean quantitative estimates of particular perils, the fact that high quality data do not go back far is a problem. In econometric investigations, simply counting degrees of freedom is not enough. When the data generating process is vulnerable to low frequency shocks, a well known problem in financial markets, a long span of data is needed – forming a view on the chances of shocks hitting requires a long spell of history. But high frequency observations are mostly limited to a decade or two. If this short period is exceptionally benign (such as the 14 years from 1992 to late 2006 in the North Atlantic economies), the problem is even more serious. Risk managers, banks and financiers all become increasingly optimistic as the years roll by. Politicians are lobbied. Regulators, whose costs are usually borne by the institutions they regulate, face growing pressure to slim down their operations, and lighten their scrutiny and their rules.

Econometrically, 'discounted least squares learning' has its uses, especially if there is an enduring shift in some intercept or slope coefficient in a model. But it can also be very dangerous, when the discount rate applied to older data is large, the issue at hand relates to second moments, and the model in question is subject to low frequency shocks. In this situation, a protracted spell of lower turbulence may cause observers, market participants and regulators to think that the world has become safer when it has not. The relevance of this to current events can hardly be overstressed. It implies that it is in longer periods of seeming calm that the seeds of the worst financial crises are likely to be sown. Furthermore, Basel type risk asset ratios that appear to be neutral to the cycle can become a factor that aggravates it.

OTHER ISSUES TO BE RESOLVED

The Future of the Tripartite

The House of Common's Treasury Committee's report on Northern Rock, like many commentators, criticised the tripartite for being too slow to respond during the Northern Rock crisis. This is always going to be a problem when there are three institutions which must be consulted at a time when immediate, decisive action is critical. Somebody must take the decision. But here things get tricky. In principle the BoE has the liquidity needed for any bailout but in reality it is dependent on HMT for funding or indemnity. The FSA possesses the data to judge banks' quality.

The Special Resolution Regime (SRR) in the 2009 Banking Act specifies a choice of stabilisation options. A troubled bank can be purchased by a private concern, either directly or via a bridge bank, temporarily nationalised by the Treasury, or declared insolvent and put into administration.[21] The choice of options will depend on the objectives of the exercise. If it is a one-off with a straightforward set of problems, the bank is likely to be sold on to another bank. If the stability of the entire UK financial system is at stake (as it was in 2008), several of the options may be exercised, depending on the status of the problematic banks.

Many hoped the 2009 Banking Act would give the BoE the lead role in deciding how to deal with troubled banks. Though the BoE established a new Special Resolutions Unit to lead the work, it is clear that key decisions must be taken by the tripartite:

> Before determining which of the stabilisation options to use, the Bank of England must consult the FSA and the Treasury (HMT, 2009).

Effectively, the FSA decides if a bank is in enough trouble to trigger the SRR and all three bodies choose the option to be implemented by the BoE. In a recent Annual Report of the BoE (2009), the Governor expresses regret that new Act does not allow for earlier intervention, while the chairman implicitly questions the lead role played by the FSA as opposed to the BoE.[22]

Thus, beyond formalising procedures for a troubled bank, the 2009 Act fails to provide clear lines of decision-making when it comes to dealing with them, and the status quo prevails. One cannot be confident that it would have stopped the apparent dithering associated with the run on Northern Rock.

Nor is the SRR considered sufficient to address the failure of an institution with a large investment banking arm. The Lehman collapse is a good illustration of the problem. The US parent went into chapter 11 bankruptcy which, by protecting the firm from creditors, allows some trading to continue. By contrast in London (and throughout Europe and Asia) the Lehman's subsidiary, subject to UK insolvency law, went into administration, so all activity had to cease immediately. The assets of banks, fund managers and hedge funds with trading relationships were frozen, including a high percentage of the $40 billion held at Lehman as collateral for counterparty trades. Lehman's administrators admit that it could be years before outstanding trades and positions are settled. HMT (12 May 2009) issued proposals for reforms that address these issues. First, investment banks would have to have contingency plans (continually monitored by the FSA) on how they would unwind their trading positions should they or their parent bank fail. Second, insolvency rules would be strengthened to ensure the swift return of collateral or equivalent to the bank's clients. Those with derivatives or financial bets can also expect rapid feedback on their positions. However, HMT's paper does not address a key problem. Months of frozen interbank markets were the consequence of rational reaction by global bankers to the Lehman collapse. If one of the top investment banks could fail so quickly when it was thought to be healthy, what bank could be trusted with an interbank loan? Second, the US authorities sent out a strong signal, even if unintended: not every bank would be bailed out.[23] Though the long-term effects of this decision might be reduced moral hazard, in the short term it added to market uncertainty and global chaos.

The number of global MoUs has mushroomed over the last two decades and are most common among central banks and supervisors from different countries. However, there is little evidence that they played a role in stabilising a global meltdown. Policymakers in different countries took largely independent decisions, apart from the coordinated central bank rate cut by the BoE, Fed, ECB, Bank of Canada and Riksbank (Sweden).[24] Other policy action to address the crisis was due to ad hoc cooperation than any cross-border MoU.

Storing up Future Moral Hazard Problems

Several factors will contribute to increased moral hazard post-crisis. The British government announced two bailouts in October 2008 and January 2009. The October 2008 rescue plan focused on helping banks to improve their tier 1 capital ratios, which led to the part nationalisation of HBOS, Lloyds TSB and RBS.[25] A credit guarantee scheme was also introduced, whereby banks (for a fee) obtain a government guarantee on new issues of short and medium term debt, for up to £250 billion. Up to £200 billion was made available through the BoE's special liquidity scheme, which introduced a discount window: banks can swap illiquid assets for risk free government securities. The second bailout announced in January 2009 introduced the government's troubled assets purchase scheme. Banks can insure problem assets though they are liable to the equivalent of an excess (first loss amount) and 10 per cent of the residual assets. The credit guarantee scheme was extended to the end of 2009 and expanded to include more triple A-rated asset-backed securities, notably mortgages and consumer debt. The maturity date of the BoE's discount window was also extended.

Second, UK deposit insurance is more generous. At the time of the Northern Rock run, the Financial Services Compensation Scheme insured 100 per cent of up to £2000 in deposits; then 90 per cent of deposits up to £35 000. The 10 per cent co-insurance meant a maximum pay out of £31 100. In October 2007, Chancellor Darling scrapped the 10 per cent co-insurance and raised the ceiling to £50 000. It became law when the Banking Act took effect in 2009. However, since Northern Rock, the government has made it clear that it will protect all depositors. For example, when the London Scottish went into administration in December 2008 the government immediately guaranteed all deposits even though the bank was a minnow – 10 000 individuals' deposits totalling £273 million.[26] However, the government feared that anything less than a 100 per cent deposit guarantee would provoke bank runs at other larger banks. Though 100 per cent deposit insurance is the only sure way of stopping a bank run, it gives depositors (especially wholesale) little incentive to monitor bank activities, and may also tempt them to switch funds to less sound banks offering higher deposit rates. Third, while senior management at the most troubled banks have gone and have publically apologised for their errors, they are hardly destitute![27] Most were extremely well paid with generous severance schemes and substantial pensions. Goodwin, aged 50, was allowed to draw on a pension with an annual payout of close to £700 000.

Government rescues, 100 per cent deposit insurance, and the nest eggs of failed executives are bound to have an effect on future moral hazard and therefore, on risk-taking behaviour. It would be simplistic to argue future CEOs will deliberately engage in highly risky ventures because of today's massive bailout. However, should senior management find themselves in increasing financial difficulty, the go for broke option is appealing. The only way of addressing this issue is to ensure regulators are extra vigilant in their scrutiny of banks, especially after a decade or so, when the current crisis will be but a distant memory.

Governance and Compensation

Bank shareholders have paid dearly for the near collapse of the banking system. The likely consequence is far greater scrutiny of the decisions taken by senior management and more careful choice of non-executive directors. Shareholders will insist on changes to compensation packages, especially bonuses. Pre-crisis a typical bonus scheme for senior executives involved some 10–12 per cent of net short-term profits, encouraging them to focus on short-term profits, resulting in greater risk-taking and lower long-term profitability. This short-termism is more serious in the financial sector because of the maturity structure of most assets – the effects of most decisions do not affect profitability for a number of years, in contrast to other sectors such as manufacturing. Share options have been a particular failure, encouraging senior executives to put their energies into boosting the share price at the time of exercise, ignoring the long-term consequences for the bank. It is unwise to leave this matter to government. The Sarbanes-Oxley Act was a knee-jerk reaction to Enron and Worldcom and criticised for being excessively bureaucratic. But shareholders do have options.

One of the most sensible comes from Burton Malkiel. He recommends that executive bonuses be paid in restricted shares. Senior executives would be required to hold them throughout their tenure and for several years later. Governments could encourage such schemes by making them deductible from corporate tax provided they create the right incentives for employees. At RBS, the British government used its 68 per cent ownership to exert pressure on bonuses. In 2009 it was agreed that senior management's bonuses will be given in subordinated debt to be repaid in three years. As the most junior form of unsecured debt, managers lose it all if the bank goes under, but unless it is done on a rolling basis, three years may not be sufficiently long to encourage greater attention to the long term.

Shadow Banking

The shadow banking sector, especially hedge funds and private equity firms, stand accused (mainly by politicians) of contributing to the crisis by destabilising the financial sector. The FSA temporarily banned short-selling in late October 2008 because of claims it was destabilising the market for certain bank shares, such as HBOS and RBS. Subsequent investigations proved this to be untrue. An investigation by the US Senate could find no evidence that their activities contributed to volatile oil prices.

The hedge fund LTCM (Long Term Capital Management) had to be rescued by a lifeboat organised by William McDonough, President of the Federal Reserve Bank of New York. There were fears that had it been allowed to fail, the global financial markets would have been severely disrupted because of the exposures of many top global banks, especially investment banks, including Lehman Brothers, Bear Stearns, and Goldman Sachs. However, this is a case for limiting the exposures of global banks in hedge funds, which can be done within the scope of existing bank regulation. Some of our continental EU neighbours have come out in favour of extensive regulation of the shadow banking sector, especially hedge and private equity funds. These same countries aspire to be leading financial centres and increased regulation would notably improve their competitive advantage against London. Reining in their activities at a time when banks are unable (and in some cases unwilling) to lend would only serve to further reduce funds available for investment. In the current climate, private equity is desperately needed as a source of finance. Also, strangling these firms (in the absence of any evidence of wrongdoing) could mean the EU suffers if these firms relocate to countries outside it, such as Switzerland.

Capital and Other Ratios

Asking banks to set aside more capital during this crisis makes capital ratios such as the Basel risk assets ratio even more pro-cyclical than they already are. Given the earlier remarks on short data spans, whether minimum capital ratios are retained and merely refashioned, or replaced by something more delicate and appropriate, anti-cyclicality should become a key feature.

In practice, it appears the authorities are doing the reverse. In 2008, the FSA demanded banks raise their tier 1 capital ratios to 8 per cent to ensure they had sufficient capital to cover for potential future losses, though it has eased up somewhat recently. With the announcement of the second rescue plan in January 2009, the FSA said some of the capital could be used for current problems and suggested that 6 per cent might be acceptable for tier 1.

In the US, stress tests results announced in May 2009 showed that ten of the top 19 banks (by assets) would have to raise a total of $75 billion in capital.[28] Six of the banks sold close to $20 billion of common stock just over a week later and the full amount is expected to be raised within two quarters. Only General Motors Acceptance Corporation is likely to face nationalisation.[29] The tests have been criticised for being too soft – for example, tier 1 core capital was 4 per cent compared to the 6–9 per cent range suggested by the IMF.

However, this laxness may be a good thing because it contributes to counter-cyclicality. As Llewellyn (2009) has pointed out there is no hard and fast rule for capital ratios:

> There is a case for a graduated response . . . there is no magical capital ratio below which an institution is in danger and above which it is safe.

CONCLUSION

Based on this chapter's scrutiny of events in the UK there is no real need for radical regulatory reform. So what does need to change? This review offers two key messages. First, the FSA must be proactive in enforcing rules and regulations, using its existing tools. However, constitutionally enshrined independence to protect the FSA from politicians and/or the institutions that fund it is essential. Improved expertise and reorganisation to discourage a silo-like mentality will help to achieve these objectives. There is no need to increase the regulatory burden on private equity or hedge funds.

Second, credit risk is the Achilles heel of the financial system, and hardly unique to this crisis. Bankers must focus on good risk management, especially credit risk, and be wary of the perils of data limitations. Other issues at the fore include the continued ambiguity of the tripartite arrangements. Further clarification is essential, making one of the three members responsible for taking decisions on illiquid/insolvent banks. Shareholders, especially institutions, must be better informed and assertive. The extensive (and costly) bank rescues, changes in deposit insurance and top managers' nest eggs pose notable challenges for future moral hazard which necessitate even greater vigilance. The popular clamour for more regulation is understandable, but arguments for it are not compelling.

NOTES

1. Presented at the conference in honour of David Llewellyn at Loughborough University on 16 June 2009.
2. In the area of financial regulation, see, among many publications, Llewellyn (1999, 2009) and Llewellyn et al. (1998).
3. Lord Turner (2009a).
4. And prior to the shift in focus to 'principles based regulation' – abandoned in 2009.
5. Source: FSA (2008a).
6. Source: Turner, A. (2009c). Though it is unclear from the chart used to report loan to income, it is believed this ratio is annual new mortgages/household income. According to Turner up to 40 per cent of new mortgages had loan to value ratios equal to or above 95 per cent in the 1980s and 1990s.
7. Liars' loans can include loan applications where no income or assets are stated or, if declared, are not verified. They were originally designed for individuals where it might be difficult to verify a stable income such as the self-employed or those dependent on gratuities. In 2002, the FSA had threatened to ban them but were dissuaded from doing so by the mortgage industry. In 2003, the BBC's *Money Programme* reported on the practice of self-certification at B&B (owned by HBOS).
8. Source: Rupert Jones, 'FSA may end "liar loan" mortgage fraud', www.guardian.co.uk, 12 May 2009, reporting on a speech by Jon Pain, FSA Managing Director, retail markets.
9. FSA (2008b).

10. Using the definition employed by the Financial Services Compensation Scheme, the five banks in default in 2008 are B&B, Heritable Bank (a Landsbanki subsidiary which was subsequently sold to the Dutch bank, ING), London Scottish Bank, Kaupthing, Singer and Friedlander Banker, and Landsbanki, which in the UK operated as a branch of Icesave.
11. Specifically the Chancellor invoked sections 4 and 14 of Schedule 3 to the Anti-Terrorism, Crime and Security Act 2001 – the Treasury believed actions by non-UK citizens/governments would be to the detriment of the UK's economy. Source: House of Commons (2008).
12. The retail property division made a profit of £1.3 billion.
13. FSA (2009).
14. On 8 June 2009, £4 billion of preference (non-voting) shares were repaid by Lloyds following the issue of new ordinary shares, underwritten by the Treasury. All were either purchased by existing shareholders or bought on the open market, leaving the government shareholding at 43 per cent. The repayment of preference shares means Lloyds no longer has to pay interest on them and can resume paying dividends to ordinary shareholders.
15. Dunfermline's social housing loan portfolio was placed in a bridge bank wholly owned by the Bank of England; its commercial loans and acquired mortgages were placed in administration.
16. Barnsley merged with Yorkshire Building Society; Catholic with Chelsea; Cheshire & Derbyshire with Nationwide. Britannia Building Society merged with Cooperative Financial Services in April 2009.
17. Speaking to the House of Commons Treasury Select Committee (2009), p. 31.
18. The Building Societies (Funding) and Mutual Societies (Transfers) Act 2007.
19. Though volatile interbank markets were never going to provide a dependable cheap source of funds, unlike retail deposits.
20. *Evening Standard*, 2 June 2009.
21. A bridge bank is a short-term solution used to achieve the transfer of the bank to a private purchaser. It holds the bad assets which are excluded from the private deal, and are either sold or wound up. The Bank Administration Procedure is an alternative temporary undertaking, used when a part of the problem bank cannot be transferred to the private buyer or the bridge bank because, for example, it is insolvent. The Bank of England can apply to the courts for special administration of this residual bank so it can continue to provide essential services while the rest of the bank is bought by a private concern, either directly or via a bridge bank.
22. Sir John Parker, chairman of the Non Executive Board at the BoE.
23. The US authorities had hoped for a market takeover, which only fell apart at the last minute.
24. These central banks cuts their individual benchmark rates simultaneously by 50 basis points on 5 October 2008.
25. Under the recapitalisation scheme Abbey, Barclays, HBOS, HSBC, Lloyds TSB, Royal Bank of Scotland, Standard Chartered and Nationwide Building Society could apply for up to £25 billion of permanent capital to raise tier 1 capital ratios. A further £25 billion was made available on a standby basis and for other banks.
26. London Scottish Bank was closed by the FSA after failing to meet new capital requirements. Manchester-based, and established in 1895, it had a long history in UK sub-prime, granting small (on average £500–1000) short-term unsecured 'doorstep' loans for up to six months at high interest rates, reflecting a hefty risk premium. Interest and principle were collected weekly. The bank expanded into other forms of direct lending by purchasing specialists such as Call 4 Cash and the Personal Loan Centre and also right to buy, unsecured mortgages for council flat tenants (until early 2008). It also operated a profitable debt collection business, Robinson's Way. It began taking retail deposits in 2004 and, when closed, had 10 000 depositors (worth £273 million).

27. For example, at RBS: Sir Fred Goodwin (ex-CEO), Sir Tom Mckillop (ex-chairman); Northern Rock: Adam Applegarth and the board; HBOS: Andy Hornby (CEO), Sir James Crosby (ex-CEO, who resigned his post as deputy chairman at the FSA), and Lloyds: Sir Victor Blank (chairman – has announced he will resign in 2010).
28. The ten top US banks are Bank of America ($33.9 billion), Wells Fargo ($13.7 billion), GMAC ($11.5 billion), Citigroup ($5.5 billion), Regions Financial ($2.5 billion), SunTrust ($2.2 billion); Morgan Stanley ($1.8 billion), KeyCorp($1.8 billion), Fifth Third ($1.1 billion) and PNC Financial ($0.6 billion). Those exempt include JP Morgan Chase, Goldman Sachs, MetLife, US Bancorp, Bank of New York Mellon, State Street, CapitalOne, BB&T, and American Express.
29. Source: *Economist* (2009), p. 87–8.

REFERENCES

Bank of England (2009), Annual Report, accessed 5 October 2010 at www.bankofengland.co.uk/publications/annualreport/.

Blair, A. (2005), *Risk and the State*, speech to the Institute of Public Policy Research, June, London.

Buiter, W. and A. Sibert (2008), 'The Icelandic banking crisis and what to do about it', CEPR Policy Insight no. 26, October, accessed 5 October 2010 at www.cepr.org/pubs/PolicyInsights/PolicyInsight26.pdf.

Centre for the Study of Financial Innovations (CSFI) (2005), *Banking Banana Skins 2005*, London: CSFI.

The Economist (2009) CSFI (2008), Banking Banana Skins 2006, London: CSFI 'Stress tests – hospital pass', 16 May.

Financial Services Authority (FSA) (2004), 'FSA fines Bradford and Bingley £650000 for precipice and with profits bonds mis-selling', accessed 5 October 2010 at www.fsa.gov.uk/Pages/Library/Communication/PR/2004/112.shtml.

FSA (2008a), 'Peer group comparisons in ARROW letters', accessed 5 October 2010 at www.fsa.gov.uk/pubs/other/arrow_peer.pdf.

FSA (2008b), 'The supervision of Northern Rock: a lessons learned review, March, Internal Audit Division report, accessed 5 October 2010 at www.fsa.gov.uk/pubs/other/nr_report.pdf and www.fsa.gov.uk/pages/Library/Other_publications/Miscellaneous/2008/nr.shtml.

FSA (2009), 'Statement re: HBOS', accessed 5 October 2010 at www.fsa.gov.uk/pages/Library/Communication/Statements/2009/letter_chancellor.shtml.

Her Majesty's Treasury (2009), 'Banking Act 2009: Special Resolution Regime Code of Practice', accessed 5 October 2010 at www.hm-treasury.gov.uk/d/bankingact2009_codeofpractice.pdf.

House of Commons (2008), 'Banking Crisis: the impact of the failure of the Icelandic Banks', accessed 5 October 2010 at www.publications.parliament.uk/pa/cm200809/cmselect/cmtreasy/402/40206.htm.

House of Commons Treasury Select Committee (2009), 'Banking crisis – dealing with the failure of UK banks', seventh report, 21 April, accessed 5 October 2010 at http://www.publications.parliament.uk/pa/cm200809/cmselect/cmtreasy/416/416.pdf.

Llewellyn, D.T., C.A.E. Goodhart, P. Hartmann, L. Rojas-Suarez, and S. Weisbrod (1998), *Financial Regulation: Why, How and Where Now*?, London: Wiley.

Llewellyn, D.T. (1999), 'The economic rationale for financial regulation', Financial Services Authority Occasional Paper 1, April, accessed 5 October 2010 at www.fsa.gov.uk/pubs/occpapers/OP01.pdf.

Llewellyn, D.T. (2009), 'The global financial crisis: incentive structures and implications for regulation', in P. Booth (ed.), *Verdict on the Crash: Causes and Policy Solutions*, London: Institute for Economic Affairs.

Turner, A. (2009a), 'The financial crisis and the future of financial regulation', The Economist's Inaugural City Lecture, 21 January, accessed 5 October 2010 at www.fsa.gov.uk/pages/Library/Communication/Speeches/2009/0121_at.shtml.

Turner, A. (2009b), *The Turner Review: A Regulatory Response to the Global Banking Crisis*, London: Financial Services Authority.

Turner, A. (2009c), 'The mortgage market: issues for debate', speech at the Financial Services Authority Mortgage Conference, 12 May 2009, accessed 5 October 2010 at www.fsa.gov.uk/pages/Library/Communication/Speeches/2009/0512_at.shtml.

PART FIVE

Information, shareholders and projects

13. Asymmetries in financial information, risk and know-how: the roles of disclosure rules, financial safety nets and market discipline

Morten Balling

INTRODUCTION: FINANCIAL MARKETS ARE NOT INFORMATIONALLY EFFICIENT

In financial theory, perfect capital markets are defined as being informationally efficient. In perfect markets, information is supposed to be costless and to be received simultaneously by all market participants. The definition of efficient capital markets is less restrictive. In efficient markets, prices are assumed to reflect all available relevant information. There are model versions with different degrees of market efficiency where it is possible to analyse the implications of the costs of information and delays in the distribution of information. A lot can be learned from theoretical models that assume capital market efficiency. According to random walk theory for example, investors are unable to earn an extra profit by studying the information flow from banks, listed companies and other data sources.[1]

In the real world, people and institutions have access to very different information sets and they do not receive the information simultaneously. Many have to pay for financial advice. They are exposed to different risks, and their knowledge about banking, finance and economics varies considerably. When people have different information, different risk exposures and when there are large differences in their understanding of banking and finance issues, we must expect them to behave differently. Asymmetries in information, risk and know-how have several explanations. Modern market economies are characterised by specialisation and division of labour between people and institutions with different types of expertise. Already in 1776, Adam Smith explained that the wealth of nations depends on division of labour. Of course, specialisation and division of labour imply a lot of asymmetries. In order to ensure incentives to innovate, we have laws concerning protection of immaterial rights, patents and rules on proprietary rights and confidentiality. So a lot of asymmetries are considered to be appropriate and we accept that they imply unequal opportunities for people to act in the market economy.

Financial regulation has strong implications for market efficiency and the asymmetries that we discuss here. Accounting and disclosure rules obviously have implications for asymmetries in financial information. When financial institutions are required to disclose information to the public, it implies a reduction of the information gap between the institutions and the investors and depositors. One could say that the political intention is to reduce the degree of market inefficiency. Financial safety nets in the shape of deposit guarantee schemes have implications for the distribution of risk among the depositors and other market participants. In turbulent times, financial safety nets may even have implications for taxpayers. One could also argue that a strengthening of financial safety nets reduces market efficiency in the sense that fewer market participants have incentives to contribute to the formation of a market price of risk. By affecting these asymmetries, both disclosure rules and financial safety nets have implications for the abilities and incentives of market participants to monitor financial institutions and to exercise market discipline.

Regulation and supervision of financial systems differ from country to country. It is beyond the scope of a short book chapter to try to give an overview from an asymmetry perspective of regulation in a number of countries.[2] Below, references are given to quotations concerning asymmetries in a small sample of documents from standard setting international organisations namely the EU Commission, EU Council, EU Parliament and the Basel Committee. To a large extent, provisions in EU Directives concerning disclosure and financial regulation have been implemented in the legislation of Member States, and the Basel principles are followed by most countries in the Western world despite their non-binding character.

ASYMMETRIES IN BANK PERFORMANCE RELEVANT INFORMATION

Bank performance relevant information (BPRI) is a very broad concept. It covers interest rates paid and received by the bank, fees for all types of bank services, returns and losses on the bank's loans and investments, the size of transactions and balance sheet items, funding cost items, operational cost items, risk exposures of all kinds, and leverage and capital adequacy. In short, it covers all evidence and budget estimates with an expected impact

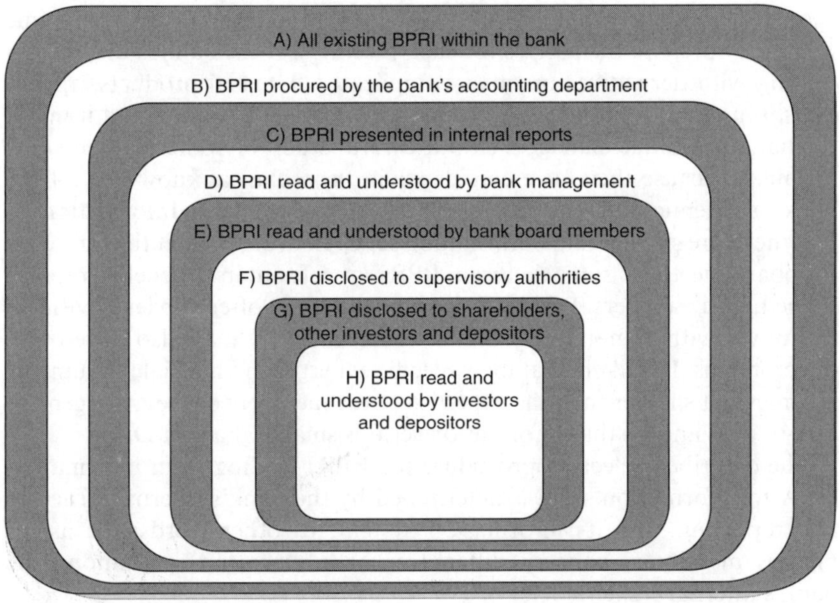

Figure 13.1 Asymmetries in bank performance relevant information (BPRI)

on the bank's earnings structure, risk level and balance sheet. The picture of asymmetries in BPRI in Figure 13.1 is strongly simplified. It ignores, for example, all information which is not generated within the bank. It ignores that investors can procure decision support from rating agencies and from providers in the market for financial information like ThomsonReuters. The figure can, however, be used to illustrate how disclosure rules affect the information sets available to different bank stakeholders.

Information set A represents all existing BPRI within the bank at a given time. This information is distributed among all bank employees but no single person or department in the bank possesses all of it. The bank's accounting department does not procure all performance relevant information. For example, lending officers typically do not report all details of their knowledge about customers' plans to the accounting department. Information set B is therefore smaller than information set A. When internal reports are written, some aggregation is needed. Transactions and balance sheet items are added together by type so that sums can contribute to an overview of the bank's situation. Information set C is therefore smaller than set B. Bank managers who have the duty to read the internal reports and to discuss them in meetings before decisions are taken, are often busy people and it is likely that they skip a few tables and pages from time to time when they prepare themselves for such meetings. If the bank is involved in trading with derivatives or other complicated financial products, appendices in internal reports can be quite mathematical in nature and it might be that some bank managers skip a careful study of some mathematical formulas because they have confidence in the technical know-how of the bank's academic staff who have prepared such appendices. Information set D is therefore smaller than information set C. In order to limit the time used for board meetings, some details in BPRI are left out in the enclosures sent to the board members. Besides, board members are often top level business executives with demanding jobs elsewhere and they may also have other directorships. It is likely that their specific expertise in financial instruments is somewhat smaller than the expertise of the members of the management board. This implies that information set E is smaller than set D.

The described selection procedure for BPRI leading from information set A to information set E is determined by the bank's internal structure and reporting, and its information system. In other words, the asymmetries mentioned concern differences in information sets among the bank's internal stakeholders.

BPRI is, however, also to some extent disclosed to external stakeholders. Based on banking laws, supervisory authorities have issued very detailed reporting forms that banks have to comply with. In European countries, these reporting requirements in many respects follow EU Directives and the Basel core principles for effective banking supervision. Regular reports to the supervisory authorities are probably in most cases presented to the board of the bank before they are sent to the authorities but such reports represent only a minor part of the information available to the board. We can therefore observe that information set F is smaller than information set E. For banks operating in several jurisdictions, there might be important asymmetries between the information sets available to supervisory authorities in host countries and home countries respectively.[3]

Accounting laws and stock exchange regulations provide the framework for disclosures to the public. The provisions in this regulation and in international accounting standards that are in many cases referred to as the reference standard, require in most cases less detailed reporting than is provided to the supervisory authorities, so the information set available to shareholders, other investors and depositors (set G) is smaller than information set F. Market discipline is supposed to be exercised by the shareholders, other investors and to some extent depositors. Figure 13.1 illustrates that external stakeholders have much less information to base their decisions on than internal stakeholders like board members who have governance duties in the bank. Even though the information flow to external stakeholders is much smaller than the flow to internal stakeholders, it is questionable how many of the external stakeholders actually read and use the available information as the basis for their decisions. A typical annual report from a middle sized bank contains between 100 and 200 pages with lots of tables and footnotes, some of which are rather technical. Based on conversations with a small sample of Danish bank shareholders, it is the author's impression that less than 10 per cent of the shareholders read annual reports fully. Some shareholders do of course also procure information from the bank's website on a quarterly basis, but serious monitoring by shareholders of bank performance happens probably only in relatively few cases.

Investors, depositors and supervisors base their decisions on the picture they have of the bank's performance. Such a picture is always incomplete. It depends on the set of BPRI available to the person or institution in question. Figure 13.1 illustrates that there are asymmetries in information. In addition, the value of the assets of a bank always depends on uncertain future cash flows that nobody can predict accurately. It follows that bank managers, shareholders, depositors and supervisors may have different perceptions of a bank's performance.

Let me now turn to a few examples of recent disclosure rule and safety net initiatives taken within the EU framework and the Basel framework respectively.

RECENT INITIATIVES TAKEN WITHIN THE EU FRAMEWORK: DISCLOSURE

The number of EU documents with provisions that are relevant to financial regulation and supervision is very large. The documents referred to below, represent only a small sample.[4]

Directive 2006/48/EC (European Commission, 2006)

This directive relates to the taking up and pursuit of credit institutions. If we include the annexes, the directive contains 200 pages, most of them written in heavy legal language. In the introductory remarks there are several provisions about exchange of information. An example is provision 23:

> It is appropriate to allow the exchange of information between the competent authorities and authorities or bodies which, by virtue of their function, help to strengthen the stability of the financial system. In order to preserve the confidential nature of the information forwarded, the list of addressees should remain within strict limits.

In Figure 13.1, this EU provision refers to information set F, BPRI disclosed to supervisory authorities. Financial supervisors should be allowed to share their information with other supervisory authorities or central banks but not with the general public.

Annex 12 of Directive 2006/48/EC has particular relevance to the discussion of asymmetries. The headline is 'Technical Criteria on Disclosure'. In the introduction to the annex, there are definitions of material, proprietary and confidential information respectively. Information is material if its omission or misstatement could change or influence the assessment or decision of a user relying on that information for the purpose of making economic decisions. Information is proprietary to a credit institution if sharing that information with the public would undermine its competitive position. It may include information on products or systems which, if shared with competitors, would render a credit institution's investments therein less valuable. Information shall be regarded as confidential if there are obligations to customers or other counterparty relationships binding a credit institution to confidentiality.

A credit institution is of course not obliged to disclose proprietary or confidential information to the public. So this kind of information should not be included in information set G in Figure 13.1. However, Annex 12 contains a long list of material information that should be disclosed and included in information set F and to some extent also in information set G. Important examples are: the risk management objectives and policies of the credit institution, main features of its own funds items, its assessment of the adequacy of its internal capital, its risk-weighted exposure, and its exposures to counterparty risk.

Directive 2007/14/EC (European Commission, 2007)

This directive contains implementation rules for Directive 2004/109/EC on the harmonisation of transparency requirements in relation to information about issuers whose securities are admitted to trading on a regulated market. It follows from the introductory text that the directive seeks to ensure that, through the disclosure of accurate, comprehensive and timely information about security issuers, investor confidence is built up and sustained. Provision no. 15 in the transparency directive has the following text: 'Dissemination should involve the active distribution of information to the media with a view to reaching investors'. Issuers should ensure that minimum quality standards for the dissemination of regulated information are met. In this context, Directive 2007/14/EC refers to international accounting standards. The formulation in the directive's provision 15 seems to reflect a certain concern among the EU rule-makers that there might be a considerable difference between information set G (information disclosed to shareholders, other investors and depositors), and information set H (information read and understood by investors and depositors).

Regulation (EC) No. 1126 (European Commission, 2008)

On 13 October 2008, the International Accounting Standards Board published an adjustment of IAS 39 with standards for measurement of financial instruments (IASB, 2008). On 3 November 2008 the European Commission published Regulation (EC) No. 1126 which adopted the changes of IAS 39 with the effect that listed companies – including listed banks – could apply the new rules for recognition and measurement in their 2008 disclosures. According to the new rules, under certain conditions it is allowed to reclassify financial assets and liabilities from categories with fair value measurement to categories with amortised cost measurement. Because of regulation 1126, banks that had suffered large losses because of falling securities prices in the fall of 2008 could to some extent postpone the effect of those losses on their profits and own funds. In the context of Figure 13.1, a bank could in information set G draw a 2008 picture of its earnings and balance sheet performance which was less alarming for shareholders and depositors. Some, but not all banks, used this opportunity to manage their disclosed figures. This did not make comparative analysis of bank performance easier for investors.

RECENT INITIATIVES WITHIN THE EU FRAMEWORK: FINANCIAL SAFETY NETS

Financial safety nets usually include prudential regulation and supervision, a lender of last resort and deposit insurance. The institutional structure varies from country to country and so does the distribution of powers and responsibilities among central banks, financial supervisors and deposit insurance providers. A recent initiative within the EU framework concerns strengthening and harmonisation of deposit insurance schemes.

Directive 2009/14/EC (European Commission, 2009a)

Since 1994, Directive 94/19/EC has provided for basic coverage for bank depositors in Europe. In the fall of 2008, the EU Council decided to take measures to improve this part of the European financial safety nets. In March 2009, the European Parliament and the Council adopted Directive

2009/14/EC, which amended the 1994 directive on deposit guarantee schemes as regards the coverage level and the payout delay. The minimum coverage level was increased from €20 000 to €50 000 by 30 June 2009. And by 31 December 2010, coverage for the aggregate deposits of each depositor should be set at €100 000, unless a Commission impact assessment concludes that such an increase and such harmonisation are inappropriate and are not financially viable for all Member States in order to ensure consumer protection and financial stability in the EU, and to avoid distortion of competition between Member States. In the event that the impact assessment reveals that such an increase and such harmonisation are inappropriate, the Commission should submit appropriate proposals to the European Parliament and the Council.

The EU Commission's initiative concerning deposit guarantee schemes has been supported by the high-level group on financial supervision in the EU, chaired by Jacques de Larosière.[5] According to the group, the crisis has demonstrated that the current organisation of deposit guarantee schemes in the member states was a major weakness in the EU banking regulatory framework. In integrated financial markets, deposit guarantees may have implications for cross-border capital movements. In 2008, changes in Icelandic and Irish financial safety nets provided interesting cases. Concern for this, and for unwanted competition among national regulators, is reflected in recommendation 14 in the de Larosière Report.[6]

> Deposit Guarantee Schemes (DGS) in the EU should be harmonised and preferably be prefunded by the private sector (in exceptional cases topped up by the State) and provide high equal protection to all bank customers throughout the EU.

The recommendation illustrates that the authors of the de Larosière Report want to limit asymmetries in risk protection between the EU countries.

RECENT INITIATIVES TAKEN WITHIN THE BASEL FRAMEWORK

The Basel Core Principles are used by countries as a benchmark for assessing the quality of their supervisory systems. In the Basel documents on the core principles, it is recognised that an effective system of banking supervision needs to be based on a number of external elements or preconditions.

Among the external elements mentioned are 'effective market discipline' and mechanisms for providing an appropriate level of systemic protection or a public safety net. Effective market discipline depends on adequate flows of information to market participants, appropriate financial incentives to reward well-managed institutions, and arrangements that ensure that investors are not insulated from the consequences of their own decisions.[7] In handling systemic issues there is a trade-off to make between preserving confidence in the financial system and avoiding contagion, and the need to minimise the distortion to market signals and discipline.

Some of the 25 Basel Core Principles list information on risks that should be available to supervisors. These principles are therefore recommendations concerning the formulation of disclosure requirements about risk information in set F in Figure 13.1. The lists of risks include credit risk, country risk and transfer risk, market risk, liquidity risk, operational risk and interest risk in the banking book. Information on such risks is also relevant to private market participants that are supposed to exercise market discipline but perhaps in a less detailed form.

Basel II, Pillar 3

The purpose of Pillar 3 which has the headline 'market discipline' is to complement the minimum capital requirements (Pillar 1) and the supervisory review process (Pillar 2). The Basel Committee wants to encourage market discipline by developing a set of disclosure requirements which will allow market participants to assess the performance and risk of each institution. Supervisors should have the authority to require banks to provide information in regulatory reports, and some of this information should be made publicly available, that is accessible to private market participants. Proprietary and confidentiality rules mean, however, that there will always be asymmetries between the information set F available to supervisors and set G available to private market participants.

One should also remember that there are costs involved when more information and more disclosure are required. The Basel Committee therefore recognises the need for a Pillar 3 disclosure framework that does not conflict with requirements under accounting standards which are broader in scope. The choice of an appropriate medium depends on whether the disclosures are made under accounting requirements or not. The overriding principle is that it should be made as easy as possible for investors to procure the relevant information on bank performance and risk. In accordance with international accounting standards, banks should be obliged to disclose material information.

In January 2009, the Basel Committee published proposals for enhancing Pillar 3.[8] Based on the experiences during the financial crisis, the proposals are focused on disclosures related to securitisation, off-balance sheet exposures and trading activities. The Committee believes that enhanced disclosure will help to prevent a recurrence of market uncertainties about the strength of banks' balance sheets related to their capital market activities.

IMPLICATIONS FOR MARKET DISCIPLINE

Assumptions Concerning the Behaviour of Market Participants

When we use the expression market discipline, we assume that banks operate in markets in which different providers of funds are active on the supply side. We assume that there are markets for demand deposits, saving deposits, certificates of deposits, interbank deposits, subordinated bank capital (maybe in the form of bank bonds) and stocks. And we assume that the different providers of bank funds keep an eye on the receiving banks' performance and take action if they are not satisfied with the development. Recent runs and interbank dysfunctions illustrate that bank fund providers do react when they realise that they are exposed to more risk. We assume further that bank managers feel that they are monitored and that they therefore try to satisfy the different stakeholders when they decide on the bank's strategy.

Like other investors, providers of bank funds are interested in expected return and risk. The menu of choices between expected return and risk that a bank can offer depends on the bank's own lending policy, portfolio choices, its degree of leverage and loan/deposit ratio, for example.

If bank fund providers want to exercise market discipline, they must form an opinion concerning the quality of the lending and trading operations of the bank. They must read the annual reports published by the bank and follow the press releases of the bank during the year. They must also procure information about the risk premia the bank is currently paying in the market. Spreads in the interbank market contain information on the risk of the borrowing bank in the view of other banks. If the bank in question is rated by a rating agency, the (re)classification of the bank by the rating agency may be useful investor information.

Banking is, however, an opaque industry. It is difficult for external observers – even experienced rating agencies – to evaluate bank performance. Morgan (2002) has compared the dispersion of Moody's and Standard & Poor's ratings of banks.[9] The idea is that if bank performance is harder to observe, the rating agencies should disagree more often over bank bond issues than over other issues. The evidence shows that they do. The author therefore concludes that banking firms are more opaque than other sorts of firms and that the veil between them and outsiders seems inherent to the business.

Since procurement of information and analysis is rather time consuming and in some cases costly, many bank fund providers will probably be content with seeking advice from investment analysts in the financial industry or with reading the business section of a newspaper whose journalists comment on new information on bank activity and financial results.

Financial Skills and Financial Literacy – Recent Initiatives

Both authorities and individual researchers have recently proposed educational initiatives in order to reduce asymmetries in financial know-how. In reports from HMT and the FSA there are several proposals for improving financial literacy and financial skills.[10] It is recommended that the financial industry should work with the government to assess the likely size and skills profile of the financial services workforce. A higher skill level could lead to better quality of the advice given to depositors and investors. The Organisation for Economic Cooperation and Development (OECD) and the US Treasury Department have also recommended measures to improve financial literacy, focusing on consumer protection perspectives.[11]

Preservation of Incentives and Scope for Action

Bank fund providers have different incentives to monitor bank performance. The strength of the incentives depends on the design of the financial safety net. The more bank fund providers are protected against losses, the weaker their incentive to exercise market discipline.

If bank fund providers are not satisfied with the performance of a bank they are supposed to take action. But what is the scope for action? The answer depends on which type of bank fund provider we are looking at. Retail depositors can move their money to bank X if they are not satisfied with bank Y. In a dramatic situation, they can 'run'. Bank shareholders can sell their shares and invest in other securities. But, since there are voting rights attached to shares, bank shareholders can also use their influence at the shareholder meeting. They can criticise bank managers and directors and try to replace managers and directors with people that are supposed to be more performance oriented. There is a clear overlap between corporate governance and market discipline. A BIS report has underlined the importance of transparency for sound and effective corporate governance.[12] If shareholders do not receive sufficient information on the ownership structure and control structure of the bank, and on bank performance, it is difficult for them to effectively monitor and properly hold accountable the board of directors and senior management. It is difficult for them to evaluate the competence of bank board members and their ability to ensure satisfactory bank performance. Financial expertise is highly desirable but to elect retired bankers to the board is not a good idea in all cases.[13] In some banks, the articles of association have ceilings on the number of votes that can be cast by an individual shareholder at the general meeting or other provisions that may entrench the incumbent bank board. Voting power limitations may seriously hurt market discipline exercised by shareholders.

In addition to disclosure rules in accounting laws and stock exchange regulations, there are disclosure recommendations in corporate governance codes. According to Principle VI.F in the OECD Principles of Corporate Governance, for example, board members should have access to accurate, relevant and timely information. Principle V.A.6 recommends disclosure of material information on foreseeable risk factors and the annotation adds that disclosure about the system for monitoring and managing risk is increasingly regarded as good practice. If companies comply with these recommendations, the ability of the shareholders to pose critical questions to managers and board members about performance is improved.

It seems to be a precondition for the efficiency of market discipline that at least some of the bank fund providers are exposed to risk. Financial safety nets should therefore not cover all fund providers completely. In most jurisdictions, it is accepted that bank shareholders should be exposed to losses when their bank defaults. There is, however, a strong global trend towards better protection of bank retail depositors. Deposit insurance reduces the incentive of depositors to monitor their banks. However, Demirgüc-Kunt, Kane and Laeven (2008) describe how a certain degree of depositor incentives to monitor can be preserved.[14] Market discipline exercised by depositors can be improved by: (a) limiting coverage; (b) excluding particular types of deposits (such as interbank deposits); (c) introducing co-insurance by depositors; and (d) setting coverage limits per depositor rather than per account. Similar views can be found in the UK Turner Review.[15]

CONCLUDING REMARKS

In this chapter, the focus is on the roles of disclosure rules, financial safety nets and market discipline. Recent initiatives taken within the EU framework and the Basel framework aim at making financial markets more transparent and at improving the protection of depositors and other private market participants. They aim at improving financial stability. We have to be realistic, however, about how much can be achieved by such measures. Disclosure rules cannot (and should not) remove all information asymmetry. They can, however, make the distribution of information more even and enhance the ability of depositors and shareholders to monitor banks and exercise market discipline.

Financial safety nets cannot remove all risks from the financial system. Financial safety nets can redistribute risks so that risk exposures are allocated to people and institutions that are most able to bear them. In extreme cases, financial safety nets transfer the ultimate risk to the taxpayers.

Improved disclosure will certainly contribute to a reduction of information asymmetries and higher efficiency in financial markets. We should remember, however, that availability of more financial information does not in itself ensure a better understanding of the performance of banks and banking systems. More information and transparency helps, but the perception by bank board members, private market participants and supervisors will still be incomplete. The chapter refers to some recent initiatives to improve the level of skills in the financial sector and more generally the level of financial literacy in the population.

It is realistic to contend that neither investors nor supervisors have a complete perception of the performance of individual banks or of the financial system as a whole. Thus, all market participants and authorities must base their decisions on partly uncertain information and on an incomplete perception of financial institution and system performance. Incomplete perception by market participants means that there are limits to what we can expect market discipline to do to improve performance. But the incomplete perception by supervisory authorities of financial institution and system performance mean that there are also limits to what we can expect supervisors to do. In the real world, private as well as public decisions are made under uncertainty. In democratic societies, parliaments have the authority to assign power to supervisory institutions but it seems to be appropriate to choose a financial system in which the power to exercise discipline on financial institutions is diversified among supervisors, investors and depositors. It seems here to be fair to draw an analogy with the main conclusion from Markowitz' portfolio theory. Diversification is a good solution when we are operating in an uncertain world that we do not completely understand.

NOTES

1. Shiller (2000), p. 174.
2. From time to time the IMF conducts surveys of the member countries' compliance with

the Basel Core Principles for Effective Banking Supervision. See, for example, Podpiera (2006).
3. In the de Larosière report (European Commission, 2009b), p. 73 it is pointed out that responsibility, information and tools are asymmetrically distributed and concentrated in the home country. The proposed solution to such asymmetry problems is more effective collaboration between home and host supervisors.
4. A good place to start if an overview of EU regulation is sought is http://eur-lex.europa.eu.
5. European Commission (2009b), p. 34.
6. European Commission (2009b), p. 36.
7. Basel Committee on Banking Supervision (2006a), Core Principles etc. p. 6.
8. Basel Committee – Basel II New Framework (2009).
9. Morgan, D.P. (2002), p. 874 ff.
10. HMT (2007) and (2009) and FSA (2006).
11. OECD (2005) and Lusardi et al. (2007) and Lusardi (2008).
12. Basel Committee on Banking Supervision (2006b), 'Enhancing corporate governance for banking organisations', p. 15 ff.
13. Kirkpatrick (2009), p. 22.
14. Demirgüc-Kunt, A., Kane, E.J. and Laeven, L. (2008).
15. FSA (2009), p. 77.

REFERENCES

Basel Committee on Banking Supervision (2006a), *Core Principles for Effective Banking Supervision,* October, Basel.

Basel Committee on Banking Supervision (2006b), *Enhancing Corporate Governance of Banking Organisations,* February, Basel.

Basel Committee on Banking Supervision (2009), *Proposed Enhancements to the Basel II Framework,* January, Basel.

Demirgüc-Kunt, A., E.J. Kane and L. Laeven (2008), 'Determinants of deposit-insurance adoption and design', *Journal of Financial Intermediation,* **17**(3), 407–38.

European Commission (2006), 'Directive 2006/48/EC of the European Parliament and of the Council of 14 June 2006 relating to the taking up and pursuit of Credit Institutions (recast)', OJ L.177, 1–200.

European Commission (2009), 'Directive 2009/14/EC of the European Parliament and of the Council of 11 March 2009 amending Directive 94/19/EC on deposit-guarantee schemes as regards the coverage level and the payout delay', OJ L. 135, 5–14.

European Commission (2007), 'Directive 2007/14/EC of March 2007 laying down detailed rules for the implementation of certain provisions of Directive 2004/109/EC on the harmonisation of transparency requirements in relation to information about issuers whose securities are admitted to trading on a regulated market', OJ L. 69, p. 27 ff.

European Commission (2008), '*Regulation (EC) No. 1126, 2008 of 3 November 2008 adopting certain international accounting standards in accordance with Regulation (EC) No. 1606/2002 of the European Parliament and of the Council*', Brussels.

European Commission (2009b), 'Report of the High-Level Group on Financial Supervision in the EU (De Larosière Report)', February, Brussels.

Financial Services Authority (FSA) (2006), 'Financial capability in the UK: establishing a baseline', London.
FSA (2009), 'The Turner Review: a regulatory response to the global banking crisis', March, London.
HM Treasury (HMT) (2007), 'Financial capability: the government's long-term approach', London.
HMT (2009), 'UK international financial services – the future', a report from UK-based financial services leaders to the government (the Bischoff Report), May, London.
International Accounting Standards Board (IASB) (2008), 'Reclassification of financial assets, amendments to IAS 39 Financial Instruments: recognition and measurement, and IFRS 7 Financial Instruments: disclosures', October, London.
Kirkpatrick, G. (2009), 'The corporate governance lessons from the financial crisis', *OECD Financial Market Trends,* **1**, 1–30.
Lusardi, A.M., M. van Rooji and R. Alessie (2007), 'Financial literacy and stock market participation', MRRC working paper, no. 2007-162.
Lusardi, A.M. (2008), *Taking Financial Literacy to the Next Level: Important Challenges and Promising Solutions,* Washington, DC: Organisation for Economic Co-operation and Development and US Treasury Department.
Morgan, D.P. (2002), 'Rating banks: risk and uncertainty in an opaque industry', *American Economic Review,* **92**, 874–88.
Organisation for Economic Co-operation and Development (OECD) (2005), *Improving Financial Literacy: Analysis of Issues and Policies,* Paris: OECD.
Podpiera, R. (2006), 'Does compliance with Basel Core Principles bring any measurable benefits?', International Monetary Fund staff papers, 53, no.2.
Schich, S. (2008), 'Financial crises: deposit insurance and related financial safety net aspects', *OECD Financial Market Trends,* 1–39.
Shiller, R. (2000), *Irrational Exuberance,* Princeton, NJ and Woodstock: Princeton University Press.

14. 'The new masters of the universe': institutional shareholder engagement and the regulation and governance of banks

Andy Mullineux[1]

INTRODUCTION

Two years is a long time in banking and finance. In 2007 it was the senior partners in private equity funds (PEFs) who were the fat cats under scrutiny in the UK. In 2009 it was the managers of the big banks that were being grilled by the House of Commons Treasury Select Committee about their large bonuses, and the managers of the large hedge funds (HFs) who were under scrutiny in both the US and the UK as a result of their short selling activities, especially of bank shares.[2]

Following the credit bubble, in August 2007 the current banking crisis began as a North Atlantic liquidity squeeze.[3] The crisis got much worse after the collapse of Lehman Brothers investment bank in mid-September 2008, which in turn precipitated the collapse of the shadow banking system.[4] The collapse of the Madoff Ponzi scheme in December 2008 and temporary bans on short selling in the autumn of 2008 put HFs under pressure.[5] The bear market on the major stock markets from July 2008 put further pressure on HFs and PEFs and raised some serious issues about the traditional UK corporate governance model; particularly relating to appropriate levels of leverage and the design of remuneration packages to achieve incentive compatibility between management and shareholders (and perhaps other stakeholders).[6]

This chapter considers lessons for the corporate governance system in the UK, and the governance of banks in particular, resulting from the rise and fall of the shadow banking system. This system was based on the interaction between commercial and investment banks with PEFs, HFs and other funds, particularly money market mutual funds, which were major suppliers of the liquid funds which the leveraging fed off.

THE RISE OF PRIVATE EQUITY – A NEW MODEL OF FINANCIAL CAPITALISM?

In the first half of 2007, pressure was increasing to tighten scrutiny of HFs, particularly through greater disclosure requirements. Concern in the US about HFs was motivated by worries about insider trading, such as warning favoured customers (including large insider shareholders) ahead of pending trades or management buyout bids, and more general malfeasance. The G7 meeting in February 2007 issued a more general warning of its concerns, some of which related to wider conflicts of interest within investment banks that had surfaced in the US in recent years. These conflicts can be reproduced between the target firm management, and HF and PEFs, which are major clients of the big investment banks, both in New York and in London (the major PEF and HF centres) and elsewhere.

The wave of private equity-led management buyouts in the mid-2000s was leveraged by funds from commercial banks through leveraged buyouts. (LBOs) Investment banks were also closely involved as advisors and prime brokers and increasingly ran their own in-house HFs and PEFs themselves.[7] The banks often made the initial 'covenant-lite' or 'cov-lite' loans and then securitised them as structured products such as collateralised debt obligations (CDOs) and effectively sold them on, often to HFs.[8] Further, the HFs frequently built up significant shareholdings in order to act as shareholder activists and prompt changes in management strategies or LBOs. Further, once an LBO bid is launched, the HFs can build shareholdings in order to profit from capital gains and influence the outcome through their shareholder voting rights.

Concern about such HF activism was famously raised in Germany by Franz Müntefering, then chair of Germany's Social Democratic Party, in 2005. He compared them to locusts, alluding to their alleged asset-stripping and workforce-cutting activities, and pressed for action to protect the social market economy in Germany from this rampant form of 'new capitalism'. It is notable that the HFs have become more activist as shareholders than most institutional shareholders such as insurance, pension and (public) equity investment funds. There is a concern that given the more narrow constituency they represent, they could be more short-termist and less strategic in their investment than traditional institutional shareholders.

As the LBO targets of PEFs got bigger in 2007 (such as the J. Sainsbury grocery store in the UK in February 2007), public concerns grew about the effects on stakeholders other than ('inside' or 'outside') shareholders. This prompted calls for more transparency about what was being done, and greater disclosure. The PEFs were urged to respond quickly if they wished to avoid regulation. Some of their managing directors claimed that they were very transparent to their (inside) backers, that they were professional, and that the public equity (stock) market had become lazy about monitoring and prompting enhanced management performance. In other words, the traditional investors were not engaging effectively enough, either by exercising their voting rights at shareholder meetings, or by using other forms of suasion. This private equity-led 'new capitalism' is a direct challenge to both the US and the UK models of corporate governance (Mullineux, 2008), and the forms of capitalism they underpin.

A report by Credit Suisse found that since 1996, European stocks with a significant family interest (in which the founding family or manager retains a stake of more than 10 per cent of the company's capital) have achieved a superior performance than their respective industrial sectors peers.[9] A similar result is found in the US. Credit Suisse has used these findings to construct a Family Value Index made up from 40 such companies, including BMW and Ericsson. Three key reasons for the superior performance are proposed by Credit Suisse. First, long-termism is engendered by the desire to pass on holdings to the children in the family. Second, there is avoidance of costly acquisition and associated leverage (debt). Third, there is strong alignment of manager and shareholder interest.

In the latter respect, there is a strong similarity with formerly public firms taken private by PEFs through LBOs. There are, however, sharp contrasts too. PEFs usually look to exit (sell their shares) after three to five years and are thus more medium term in outlook and less long-termist. They need quick and substantial financial results in order to satisfy their investors (limited partners) and must often act ruthlessly to cut costs and sell or close non-core business. They have also taken on large amounts of debt to leverage the capital from the partners of the firm and investors in their funds, and from the funds provided by HF participants in the LBO bids, by issuing bonds and taking on bank loans. (These 'leverage loans' were typically 'covenant-lite' at the height of the boom in 2006–07).

LBOs remove outside public investors from the picture, thereby resolving at a stroke the kernel of the principal agent problem and underlying corporate governance problems such as asymmetric information, conflicts of interest between insiders and outsiders, and the coordination problem faced by outside shareholders. The leveraging is effectively subsidised by the bias towards tax deductable debt relative to non tax-deductable equity, which faces double taxation of profits and dividends. Admittedly, publicly traded firms could also take on more debt, and indeed many did so to fund share buy-backs *inter alia* and were increasingly encouraged to do so by institutional investors in the run up to the credit crunch in August/ September 2007 (Mullineux, 2008b).

In a world where tax competition between countries exerts downward pressure on corporate tax rates, it is debatable whether debt interest deductibility can be sustained. Both the British and German economics and finance ministries have mooted withdrawing deductibility, but have faced strong opposition from the corporate sector and from SMEs, which tend to be more dependent on bank loans (debt) for external finance, in particular. A trade-off between reduced corporate tax revenue and reduced deductibility can be envisaged in light of the damage caused by over-leveraging in the credit crunch which gained strength from mid-2008.[10] PEFs, however, enjoy even greater tax concessions relating to the taxation of their profits as capital gains ('carried interest') and the fairness of this has been questioned in the UK and the US and is under review.

IMPLICATIONS FOR INSTITUTIONAL INVESTOR ENGAGEMENT IN THE UK AND HEDGE FUND ACTIVISM

If PEF-sponsored LBOs result in better performance for stock exchange quoted companies that have been subject to such interventions than those that have not, then there are serious implications for the corporate governance systems in the UK and elsewhere. The jury is still out and the evidence is mixed, but if the PEF interventions do improve company performance, it is important to know why so that the performance and governance of publicly quoted companies can be improved.

Institutional shareholders hold the majority of shares in the UK and their responsibilities are outlined in a set of principles overseen by the Institutional Shareholders Committee (Mullineux, 2008a). These include monitoring the performance of companies in which they invest, intervening where necessary, reporting back to clients and beneficial owners, and voting all shares held directly or on behalf of clients (where practical to do so).

As well as voting the shares (there is little disclosure on this) UK institutional shareholders' engagement with management includes dialogue and efforts to influence the election of board members (especially the independent directors), the decisions of executive remuneration committees, and appointments to internal audit committees.

The fact that there were so many underperforming publically quoted companies serving as attractive targets for a feeding frenzy of PEF activity implies that institutional shareholders were not doing a good job. Lord Myners, the UK City Minister recently accused them of being 'absentee landlords' and urged a radical review of the UK's corporate governance code by the Financial Reporting Council, which is responsible for monitoring compliance with it.[11]

The HFs have become more aggressively activist than even the most activist of institutional shareholders, often as an precursor to an LBO or the break-up of a conglomerate. There is a concern that the HF activism is more short-termist and profit seeking, and less strategic (or long-termist) than that of the institutional shareholders aiming to improve management performance and the value of their investments held on behalf of their generally more numerous and smaller investors.

As the size of the target firms for PEF-led LBOs grew, so did the public and political concern about their impact on stakeholders other than shareholders, or in other words about their social impacts. Asset stripping and cost cutting leading to job losses are feared, but disputed by the private equity and venture capital associations in the UK and Europe. It is too early, however, to draw conclusions from a medium term study of their costs and benefits. What is required for this is to observe the performance of companies over a period of perhaps three to five years following their return to publicly quoted company status and to compare it with performance over a similar period prior to the LBO.

The HFs often join the party by buying shares in target companies and selling them to PEFs participating in the LBO and there is thus a symbiosis between them. The PEFs and the HFs are lightly regulated and their portfolio companies, once privatised, do not face the pressure of quarterly or six-monthly reporting and the associated pressure to bolster share prices in the short-run. Free from this imposition, it is argued tough and more strategic decisions can be made (Jensen, 1989).

Nevertheless, as the UK LBO targets increased in scale and household names such as AA, Boots, Saga and Sainsburys became involved, pressure for more transparency increased in the UK. The PEFs responded with the Walker Code (November 2007). In turn, in 2008, the UK HFs delivered their own code in January 2008 as a result of the deliberation of the Hedge Fund Working Group chaired by Sir Andrew Large. These UK voluntary codes are overseen by the Private Equity and Venture Capital Association and the Hedge Funds Standard Board, respectively, and similar bodies in the US. The proportion of HFs and PEFs signing up to the codes is relatively small, although many of the bigger players have chosen to do so, perhaps in the hope of avoiding the tough regulation desired by many politicians. However, the UK voluntary codes and the similar codes adopted in the US by HFs in April 2008 seem unlikely to prevent the US, UK and EU authorities introducing a much tougher regulatory regime for PEFs and HFs in light of the credit crunch.

DOES PRIVATE EQUITY WORK?

The PEF LBO model is supposed to work primarily through incentivising the management through the carrot of incentive compatible remuneration packages and the stick of high leveraging (debt to equity ratios). Compensation is related to performance by including high equity stakes, normally in the form of share options. The high debt levels require cost cutting to generate the cash flow to pay the substantial regular interest payments to the banks and other creditors. This prevents accumulation of retained earnings and the temptation to wastefully invest them (Jensen, 1989). If it is that simple, and there are so many target companies, then UK-style institutional shareholders activism has clearly been a monumental failure.

However, PEFs often also bring their own professional expertise (or hire it from outside) to bear on the running of the portfolio companies under their management. A recent study by Archarya and Kehoe (2008), based on a sample of LBOs, finds that the improved performance (the 'alpha') above what might be expected of the relevant industrial sector (the 'beta') is partly due to increased leverage and the choice of potentially good, but underperforming targets, but primarily due to improved operating margins. This, in turn, is attributed to better management, not just due to incentivisation but as a result of improved expertise through the inclusion of experts on the board. The increased focus of managers could also result from relief from regular reporting and an ability to concentrate on profitability rather than other social responsibility and environmental distractions (such as 'sustainability') relating to the interests of stakeholders other than the inside shareholders.

The poor management of UK corporations has frequently been cited as a problem and it is one that institutional shareholders clearly need to focus upon. The relief from concerns about social responsibility and responsibility for outside shareholders is only temporary for companies from which the PEFs exit using initial public offerings (IPOs) and trade sales to public companies. What really matters is how the companies perform after the PEFs appointed experts have left the board. This is why the performance in the three to five years before the private equity intervention and after the IPO needs to be compared. Comparing the company valuation before and after the private equity intervention (the direct perceived value added by the PEFs), as is traditionally done, says little or nothing about the sustainability of the effects of the interventions. Such perceived gains from PEF intervention may owe more to the bull market conditions of rising share prices. In a bear market, as at present, with falling prices, the PEFs are forced to actively manage their portfolio companies for longer. In the current bear market, there have been few IPOs of portfolio companies and many are struggling to manage their heavy debt loadings. Further, it is only the top tier of the PEF firms that outperform market indices; which implies that genuine managerial talent is scarce.

PEFs may have thus enjoyed particularly benign, or golden, conditions in the 2003 to 2007 period due to low interest rates and a consequently high appetite for return (and thus associated risk), and also due to unduly favourable capital gains tax treatment and a period of almost continuously rising stock prices, which makes exiting at a profit easy as a result of buying and holding companies. Such factors may account for the high profitability of their interventions, and thus their incentive to intervene, but have less to do with whether or not they actually improve corporate performance in the medium term. They may also explain why PEFs were able to raise the funds and bear the debt necessary to mount increasingly large LBOs. Further, a small number of successful, large LBOs is less costly to manage (in terms of staffing and other costs) than a large number of smaller LBOs. It is the smaller LBOs that the PEFs must now pursue.

A report by the British Private Equity and Venture Capital Association, in conjunction with the accounting firm Ernst and Young, in January 2009 attributed half the profit in the 2005–07 boom years to taking on large amounts of cheap debt and less than one fifth to operational improvements in the companies under their management. Of the 330 per cent return on 14 of the biggest deals, 100 per cent come from rising share prices, 167 per cent from use of extra debt (such as leverage loans from banks) and 62 per cent from strategic and operational improvements.

There is also a concern that the incumbent management might be tempted to sell out too cheaply in response to LBO bids led by PEFs. In other words, as insiders the management is tempted by the promise of significant salary increases to recommend a sale at a price that sells the outside shareholders short.

In the downturn the high debt levels are proving to be a heavy burden for the PEF portfolio firms and in March 2009 a number of the large PEFs began making large write-offs. Others began lending to their portfolio firms during bankruptcy proceedings, raising the possibility that they might be tempted to push portfolio companies into bankruptcy prematurely. In 2008 PEFs had already started to buy at a discount leverage loans from banks, which are sometimes to their own portfolio companies, using new loans from banks. Along with HFs, PEFs are expected to participate in the US Troubled Asset Loan Fund and similar schemes operated by the Bank of England and other central banks, and thus to borrow money from the central bank to buy toxic assets and distressed loans. Potential conflicts of interest in such activity and wider vulture fund activity, especially when their own portfolio companies are involved or the HF prime brokers are involved, need to be carefully monitored.

PEFs, HFs AND THE CREDIT CRUNCH

With the distraction of the North Atlantic liquidity squeeze and the Northern Rock debacle in Autumn 2008 (Mullineux, 2008a, b, c), the public glare faced by the senior partners of PEFs and HFs was diverted. However, as the banking crisis deepened, banks tried to sell their impaired loans to PEFs and in the late spring/early summer 2008, the PEFs began to buy assets from the banks at a discount. Meanwhile the HFs began shorting (short selling) the stocks of banks that ran into difficulties and which were trying to raise new capital (using rights issues to existing shareholders in the UK). This caused Abbey National (Santander) to reprice a share issue. The shorting prompted the UK and US authorities (and other countries such as Australia) to step in with emergency rules designed to halt the shorting of bank shares. This may be seen as further evidence of special protection for banks in a time of high financial fragility. The fact that HFs can potentially aggravate financial instability did not go unnoticed and led to calls for a significant tightening of their regulation in the EU, the US and the UK.

Two HFs (most notably TPG-Axon) bought shares in Northern Rock in August/September 2007 in anticipation of a private deal that would raise the share price. They were ultimately disappointed as no private deal transpired and the UK government 'temporarily' nationalised the bank in November 2007. The HFs challenged the share price offered by the government and stood to make a substantial loss. The government arranged for an independent evaluation of the price it should pay for a bank that would have failed without its support (via the Bank of England). The challenge turned out to be unsuccessful.

The bank liquidity squeeze that started in August 2007, and the associated decline in appetite for risk as a result of the US sub-prime mortgage market crisis, terminated the boom in large LBOs. Indeed some of the larger LBOs, for which leveraged financing had not been arranged and agreed prior to the onset of the liquidity squeeze, struggled to complete or were abandoned. Further, as the credit crunch proper took hold in the second half of 2008, the more highly leveraged companies, including PEF portfolio companies, began to struggle to maintain their access to bank funding.[12]

As 2008 progressed, especially after the collapse of Lehman Brothers in mid-September and the subsequent collapse of the shadow banking system, it became clear the PEFs no longer had ready access to bank funding to leverage and launch large scale LBOs. Banks also widened their interest margins and risk spreads and began to reimpose covenants, reducing the incentive to borrow despite dramatic central bank interest rate reductions.

The PEFs were left holding larger portfolios of firms than they normally would because exiting became more difficult, either via IPOs (due to falling stock prices) or trade sales (due to liquidity hoarding and lack of access to credit). As the recession deepened alarmingly after September 2008, the trading conditions of the portfolio companies (especially in the retail sector due to falling consumption) worsened dramatically and losses began to be incurred. Investors began to withdraw funds as far as possible and some PEFs responded by tightening their lock-in conditions. Nevertheless, many PEFs had unused funds which looked increasingly difficult to make returns on, and expected returns were clearly likely to be less than in the boom years that preceded the onset of the crisis in Autumn 2007. The PEFs will thus have to seek smaller targets, and in doing so return to their roots, as it were. Some of the larger firms have focused on financial sector acquisitions, however, and as the credit crunch evolves there seem likely to be some rich pickings. The field for vulture fund activity is of course much wider because the recession is becoming increasingly strewn with corporate carcasses. The rapidly declining performance of the funds under management has not only reduced profits accruing to the partners, but induced pressure from investors for fee reductions.

The outlook for the HFs seems even bleaker than for the larger PEFs. The smaller PEFs, particularly the previously underperforming ones, can be expected to wither away. The HFs were desperately trying to staunch withdrawals of funds after market trading conditions deteriorated dramatically in the second half of 2008. The temporary bans and generally increased restrictions on the shorting activity that lies at the heart of their most popular trading strategies was damaging, but other trades (such as the so-called 'carry trade' on currencies and commodity related trades) also led to losses as market conditions changed dramatically in the second half of 2008. Numerous HFs are expected to close and the survivors are already feeling substantial pressure from investors to reduce their fee structure of 2 per cent of money under management plus 20 per cent of profits.

Last, but not least, the Madoff scandal that erupted in December 2008 undermined the 'funds of (hedge) funds' industry. Madoff was essentially operating a Ponzi scheme, drawing on money from numerous investment funds and wealth managers, including funds of hedge funds seeking the highest return (which Madoff's funds consistently reported). Due diligence was badly executed and negligence claims on custodians (such as UBS) soon merged. The securities regulators were clearly asleep at the wheel, or worse, induced to turn a blind eye as has been insinuated about the US Securities and Exchange Commission (SEC) in the light of the number of red flags raised by others and reported to it. Madoff was particularly secretive about his investment strategies (which he could presumably argue was necessary to prevent others copying), but interestingly the major investment banks that ran their own internal HFs chose not to invest in the Madoff funds.

The already battered HF industry was thus badly damaged by the Madoff affair and tougher regulation, already mooted in 2007, now looks inevitable. The case for tougher regulation is further enhanced as a result of the HFs' involvement in the shadow banking system that collapsed following Lehman's demise in mid-September 2008.

PRIVATE EQUITY AND THE ANGLO-SAXON CORPORATE GOVERNANCE MODEL

The rise of PEF-driven LBOs introduced a new model of financial capitalism to compete with the US and UK models. This development was driven in part by the advantageous treatment of deferred capital gains (profits) made by partners of the private equity firms (carried interest), the fairness of which is being reviewed by the tax authorities in both the US and the UK.

More fundamentally, the new financial capitalism relied not only on high leveraging, but also on generous performance-focused remuneration packages for managers aimed at aligning their interests with those of the (private) shareholders who intend to sell out in the medium term to secure their profits and make payments to the investors in the private equity funds that they manage. Supplementary imported expertise was also a key component of the improved performance prior to the firm being returned to public ownership, as we have noted.

The question thus arose, why had the US and UK corporate governance models not adopted similar strategies involving high leverage, incentive-compatible management remuneration packages and hiring better managers and directors? If a highly leveraged capital structure is genuinely advantageous (and not simply a by-product of the tax deductibility of debt servicing costs and unusually freely available credit at abnormally low real interest rates), then why had the institutional investors in the UK, for example, not required the managers of companies in which they invest to adopt a similar structure? And why had they not imposed incentive-compatible management pay structures and demanded an improvement in the quality and expertise of executive and non-executive directors? Is this simply a failure of the UK's corporate governance model, or is it also a failure of management and director training? As the credit crunch and the resulting recession evolved, it became clear that the institutional shareholders had indeed encouraged an increase in leveraging, so much so that medium to large sized companies found it increasingly difficult to replace expiring credits as 2008 wore on and we moved into 2009.

It also became clear that executive fat cat pay had indeed grown more rapidly than the pay of other workers in the UK and the US, and this was particularly the case for the banks. Unfortunately, excessive risk-taking by banks was incentivised and the institutional shareholders failed to make provision for clawbacks of remuneration where performance fell short.

Corporate finance theory (Modigliani and Miller, 1958) demonstrates that the capital structure or degree of leveraging should have a neutral effect on performance (leaving aside distortions such as tax). Against this, however, Jensen (1989, p. 61) argued that the public company had outlived its usefulness due, in part, to the inherent conflicts of interest between managers (agents) and shareholders (principals) and the wider coordination (of dispersed shareholders) problem (Berle and Means, 1932). The conflict of particular relevance to Jensen's argument relates to the use of retained profits. Higher debt levels impose more discipline by reducing free cash flow in order to meet higher interest payments. As a result, more profitable investments should be made. Institutional investors that fail to assure that retained profits are invested at least as profitably as they might be elsewhere are failing in their fiduciary duty to investors.

However, high debt levels have serious implications for other stakeholders since higher leverage is associated with higher default risk and thus threatens the job security of current workers and the security of their pension schemes as well. During the restructuring of a firm after an LBO, there is also a threat to the job security of current employees (although PEFs claim that they are on balance net job creators). Hence, as larger firms became involved as the targets of LBOs, the PEFs came under greater scrutiny, in line with the actual or potential social impact of their intervention. There has been increasing concern expressed by the UK's Pensions Regulator and Pensions Protection Fund, for example, about the implications for past and current employee pensions. Pension scheme trustees have been encouraged to be vigilant and a number of potential LBOs were aborted when the PEFs found the conditions imposed by the funds' trustees in the form of a top-up of underfunded schemes, too costly to comply with. As the recession has deepened and elongated, and share prices have fallen and dividends have been cut, the company pension fund deficits have increased. This has resulted in an unanticipated (poison pill) protection against LBOs and other takeovers, but threatened the viability of some firms with the possible consequence of more losses, failures and unemployment.

In the UK, mergers and acquisitions are covered by the Takeover Code of Practice overseen by the Takeover Panel. The proposed disclosure requirements for PEF-led LBOs, or an enhanced version of them, might reasonably be brought within the framework. The UK government has also been urged to review the powers of the Pensions Regulator and pension scheme trustees so that the visibility of pension funds are not threatened by LBOs.

Mullineux (2008a) finds that there is no common Anglo-American system of corporate governance, or financial capitalism. Capitalism itself evolves in response to competitive forces (such as globalisation) within the context of institutional structures that currently differ substantially. Competition between the systems (Albert, 1993) is likely to lead (eventually) to convergence on a hybrid system (Mullineux, 2007). The emergence of the PEF-led LBO challenge to public company governance structures and HF activism seems likely to influence the convergence path, if not the destination.

The symbiosis between institutional shareholders, HFs and PEFs, and its implications for corporate governance in the continuously evolving and adapting capitalist system, clearly needs further investigation. There are marked differences in the importance of PEFs between the US and the UK, and the UK and other European countries. It is to be noted, for example, that in the run up to the current crisis, institutional shareholders were increasingly keen investors in PEFs and HFs as alternative, portfolio diversifying investments and that shorting by HFs relied on the willingness of institutional shareholders to lend them shares (for a fee).

On a more optimistic note, post-crisis, the PEF focus may return to small and medium sized companies. This would lead to a healthy injection of equity into such companies and to IPOs on junior stock markets, such as AIM in London (if it survives the crisis) leading, after successful growth, to graduation to the London Stock Exchange.

THE NEW FINANCIAL CAPITALISM

The nexus of commercial and investment banks, PEFs and HFs, along with money market mutual funds, formed the core of a shadow banking system that contributed to a massive increase in the leveraging of the mainstream banking system's capital and liquid reserves over the last 20 to 30 years. The LBO-related PEF and HF activity was just part of leveraging processes and clearly benefited from the easy access to loans in a system that allowed commercial banks to lend funds far in excess of their retail deposits. Like the mainstream commercial banking system, the shadow banking system engaged in maturity mismatching (transformation) by borrowing short to lend long and in so doing increased (funding) liquidity risk and the supply of credit (Niehans, 1978, Chapter 9). Securitisation acted as an accelerator and the prices of the securities depended on the expected future receivables on the underlying assets. The use of derivatives as CDOs further compounded the financial alchemy.

Alongside this process, market (asset) price-related risks were accumulating as a result of cross holdings of securities within the wider banking system. The house of cards, or dare I say pyramid[13] (for this can be viewed as a massive pyramid scheme, or perhaps more accurately, a Ponzi scheme), collapsed in September/October 2008. It had become clear as 2008 progressed that the liquidity squeeze that ensued in August 2007 was not going to be quickly and easily resolved despite massive central bank intervention. After the collapse of Lehman's in September 2008, a full-blown systemic banking crisis erupted, securitisation ground to a halt, and the shadow banking system collapsed.

From a corporate governance perspective there are numerous issues to be considered. What were the banks' internal risk managers doing and why were they ignored or replaced when they warned the management that risk was excessive and increasing, as in the case of HBOS? Why were the institutional shareholders asleep at the wheel? Were they relying on the supervisors to monitor the banks? What were the supervisors doing? Why were the auditors approving banks as going concerns? How were the risk promoting pay schemes for managers (and traders) allowed to develop? What in particular were the non-executive directors doing and did they (and some of the chief executives and chairmen of banks) have sufficient banking expertise? Paul Myners, whose 2001 Myners Report on institutional investment contributed to the UK's Combined Code on corporate governance, was appropriately appointed to the post of a City Minister in 2008 and soon began to ask hard questions along these lines. HMT has since appointed Sir David Walker to undertake a review of the corporate governance of banks and to report in December 2009.

It is clear that the banking and wider financial sector regulatory and supervisory systems are part of the governance system for banks, and a wide ranging regulatory review that encompasses the regulation of HFs, PEFs and credit rating agencies is also underway in the UK and at the EU level as well as in the US at the International Financial Stability Board and elsewhere.[14,15]

There is also plenty of scope for a wider, post-crisis review of issues pertaining to the corporate governance of non-financial institutions (including institutional shareholders). One thing is clear, the prevailing models have been revealed as totally inadequate in the UK and the US. The institutional shareholders must share responsibility with the regulators and supervisors of the financial system, and cannot or should not rely on the latter to do their job.

The role of auditors, especially of banks, also needs to be reviewed in the UK. The representatives of the institutional shareholders, the Association of British Insurers (ABI), the National Association of Pension Funds (NAPF) and the Investment Managers Associations (IMA) claimed that they had tried to engage regarding inappropriate remuneration packages, excessive risk taking and the poor quality of non-executive directors, but the bank boards refused to hear their voices. Recent high profile events involving Barclays Bank (in 2008) and Rio Tinto (in 2009), for example, have shown that institutional shareholders are finding it difficult to protect shareholder pre-emption rights when boards decide to ignore their protestations, eschew an ordinary share rights issue, and raise capital from outside Sovereign Wealth Funds (SWFs) or foreign companies, leading to dilution of their shareholding. This makes them look weak and implies they lack the necessary powers under current corporate governance arrangements. Simply shouting louder does not seem likely to be sufficient to solve the problem. The Chairman of ABI and IMA, Keith Skeoch, has, however, promised to promote more active engagement.

Since the 2001 Enron Scandal in the US there has been concern about the conflicts of interest involved in accounting firms providing both auditing and consulting services to the same client firm. The 2002 Sarbanes-Oxley Act attempted to resolve the issue in the US, and the UK established a Financial Reporting Council (FRC), which also oversees the (voluntary) Combined Code on corporate governance, to supervise the previously self-regulated UK auditors. The UK authorities did not require the FRC to go as far as the US authorities in restricting accounting firms from providing various consulting services to the clients they were auditing. The UK arms of the major accounting firms have not taken kindly to the FRC expressing concerns about ethical conflicts arising in the audits it has recently reviewed. As regards corporate governance in general, and of banks in particular, the FRC feels the Combined Code remains comprehensive, but the practical application of its rules are lacking.

It should be noted that the auditors of banks in the UK are responsible for appraising their internal risk controls and judging whether banks (and their borrowers) are going concerns and thus able to raise sufficient funding to continue in business until the next audit. This must have become increasingly difficult for them to do post-September 2008. Qualification of a bank's accounts or even weaker comments would, however, be likely to precipitate the banks rapid demise (or nationalisation). Consequently the FSA briefed the banks' auditors on what was involved in January 2009 and presumably assured them that the Bank of England and the government (taxpayer) would assure that the banks (and perhaps also their major borrowers) would receive adequate funding. As their major clients cease to be going concerns, because the banks refuse to provide funding, the banks face losses on their loans to these clients. The Bank England's lender of last resort window has thus also been extended to buying commercial paper, notes and bonds.

There may, be a bigger problem however, in relying on one group of financial institutions (institutional investors) to govern others (the banks). As fund management becomes more outsourced and professionalised, there is a danger that competition will also drive the professional managers into risk seeking, short-termist behaviour.

CONCLUSIONS

The activity of PEFs and HFs laid down a challenge to publicly quoted companies and the institutional shareholders that are their major shareholders. Aided and abetted by cheap debt, with interest payments which are tax deductable, many public companies increased their debt to equity (leverage) ratios as they got caught up in the new leveraging trend of the times. Jensen (1989) seemed to be the guru for these developments.

The practice of copying PEFs in trying to achieve remuneration packages that align the interests of managers and shareholders – by paying salaries and pensions partly in the form of stock options – was also widely adopted. To the extent that institutional shareholders influence executive remuneration committees, they were complicit in this. This was particularly true in the case of the big banks. Investment banks had long used such incentive-compatible pay packages for executives and, in addition, designed bonus packages to reward successful traders and deal makers. As the HFs developed, the investment banks became their prime brokers and over time developed their own in-house HFs and PEFs and increasingly engaged in proprietary trading on their own accounts, rather than as brokers and dealers on behalf of clients. Following the 1986 Big Bang reform of the UK stock exchange, and the repeal in 1999 of the 1933 US Glass-Steagall Act which separated commercial from investment banking, commercial and investment banking became increasingly enmeshed. As a result, remuneration packages typical in investment banking seem to have been adopted by commercial bank parents, leading to the sort of executive remuneration packages that scandalised public opinion during the crisis.

Having been well rewarded in the good times (while senior PEF partners were facing public disapproval about excessive remuneration), bank management angered the public by continuing to pay bonuses even as and after they were being bailed out by the Bank of England and the government (taxpayer). To cap it all, failure was seen to be rewarded when the former chief executives, who had been persuaded to step down prematurely (without being sacked for mismanagement) received large, eye-watering pension pots. There was seemingly no provision to claw-back money from banks whose decisions had turned out to be disastrously bad.

The fee-based culture even permeated through to the retail banking divisions, leading to a proliferation of mis-selling scandals regarding products such as endowment mortgages and pensions protection insurance (PPI). It is this imbalance between the excessive risk taking and the underpricing of risk which lies behind the subprime mortgage crisis (itself aggravated by the fees earned by the brokers who also originated the subprime mortgages) and the CDO crisis.

The CDOs were issued on the back of securities backed by receivables from pools of subprime mortgages. The investment bankers helping to create the asset backed securities and the CDOs were, of course, also incentivised by the prospect of fee income and aided and abetted by the credit rating agencies that awarded top level credit ratings to some subprime-backed securities, and indeed help to design them.

Fundamental issues have been raised about the internal controls and corporate governance of banks and by implication about the regulation and supervision of banks, given the need to protect their depositors and taxpayers against the sort of abuses that are at the root of the current crisis (Mullineux, 2006). The UK government has appointed Sir David Walker to report by Christmas 2009 on the corporate governance of banks and Lord Turner, the new chairman of the FSA, reported in April 2009 on his review of the regulation and supervision of banks and the wider financial system.[16,17] Lord Turner and his chief executive, Hector Sants, have made it clear that the previous light touch regime of regulation is to be replaced with a much tougher regime. The FSA has also said that it will take remuneration structures into account when assessing bank risk management systems (and also their future liquidity and capital adequacy requirements) and has drafted a code on remuneration policies that requires bonuses to reflect risk created as well as profits made, regulatory compliance, and partial deferral of payments to facilitate claw-backs. It proposes a separate structure for the remuneration of compliance officers and risk managers.

In addition, thought should be given to whether the role of the FSA is too wide. As well as prudential supervision, it has responsibilities for financial product and service regulation and raising financial literacy. It requires banks and financial product services providers to treat customers fairly. The UK banks have been found by the Competition Commission, the Office of Fair Trading, the Financial Ombudsman Service and the Banking Codes Supervisory Board (BCSB) to have fallen short in this respect on a number of counts.

The big UK banks have been bailed out by the government because they are utilities providing access to the payments system and credit to households and SMEs. Such access can be viewed as a citizen's right in a modern society in much the same way that access to clean water and electricity is. Banks should thus be regulated as utilities (Mullineux, 2009) to ensure that access is generally available, products are sound, and pricing is fair. To achieve this, it would make sense for the regulator, which might be called BankCom, to take on the job of raising financial literacy too. The arguments seem easy to extend to retail insurance products and services, so we may in fact need BankInCom. The FSA would then be freed to concentrate on microprudential regulation designed to assure that banks and other financial institutions do not take excessive risks. The Bank of England would, in turn, be responsible for assuring overall (systemic) financial stability, as far as that remains possible in a single country, especially a relatively small one containing a very large international financial centre.[18]

NOTES

1. The term 'masters of the universe' was coined by Tom Wolfe in his novel on finance capitalism in the 1980s in New York entitled, *The Bonfire of the Vanities* (1987, New York: Farrar, Straus and Giroux). The 'masters' in the book were bond traders and their like. The new masters referred to here are private equity and hedge fund managers and the investment banking deal makers and traders that worked with them.
2. Short selling involves the selling of stocks borrowed (for a fee) in the hope that they can be bought back at a lower price, at a later date, so that a profit can be made.
3. The credit bubble (or boom) had its origins in cheap money, in part because interest rates were cut and held low following crises in 1997 and 2001 and in part because of large and cheap capital inflows into trade deficit countries such as the US and UK from oil producing and Asian countries which were running large trade surpluses.
4. The shadow banking system was a complex financial network of commercial banks and their off balance sheet vehicles (such as Conduits and Structured Investment Vehicles or SIVs), investment banks, hedge funds, private equity funds and mutual funds *inter alia.*
5. Ponzi schemes are speculative funds whose outstanding debt grows (due to high interest promises) even if no new income yielding assets are purchased. To prevent collapse new money must be raised by the fund at increasingly fast rates. See Minsky (1982, Chapter 2) for further discussion. Pyramid schemes are related, but typically there is simply no attempt even to develop a fund of assets to underpin the scheme.

6. Leverage here is taken crudely to mean the debt to equity ratio.
7. A prime broker is typically a division of an investment bank that provides broking services for hedge funds (such as buying and selling shares), credit and perhaps also custody (holding shares and portfolio management) in return for fees (and interests if credit is supplied).
8. 'Covenant-lite' or 'cov-lite' loans are loans made with few conditions (covenants) imposed on the borrowers. There was a great deal of competition among banks for leveraged loan business in the credit boom.
9. See *Financial Times*, 30 January 2007, p. 30.
10. The credit crunch has been adopted widely as the name for the current liquidity and solvency crisis in banking and the associated major recession (possibly a depression). Previously the term was used more commonly in the literature to refer to the tighter rationing of credit advanced to SMEs as credit risks increased in the recession; which in turn helped deepen the recession (Kliesen and Tatom, 1992).
11. See *Financial Times*, 22 April 2009, pp. 17–18.
12. See endnote 9.
13. For this can be viewed as a massive pyramid scheme, or perhaps more accurately, a Ponzi scheme.
14. The Turner Review, led by the new chairman of the FSA and due to report in April 2009, www.fsa.gov.uk.
15. See the report for the European Commission issued by a group chaired by Jacques de Larosiére on 25 February 2009.
16. Sir David Walker's report was subsequently published as Walker and Associates (2009). See www.fsa.gov.uk.
17. See www.fsa.gov.uk
18. Or macro-prudential regulation.

REFERENCES

Acharya, V. and C. Kehoe (2008), 'Corporate governance and value creation: evidence from private equity', London Business School working paper.

Albert, M. (1993), *Capitalism Against Capitalism*, London: Whurr Publishers.

Berle Jr, A. and G. Means (1932), *The Modern Corporation and Private Property,* Chicago: Chicago Clearing House.

Bush, T. (2005), '*Divided by a* common language where economics meets law: US vs non-US financial reporting models', in the ongoing *Dialogue in Corporate Governance series Beyond the Myth of Anglo-American Corporate Governance*, Institute of Chartered Accountants in England and Wales (ICAEW), June.

Dow, C. (1998), *Major Recessions: Britain and the World, 1920–1995*, Oxford: Oxford University Press.

Group of Thirty (2009), 'Financial reform – a framework for financial stability', paper from the working group on financial reform, January, Washington, DC.

Jensen, M. (1989), 'The eclipse of the public corporation', *Harvard Business Review*, (September–October), 61–74.

Kliesen, K.L and J.A. Tatom (1992), 'The recent credit crunch: the neglected dimensions', *Federal Reserve Bank of St Louis Review,* (September–October) 18–36.

La Porta, R., F. Lopez-de-Silanes, A. Shleifer and R.W. Vishny (1998). 'Law and Finance', *Journal of Political Economy*, **106**, 1113–55.

Llewellyn, D.T. (2006), 'Issues on the governance of mutuals in the financial sector', paper commissioned for the Myners Enquiry into Governance of Life Mutuals.

Masulis, R.W. (2006), 'The law and economics of self-dealing', keynote speech to the The 19th Australian Finance and Banking Conference, University of New South Wales, December, Sydney.

Minsky, H.P. (1982), *Can it Happen Again?*, Armonk, NY: M.E. Sharpe.

Modigliana, F. and M. Miller (1958), 'The cost of capital corporate finance, and the theory of investment', *American Economic Review*, **48**, 261–97.

Mullineux, A. (2006), 'The corporate governance of banks', *Journal of Financial Regulation and Compliance*, **14** (4), 375–82.

Mullineux, A. (2007), 'Financial sector convergence and corporate governance', *Journal of Financial Regulation and Compliance*, **15**(1), 8–19.

Mullineux, A. (2008), 'Is there an Anglo-American corporate governance model', discussion paper available from author.

Mullineux, A. (2008a), 'British banking regulation and supervision: between a rock and a hard place', *International Economics and Economic Policy*, **4**(4), 363–70.

Mullineux, A. (2008b), 'Lessons from Northern Rock and the North Atlantic liquidity squeeze', *The Melbourne Review*, **4**(1), 7–12.

Mullineux, A. (2008c), 'Northern Rock and the governance of banks', *inFinance*, (June), 20–23.

Walker, D. and Associates (2009), 'A review of corporate governance in UK banks and other financial industry entities', (The Walker Review), London: The Walker review secretariat, 16 July, accessed 7 January 2010 at www.hm-treasury.gov.uk/walkers_review_information.htm.

15. Minimizing collateral damage: options for financing public-private partnerships in the wake of the financial crisis

Darrin Grimsey and Mervyn K. Lewis[1]

INTRODUCTION

Writing in 2006, a former member of the Board of Governors of the Federal Reserve System, Frederic Mishkin, described the financial system in the following terms:

> the financial system [is] the brain of the economy . . . It acts as a coordinating mechanism that allocates capital, the lifeblood of economic activity, to its most productive uses by business and households. If capital goes to the wrong uses or does not flow at all, the economy will operate inefficiently, and ultimately economic growth will be low.[2]

The analogy seems an apt one, for the international financial system in 2008 experienced what may be seen as a stroke or brain seizure, although other descriptions are 'a spasm in the credit system [that] resembled a slow but ultimately devastating chain reaction' (Ferguson, 2009, pp. 9–10) or simply 'a heart attack' (Goodhart, 2009, p. 1). Inevitably, every financial shock produces casualties. While the most visible impact of this crisis is its devastating impact on the banks, the collateral damage to the rest of the system illustrates Mishkin's warning of what happens when 'capital does not flow at all'.

It is in this context that this chapter examines the impact of the global financial crisis on project financing in bond, equity and banking markets, and the consequences that follow for the raising of private finance for public-private partnerships (PPPs). In response to these financing difficulties new models of financing PPPs have been proposed involving *inter alia* staged procurement, co-funding and government support in various forms. After reviewing these alternative approaches, the chapter concludes with the questions: are PPPs worth saving and, if so, how is this to be done?

PROJECT FINANCING

The commitment of private sector finance to the construction or renovation of facilities has always been an integral part of PPPs under the project level approach using DBFOM (design-build-finance-operate-maintain) modes that has typified countries such as UK, Australia, Canada, South Africa and others. Underpinning the development of the PPP concept has been an appropriate model for channelling the supply of private finance for infrastructure projects. Structured project finance provides a vehicle for mobilizing equity and debt in infrastructure projects by fashioning the finance to the specific project, with the risks (and returns) borne not by the sponsors alone but by different types of investors (equity holders, bond holders, debt providers, quasi-equity investors). The underlying premise is that projects are income-producing and borrowings can be serviced from these proceeds. Future income from the investment is earmarked to service the borrowings, providing security to the financiers by decoupling the servicing of the loans from the financial fortunes of the owners or sponsors of the investment. A fairly standard approach is for the sponsors of a project to establish a special purpose vehicle company (SPV) to operate for the duration of the project (20 to 30 years) in which they are principal shareholders. Funding of the project and its repayment is then routed through the SPV.

Due to the low capitalization of the SPV, there is a reliance on direct revenues to pay for operating costs and cover financing while giving the desired return on risk capital. In the first instance, the senior financier of private finance looks to, and evaluates the adequacy of, the cash flow and earnings of the project as the source of funds for repayments. In the second, the senior financier will look at the security arrangements and the way that risk is transferred to the various parties that contract with the SPV and provide the services, such as the construction contract, operating services contracts, mortgages over property, financiers' direct deed, performance bonds, parent company guarantees and so on. The aim is to achieve a financial structure with minimum recourse to the sponsors, while at the same time providing sufficient support via the SPV so that the financiers are satisfied with the residual risks and confident that the senior debt is well insulated against risk, preferably leaving only exposure to major default risk and the compensation provisions on termination. In this respect, the financing of a PPP project must be engineered to take account of the risks involved, sources of finance, and accounting and tax regulations. Project design requires expert analysis of all of the attendant risks and then, usually prior to competitive tendering, a structuring of the contractual arrangements that allocates risk burdens appropriately.

A fairly typical benchmark figure that has operated in the market is for the finance to comprise around 90 per cent debt, made up of senior bank debt or bonds, plus 10 per cent equity provided by the investors in the SPV. Subordinated debt has also been used, seen as akin to equity in that the rights of holders of this debt are subordinated to other creditors (except shareholders). Because the major costs of constructing the facility are funded by non-recourse debt, the private debt markets must commit to significant sums of debt up-front. The expectation is that those with money at risk will require there to be a harder-nosed approach to project evaluation, risk management and project implementation than occurs with government funding. Usually the financiers rely on their own advisory group or occasionally outside advisors to assess the financial viability of a project and the risks attached to the revenue stream providing security for the finance. When projects are financed through the issue of bonds to the public, rating agencies are consulted to provide credit ratings for the underlying debt. These agencies are typically involved at very early stages of project formulation so that credit concerns can be addressed and a new structure developed (for example, by altering the extent of equity in the SPV). Insurers have also been used to provide credit enhancement. These 'monoline' insurers have engaged in credit risk arbitrage to create value for project financing in circumstances where the market generally would tend to overestimate the risks involved.

THE NEW FINANCIAL ENVIRONMENT

These well-developed financial arrangements have been thrown into disarray. Bond markets are moribund, credit ratings agencies and monoline insurers are under pressure, equity is restricted, and conditions in the banking markets have changed dramatically in terms of market capacity, conditionality, documentation, term (tenor) and margins. We comment on each in turn.

Capital Markets

Bonds

Bond markets are now hard to access for infrastructure projects, for PPP assets are typically in the BBB range and are highly leveraged, single asset companies. As at June 2009, the spread in US markets between the ten-year yield on BBB-rated corporate bonds (moderately risky but investment grade) and US Treasury notes was over 400 bp, admittedly down from nearly 700 bp early in 2009 but still well above the 150 bp that ruled in January 2007 pre-crisis.[3] Much of the market difficulty posed for PPPs is due to the downgrading of the monoline insurers and others providing credit enhancement or 'wrapping' (if a monoline insurer is downgraded, all of the paper it has insured must be downgraded too), although some unwrapped issues have occurred post-crisis.[4] For example, an issue of bonds in April 2009 for the Niagara PPP hospital project in Canada due in 2042 carried a spread of 385 bp over Canadian government bond yields, due largely to the A rating assigned by Standard & Poor's.[5]

Equity

Listed equity sources have dried up, and shares in those toll road projects listed on the stock market (such as ConnectEast, BrisConnections in Australia) have been severely written down. The highly-leveraged private equity-style listed fund or 'satellite' infrastructure model developed by Macquarie Bank is under question (and has been since the critical RiskMetrics Report in 2008 and the demise of 'MiniMac', Babcock & Brown, in 2009).[6] Unlisted equity sources still exist, but for smaller amounts and under stricter conditionality over matters such as termination events.

Banking Markets

Banks are now the principal source of finance for infrastructure, but conditions in banking markets have meant that lending capacity has not kept pace with demand as banks have sought to rebuild capital to cover past excesses and mounting losses on consumer and real estate loans. Faced with the need to refinance maturing bonds over the next two years ($1.1 trillion for US banks and €1.9 trillion for European banks by December 2012), in a situation in which securitization of debt remains dead, banks are trying to shrink their balance sheets, and lower future funding requirements, by applying testing new rules on loan applicants, as reflected in a number of aspects.[7] Those on the receiving end suspect an element of 'gouging' may be mixed with constrained capacity and undue caution, but the consequences are as follows.

As banks' balance sheets have shrunk, and in some cases dramatically so, the tendency has been for both credit to dry up and banks to consolidate their business activities closer to home. In turn, as credit has dried up, the terms and conditions on which banks are prepared to lend to PPPs have changed dramatically: long term loans are no longer available; shorter tenures (less than ten years in most cases and sometimes as low as three years) have led to refinancing risk becoming a major issue; margins have blown out to around 300 bp from a market that typically saw senior debt pricing at less than 100 bp.

Market capacity
The number of banks willing to participate in infrastructure financing has shrunk, not only because of capital shortages, but also because banks have retreated from overseas markets to shore up the home base – there are few truly multinational banks! Most Asia-Pacific countries rely on international lending alongside domestic banks. For example, a typical Australian PPP prior to the credit crisis may have attracted as much as 60 per cent international lending. Now, in Australia, the number of banks willing to participate in infrastructure financing has fallen to between ten and 15 depending on the project and the sponsors. Some banks will only look at a deal if there is an existing strong banking relationship with a sponsoring entity. Securing the participation of at least one and preferably two of the four domestic Australian banks is now considered necessary to complete a transaction and attract overseas banks.

Funding arrangements
In the new market dynamic, the loan syndication market remains effectively closed, with banks reluctant to provide underwritten facilities. Instead, club arrangements (multiple banks joining together) is the major source of project financing available. As a result, borrowers need to negotiate with a large group of lenders and agree on terms across all parties. The upshot is that the lowest common denominator applies as all participants accept the terms of the last lender needed to complete funding. Another feature that compounds the complexity of the negotiations is that 'hold' levels are greatly reduced, to 10–20 per cent of a project up to a maximum in the following ranges: North America, \$80–120 million per bank; UK, £40–70 million per bank; and Australia, AUD 50–150 million per bank.

Conditionality
The instability in bank funding markets has seen a raft of new measures introduced to PPP lending. 'Market flex' clauses protect the banks from market movements affecting margins in the period between when a bid is made up to financial close. 'Market disruption' provisions protect banks if their cost of funds moves relative to the relevant quoted interbank market offer rate, and can run through post-financial close into the contract phase. Underwriting conditions have also been strengthened. A 'material adverse effects' clause gives the bank the right to cancel the underwriting commitment or reprice it in certain defined conditions (such as a change in interest rates of +/−100 bp, or a fall in the stock price index of 10 per cent). Under 'refresh' arrangements, the validity of the underwriting is subject to a refresh after a specified period (for example, 30 days). The implication is

that finance packages would have to be refreshed through the evaluation phase of a PPP or project finance deal to extend the underwriting period through to financial close. With the reduction in the length of loans, refinancing is now required and there is an expectation that government will share in that risk. In practice, this risk-sharing implies that equity takes a small first loss position and the government provides a floor beyond which it takes the refinancing risk. Conversely, the upside risk can then be clawed back by the government with caps on upside gain that were previously subject to 50/50 sharing arrangements.

Documentation

Banks have also tightened their documentation requirements covering gearing, amortisation and covenants. In terms of gearing, lenders are demanding higher equity contributions from PPP sponsors. Previously PPPs were around 90 per cent leveraged due to the reassurance of the steady revenue stream from government through the unitary charge for social infrastructure, and with the application of shadow tolls and availability payments for many roads. As we write (July 2009) gearing levels for such projects are around 75–85 per cent. Projects also need to have an amortisation profile of 40–50 per cent of debt, whereas lenders used to be comfortable with little amortisation and a large balloon repayment at the end. Covenants are now more restricting. Cover ratios have increased. Lenders have increased scrutiny of construction sub-contractors and are demanding third party liquidity supports (performance bonds, letters of credit) as a matter of course.

Terms of loans

There is less enthusiasm than before for providing the 25-year plus terms of loans that are desired for PPPs. Indeed, even standby facilities are challenging to put in place, and only a limited number of banks are willing to provide this type of undrawn facility. In international project finance, there is a trend to 'mini perm' structures, which are short term (tenor) loans with strict obligations on refinancing. Often they are made with a window for refinancing, otherwise higher margins are imposed ('step up margins') and all free cash in the project is used to pay down principal ('100 per cent cash sweep'). As an illustration of the altered conditions in the market, loan terms for corporate lending in Australia have shortened markedly over the last three years. In 2006, about 18 per cent of loans had a term of 5–12 years. In 2007 that had fallen to 11 per cent and by 2008 the figure was down to 7 per cent. Loans with a term of three years or less accounted for two thirds of corporate loans in 2008 compared with about 50 per cent in 2006.

Table 15.1 Financial arrangements for selected PPP projects in the United Kingdom, January–June, 2009

Sector of project	Involved	Term of loan (years)	Initial and final pricing (bp)	Cash sweep
Waste	4	23.5	325–425	year 10
Waste	club of 4	23.5	275–300	year 10
Transport	16	27	250–350	year 7 and 19
Transport	4	32.5	200–?	–
Health	3	30	230–250	–
Health	club of 4	29	275–300	–
Education	1	26.5	275	–

Source: Ernst & Young (2009).

Margins

As noted earlier, most PPP projects fall into the BBB range, and in Australia (similar to elsewhere) the margin over base rate has widened seven-fold since 2007, from around 50 bp in mid-2007 to 350 bp in mid-2009. However, the full impact of this change has yet to be felt among borrowers since the decreases in official cash rates have kept the overall rate for BBB loans lower than it was in 2007. In the UK, there is more direct evidence for PPPs. Table 15.1 summarizes the financing arrangements for seven PPP projects brought to financial close in the first half of 2009. Margins for the bank debt range from 200 bp to 325 bp over LIBOR for the initial loan pricing to 425 bp for the final pricing over the term of the loans (ranging from 23.5 to 32.5 years). These can be compared with margins as low as 56 bp in 2006. Even as late as January–March 2008 deals were still being closed with margins in the range 55–95 bp and it was not until September–October 2008 (following the bankruptcy of Lehman Brothers) that margins widened beyond 100 bp (Ernst & Young, 2009). Will these days ever return? Some continue to see them as the market norm, and are awaiting a market rebound to 'normal' levels.

Financial Implications for PPPs

What is the appropriate pricing for a PPP? It can be argued with some justification that, while PPPs are usually rated in the BBB range, social infrastructure projects such as a PPP school or waste project have a strong government covenant very different from a corporate that is borrowing unsecured debt, exposed to systemic risk in an economic downturn. Nevertheless, certain features of PPPs do not sit well with the new market dynamics. One is the protracted bidding process. A procurement approach that requires fully costed funding commitments from a group of bidders and underwritten funding from a selected bidder (against tight timescales) is simply not practical in today's market. The reality is that too few banks are active to provide club structures for all bidders. Another problem is that most infrastructure procurement requires long-term financing, but there is little market depth at the longer end of the market at present. PPP projects cannot bear the shortened amortisation sought by lenders. Early refinancing is the obvious solution, but this brings risks for shareholders and lenders (higher pricing), with extra debt costs. These debt costs in turn become part of the PPP project and are paid for by the taxpayer through the unitary charge. Can alternative procurement approaches be forged to get around this impasse?

THE SEARCH FOR ALTERNATIVES

The current lack of funding is a global issue and is a problem that impacts on financial markets generally. PPPs are merely one manifestation of the situation. At a time when most countries are grappling with a significant need and desire to deliver infrastructure and improved services, some of which will involve PPP delivery, a range of potential, yet practical, solutions to the shortage of credit are necessary.

There is the opportunity for government to take positive steps to address the current problems. If infrastructure spending is undertaken in a strategic way it can result in expansion of productive capacity, diversification of economic capabilities and increased global competitive advantage.

In turn, this situation presents opportunities to modify the PPP model. While there is a current need to resolve the funding shortage, it is important that any changes retain the benefits of the PPP model, both during the global financial crisis and over the life of the project. Specifically, the length and longer-term impact of the financial crisis are unknown, making it imperative that any actions and policies implemented by governments consider the prospective short to long-term ramifications.

Public Financing

One possibility is to return to full public funding of infrastructure. Having decided to finance the project itself, the government could proceed via an unbundled approach with separate contracts for design, build, operate, and maintain. Construction could be commissioned by means of a fixed price (design and build) arrangement or by using a managing contractor or alliancing model (Grimsey and Lewis, 2007). Alternatively, the finance could be taken out of DBFOM, so that the PPP embraces design, build, operate and maintain (DBOM). The first, unbundled, approach is very much of the 'this is where we came in' variety, since there are well-recognized problems with traditional procurement. The second begs the question of how important the finance component is to the success of a PPP. Both of these issues are considered later in this chapter, but the more immediate issue facing public authorities is the capacity of the public sector to finance its infrastructure needs given other pressures upon the public purse, notably the bailouts and stimulus packages in response to the global financial crisis at the central government level and a declining revenue base at the state and regional government level.

The other alternatives considered below fall into two main groups. Some involve a mixture of public and private financing. The others seek to alter the procurement process in ways that seek to circumvent, or lessen the impact of the altered market conditions. We begin with the latter.

Staged Procurement

Known also as 'deferred funding confirmation', in this model procurement is envisaged to proceed with bids in two distinct stages. In stage one, bids are submitted for all components, that is DBFOM. Evaluation could occur on all aspects, recognising that financing pricing terms and conditions are not underwritten. In order to reassure itself, the government procurer could ask for due diligence and some level of underwritten debt. Then in stage two, after DBOM aspects are assessed, the procurer requests bidders to provide underwritten finance. At this point, the government may also move to a lesser number of bidders. Basically, the aim is to allow a bidding process to proceed in times of constrained financing and shortened hold periods. Such an approach may reduce the need for market flex, market disruption and material adverse effect clauses to be included. The problem is that, depending on the number of bidders proceeding to stage two, a large number of lenders may still be tied up if 'competitive tension' is sought among bidders.

Debt Funding Competitions

Known also as a 'preferred bidder funding competition', this approach is another option for a staged procurement process. The basic idea is that a preferred bidder is selected to proceed to a funding competition for senior debt. At the bidding stage, equity commitment is needed. However, committed debt is not required, no exclusive arrangement with debt financiers is allowed, and bids are evaluated on uniform assumptions about debt terms, maturity, and gearing. When a bid is selected, the government procurer and the preferred bidder would then work collaboratively to optimize a funding competition from among the financiers willing to participate. The main problem is that synergy may be lost between the bid and the financial structure as is possible at present where the deal is 'financially engineered' at the bid stage.

Government Co-funding Models

Governments may need to provide financial support to PPP projects being tendered by providing or facilitating the provision of funding beyond that available in the market through either structural changes or government support in the form of contribution, co-funding or guarantee. Most of these mechanisms alter the risk profile to which government is exposed by virtue of it taking on the characteristics of a lender in addition to purchaser *vis-à-vis* existing PPP arrangements. It is also important to take into account the consequences for taxation in structuring a co-funding arrangement, in particular considering how funds will be treated in the hands of the SPV. In some cases government support can trigger unintended tax liabilities if it is not carefully incorporated into the SPV.

There are a number of possibilities for combining government debt and private sector finance.

Supported debt model

Government funds come after financial close when key milestones are met (such as completion of construction) and a certain portion (for example, 70 per cent) of senior debt (the supported debt element) is assessed to be notionally 'risk free' and earmarked for the public sector to provide. For its part, the private sector provides construction finance, the balance of operations funding and all of the equity finance. The underlying rationale is that project risk reduces post-construction, allowing the government to take on the risk that the minimum termination payment exceeds the value of project assets. The idea is that financing costs are less than those for a 100 per cent privately financed PPP while reducing private sector demands on underwritten debt.

Government contribution model

In this arrangement, the government agrees to contribute some funds ('cash flow waterfall'/subsidy) to the SPV project company when construction is completed. This contribution reduces its own future payment obligations (via the unitary charge), while the clear commitment to the project aids financing by the private entity.

Government equity investment
In effect, the government invests with private sector investors as a joint venture. In this way, the public procurer gains greater control, but takes on greater risks. One advantage, however, is that the government stake can later be sold or refinanced as debt markets improve.

Government subordinated debt model
Under this model, the government raises debt and on-lends to the project company as subordinated debt (mezzanine finance). But this debt comes at a cost, and the premium charged on it encourages early refinancing into private debt.

Government senior debt model
Again, the government uses arbitrage in funding markets and lends to the project on commercial terms, ranking equally with private senior debt. The government tranche can later be refinanced or sold-down, allowing extra private sector finance to enter the project at that point. An arrangement along such lines was envisaged in March 2009 with the formation of the Treasury Infrastructure Finance Unit in the UK.

Government Support Models

Revenue guarantees
Market patronage risk (on toll roads in particular) is a significant, largely non-financeable risk in current conditions. Putting a floor on revenue risk would increase the pool of lenders. As an example, the Loan Guarantee Instrument for Trans-European Transport Network scheme through the European Investment Bank (EIB) covers traffic risk for seven years on core transport projects. The A4/IP4 PPP road in north Portugal benefited in this way.

Debt guarantees
The government could guarantee a tranche of SPV debt, during construction or for a specified time span. For example, since February 2009 France has agreed to guarantee 80 per cent of senior debt and bond financing for PPP and concession projects (up to a ceiling of €10 billion)

Syndication guarantees
Here the government subscribes to unallocated debt (for an underwriting fee), and allows syndication to extend beyond financial close. As an illustration, the Belgian government underwrote debt distribution and market

disruption risk for the construction of the Liefkenshoek rail tunnel project (November 2008).

WHY BOTHER WITH PPPs?

There are many critics of PPPs, especially for social infrastructure (for example, Broadbent, Gill and Laughlin (2003), Broadbent and Laughlin (2003), Pollock (2000, 2004) and Shaoul (2005)). Their response to the above suggestions for keeping the PPP concept alive would likely be: why bother? Are PPPs worth preserving?

In our view they are, despite well-publicized controversies surrounding the Cross City Tunnel saga in Sydney and the 'spectacular failure' of Metronet in the UK.[8,9] There is much evidence (outlined below) to support the view that the PPP model is a proven and effective approach to delivering infrastructure and related services. Nevertheless, in tandem the challenges posed by the financial crisis and the dislocation in finance markets run the risk of stalling projects or leading to pricing that overstates the underlying project risk, reducing the model's ability to deliver value-for-money. PPPs are most definitely not a factor in the crisis, but the crisis provides those ideologically opposed to private financing of public infrastructure with a new front on which to wage their war. The risk is that PPPs become just another piece of collateral damage in the fallout from the crisis. It would be a bad outcome if governments simply wind back the clock to traditional procurement and lose the value gained from the introduction of the PPP model, not the least of which is the demonstration effect relative to traditional procurement approaches.

The empirical support for this viewpoint comes from a number of sources. Earlier studies compared PPPs and traditional procurement in a number of aspects, notably construction performance: MacDonald (2002), HMT (2003), National Audit Office (NAO, 2003, 2009), EIB (in Thomson, 2005); projected value for money: NAO (1998, 2001), LSE/Arthur Andersen (2000), Parker and Hartley (2003), Fitzgerald Report (2004); and individual case studies: Sachs et al. (2005), Grimsey and Lewis (2004, 2005a). The results indicate that PPPs have definitely something to add for infrastructure provision in terms of delivery on time, on budget, and with expected value for money (Grimsey and Lewis, 2005b, 2007).

Adding to this evidence, two more recent studies attest to the continued strong performance of PPPs.

> Our overall conclusion is that PPPs provide superior performance in both the cost and time dimensions, and that the PPP advantage increases (in

absolute terms) with the size and complexity of projects (Allen Consulting Group, 2007).

PPP projects provide far greater cost certainty than traditional contracts and there is little variation in cost of a PPP project after the contract is signed (University of Melbourne, MERIT, 2008).

Despite these clear results and weight of evidence, the difficulties and affordability issues faced in raising private finance, allied with the idea that there may be greater use of public financing in DBOM-type structures, does raise the question: how important is private finance in PPP performance? Our earlier answer (Grimsey and Lewis, 2004) was that,

> having the privately provided finance at risk acts as a catalyst to inject risk management techniques into the project in a way that is not possible under government financing (p. 64).

While not downplaying that position, it is far from being the only factor at work in the PPP incentive structure (as we recognized at the time). A key feature inherent in the PPP model is the private sector management of the long-term cost and performance of major infrastructure assets. For this to happen, the private sector needs three things: control over design and construction; a payment mechanism with incentives for on-time, on-cost delivery; and financial costs for sub-standard performance. These features remain. Consequently, the financial market difficulties may not impinge materially upon the incentive compatibility and capacity of the PPP model to offer value for money solutions to the provision of infrastructure, although affordability remains.

A WAY FORWARD

This leaves the question of what is to be done until financial markets return to 'normal'. In turn, this question raises two issues.

What is Normality?

Can we ever again expect to see lending at margins of 55–80 bps over LIBOR on a social infrastructure project over 25 to 30 years? How much was the market driven by plentiful finance fuelled by the Greenspan credit boom unleashed in 2001–04, in which official real interest rates were reduced to their lowest level in 30 years and monetary growth raised to its highest level for 30 years (Iley and Lewis, 2007; Lewis, 2009)? In what is now undoubtedly a seller's market for finance, to what extent is project financing destined to go the same way as private equity and hedge funds, which have been pared back in the new market conditions? PPPs may have a more persuasive underlying rationale than private equity and hedge funds, but a higher overall cost of funds will inevitably lead to a market correction. Indeed, the view has been expressed that 'the issue of affordability could threaten the future of the PFI/PPP market' (Ernst & Young, 2009).

On another tack, will the capital market come on stream and see bonds once again emerge as an alternative to bank debt for project finance? The capital markets, and in particular the index-linked securities that recently dominated the Australian PPP market before the crisis set in, are a natural fit with the PPP model. These securities are attractive to pension funds that look for long term index-linked income that is backed by a secure credit risk that matches their liabilities in the form of pension payments. The return of the capital markets would also provide competition for bank debt and take many of the risk issues confronting the banks off the table. For example, refinancing risk is largely irrelevant to the longer end of the bond market. Banks would likely be in a different negotiating position when it comes to 'market disruption' and 'market flex' provisions that have crept in arguably beyond what is strictly necessary. There are encouraging signs that capital markets may be about to return; however, the big question for deals in the pipeline is when?

How is the New Market Reality Best Handled?

The issue for governments and the private sector alike is the future of the PPP market. The PPP financing models outlined above have been advanced, and in some cases adopted, to address what is currently a dissonance in market positions. Funding certainty is sought by bidders where the depth of market struggles to provide it. Long term debt is required which is increasingly less available in circumstances where PPPs cannot support short-term amortisation and the use of short-term debt produces refinancing risk. The PPP model needs to be adapted if it is to remain available, but how? Are governments prepared temporarily to lend, guarantee or provide capital contributions to projects over the next few years? The answer appears to be yes with encouraging moves made in the UK, Canada and France. Another notable step occurred in 2009 with the A$3.5 billion Victorian desalination project in Australia. A guarantee of syndication was provided by the state government to address the identified barrier to debt-raising by supporting banks to execute their typical role as syndicators. Having the public sector agree to subscribe to unallocated debt helped the project to be financed fully with private sector capital.

On the other hand, if shorter-term financing through the banks turns out to be the new market rule, then a different question is raised. Are procuring authorities willing to underwrite or share the refinancing risk? Such risk-bearing or risk-sharing may be the simplest solution for the immediate future and, significantly, does not mean that the government has to provide finance. Either the unitary charge would rise at refinancing or the procurer would benefit from lower financing costs. Either way, the public sector may be in a better position to bear this risk.

NOTES

1. The views expressed are those of the authors and should not be taken as representing the views of the organisations that they work for or in which they hold membership.
2. Weissman Center Distinguished Lecture, Baruch College, New York, 12 October 2006, cited in Ferguson (2009, p. 343).
3. Ian King of *The Times* ('351 words lit the fuse of the financial crisis') argues that the credit crisis can be dated from 7 February 2007 when HSBC issued the following seemingly innocuous statement 'HSBC Holdings plc wishes to update the pre-close trading statement issued on 5 December 2006 in respect of a single matter'. This was the first profits warning issued by the bank in its 142-year history, and admitted that slowing house prices had led to higher delinquency rates among American mortgage customers. Thereafter, in King's words, the red ink started to flow (*The Australian,* 4 March, p. 28).
4. Bond issues for PPP projects that have an underlying credit rating of BBB-plus can pay a fee for credit enhancement (or wrapping) to a monoline insurer and have a bond issue credit-wrapped so that it is priced on an AAA rating. However, this process relies on the insurer having, and retaining, its AAA rating. When Fitch downgraded US insurer Ambac, it also had to cut the rating on thousands of Ambac bonds, some of which then had to be sold off by those holders whose investment mandate prevents them from holding bonds with less than AAA rating.
5. As reported by Deirdre Fretz 'Niagara doesn't fall', http://www.pfie.com, 8 April 2009, pfi, p. 13.
6. The RiskMetrics report on the Macquarie model identified a number of faults including high fees, high debt levels, related party transactions, distributions from capital, not cash flows, overpayment for assets and poor disclosure (RiskMetrics, 2008).
7. Reported in the *Wall Street Journal* by Richard Barley. 'Lenders shrink balance sheets as huge wave of refinancing looms', WSJ.com, 7 July 2009, p. 20.
8. The two (east and west) 2.1 km 'long 80' tunnels under the Sydney CBD, along with a third ventilation tunnel, are an engineering triumph, delivered on time and on budget, but a public relations disaster. The size of the upfront payment to the public purse and its implications for the tariff levied, along with the road closures to 'return William Street to the people' were seen as putting cash into the developers' pockets and all undermined the legitimacy of the venture. The primary objectives of the project, to remove much east-west traffic from central Sydney streets, and reduce east-west travelling times, were thus compromised. A toll payers' strike saw the project company forced into bankruptcy.
9. The expression comes from the damning House of Commons Report (2008) on Metronet. Our view is that it was always optimistic to imagine that the private sector could correct years of neglect and underinvestment, the more so when Metronet grossly underestimated the task it faced. Its bid allowed £2 million on average for sub-surface

station modernization that turned out to be £7.5 million, while the bid for tube reconditioning estimated £3 million per km, but the cost was £5.7 million per km. We are indebted to Arun Aher and Gurpreet Bhatti of the University of South Australia for these figures.

REFERENCES

Allen Consulting Group (2007) *Performance of PPPs and Traditional Procurement in Australia*, Melbourne: Allen Consulting Group.

Arthur Andersen (2000), 'Value for money drivers in the private finance initiative', London: Arthur Andersen and Enterprise LSE.

Broadbent, J., J. Gill and R. Laughlin (2003), 'Evaluating the private finance initiative in the national health service', *Accounting, Auditing and Accountability Journal,* **16** (3), 422–45.

Broadbent, J. and R. Laughlin (2003), 'Control and legitimation in government accountability processes: the private finance initiative in the UK', *Critical Perspectives on Accounting*, **14** (1), pp. 23–48.

Ernst & Young (2009), 'UK infrastructure. Senior debt pricing – the impact of the credit crunch', London: Ernst & Young LLP.

Ferguson, N. (2009), *The Ascent of Money: A Financial History of the World,* London: Penguin Books.

Fitzgerald, P. (2004), 'Review of Partnerships Victoria provided infrastructure', review of Partnerships Victoria, Melbourne.

Goodhart, C.A.E. (2009), *The Regulatory Response to the Financial Crisis,* Cheltenham, UK and Northampton, MA, USA: Edward Elgar.

Grimsey, D. and M.K. Lewis (2004), *Public Private Partnerships: The Worldwide Revolution in Infrastructure Provision and Project Finance*, Cheltenham, UK and Northampton, MA, USA: Edward Elgar.

Grimsey, D. and M.K. Lewis (eds) (2005a), *The Economics of Public Private Partnerships*, Cheltenham, UK and Northampton, MA, USA: Edward Elgar.

Grimsey, D. and M.K. Lewis (2005b), 'Are public private partnerships value for money? Evaluating alternative approaches and comparing academic and practitioner views', *Accounting Forum,* **29** (4), 345–78.

Grimsey, D. and M.K. Lewis (2007) 'Public private partnerships and public procurement', *Agenda, A Journal of Policy Analysis & Reform,* **14** (2), 171–88.

HM Treasury (2003), *PFI: Meeting the Investment Challenge*, Norwich: HMSO.

House of Commons (2008), 'The London Underground and the public-private partnership agreements', Second Report of Session 2007–08, Transport Committee, London: HMSO.

Iley, R.A. and M.K. Lewis (2007), *Untangling the US Deficit. Evaluating Causes, Cures and Global Imbalances*, Cheltenham, UK and Northampton, MA, USA: Edward Elgar.

Lewis, M.K. (2009), 'The origins of the sub-prime crisis: inappropriate policies, regulations, or both?', *Accounting Forum,* **33** (2), 114–26.

MERIT (2008), *National PPP Forum – Benchmarking Study, Phase II*, Melbourne: Melbourne Engineering Research Institute, The University of Melbourne.

MacDonald, M. (2002), *Review of Large Public Procurement in the UK*, London: HM Treasury.

National Audit Office (1998), 'The Private Finance Initiative: The First Four, Design, Build, Finance and Operate Roads Contracts', HC 476, Parliamentary Session 1997–98, London: HMSO.
National Audit Office (2001), 'Managing the Relationship to Secure a Successful Partnership in PFI Projects', HC 375 Session 2001–02, London: HMSO.
National Audit Office (2003), 'PFI: construction performance', report by the Comptroller and Auditor General, London: HMSO.
National Audit Office (2009), 'Performance of PFI construction', a review by the Private Finance Practice, London: HMSO.
Parker, D. and K. Hartley (2003), 'Transaction costs, relational contracting and public private partnerships: a case study of UK defence', *Journal of Purchasing and Supply Management*, **9** (3), 97–108.
Pollock, A.M. (2000), 'PFI is bad for your health', *Public Finance*, 12 October, pp. 30–31.
Pollock, A.M. (2004), *NHS plc: The Privatisation of Our Health Care*, London: Verso.
RiskMetrics (2008), *Infrastructure Funds: Managing, Financing and Accounting: In Whose Interests?*, New York: RiskMetrics Group.
Sachs, T., C. Elbing, R. Tiong and H. Alfen (2005), 'Efficient assessment of value for money (VFM) for selecting effective public private partnership (PPP) solutions – a comparative study of VFM assessment for PPPs in Singapore and Germany', Singapore: CACS, School for Civil and Environmental Engineering, Nanyang Technological University.
Shaoul, J. (2005), 'A critical financial analysis of the Private Finance Initiative: selecting a financing method or allocating economic wealth?', *Critical Perspectives in Accounting*, **16** (4), 441–71.
Thomson, C. (2005), 'Public-private partnerships: prerequisites for prime performance', *EIB Papers*, **10**(2), 112–29.

Index